Left of Boom
Putting Proactive Engagement to Work

Eric —
Couldn't have done it
without your constant
oversight/support ☺ —
Seriously — I'm blessed to
have you in my life
Thanks

Phillip B. Wilson
Labor Relations Institute, Inc.
Broken Arrow, Oklahoma

To
Mom, my rock
Dad, my inspiration
Janet and Marissa, my life

Acknowledgements

There are a number of people without whom this book would not be possible.

This book is dedicated to the four people who are the most important in my life and without whom I would not accomplish anything. My wife, Janet, has listened to me talk about this book almost as long as we have known each other. She made great suggestions about how to structure the book – especially the sidebars about client stories. She has encouraged me every step of the way. She also gave me the greatest gift I have ever received – our daughter Marissa. Janet is my best friend and I am the luckiest man in the world to have her as my wife.

My Mom gets the lion's share of credit for anything I accomplish. She made great sacrifices to make sure that my brothers and I grew up unconditionally loved. She inspired (okay, sometimes it was more like "required") us to perform whatever we did to the best of our capabilities. In addition to whatever natural gifts I got from her, she taught me the importance of hard work, perseverance and staying positive. She is simply the greatest mother a boy has ever had.

My Dad is my inspiration, and the (dare I say "diamond-like") star I gaze at when dreaming about what my life can be. He has been a great mentor, both professionally and personally. He has inspired much of my professional work – including this book. He is my partner at work and my friend all the time. I am truly blessed to have him for my father.

Whatever clarity of thinking is found in this text I attribute to my experience as a debater in high school and college. Two of the most important influences in my life are my debate coaches, Jeanne DeVilliers and David Snowball. They taught me how to reason, persuade and communicate clearly. If this book fails in any of these regards it is due to the student, not the teachers.

Much of my thinking about employee relations issues I attribute to my mentor, Dick Wessels. I learned a lot from Dick while a lawyer at his firm. Many of these were the traditional lessons learned while bantering about mind-numbing and obscure legal issues around the office. Yet he taught me much more by letting me watch him and giving me the freedom to learn by doing. Dick gave me opportunities that I didn't deserve, that let me make huge strides up a pretty steep learning curve. Although I only worked for Dick about three years, much of what I have learned since is often a variation on a theme that I discovered while with him.

I could not have completed he actual work of this book without help from many others. Kileen Heidenreiter, Glenda Mims, Judy Barnett and Nancy Bizjack typed, proofread, commented and edited the first edition of this book.

This latest edition, about half of which is entirely new work, was edited by a very talented young writer: Meghan Jones. Meghan did a terrific editing job and this new version would not be possible without her. In addition Bryan O'Keefe, Greg Kittinger, Austin Clary and Nancy Jowske each edited and offered many valuable suggestions to white papers that became some of the new chapters of this book. Greg, Austin, Nancy and Eric Vanetti also provided valuable insights, feedback and suggestions around the approachable leadership material in this book. Nancy especially has challenged, extended, and contributed to my thinking about the topic of approachability and how first level leaders engage others. Many thanks to each of them. The book is much improved due to their help.

Finally it takes a lot more than just writing and editing to get a book out the door. Meghan and Greg Kittinger helped me get the final edition across the finish line. Thanks to both of them.

Last, but certainly not least, I want to thank Pam Vass. Pam is an HR leader at a Midwestern client and a big fan of my work. She's made the first edition of this book required reading at her company. About 3 years ago I told Pam – perhaps mistakenly –that I was rewriting this book. She's never let me forget it. Every time I've seen Pam since then the first question she asks is, "where's the book?"

Any time you take on a project of this magnitude there are times that you want to put it down and never look at it again. Pam would never let that happen – she encouraged (and yes, sometimes cajoled) me into getting this edition done. Thanks, Pam.

Preface to *The Next 52 Weeks*[1]

"Whatever you can do or dream you can do, begin it. Boldness
has genius, power and magic in it. Begin it now."
Johann Wolfgang Goethe

This book, like many others, is about transformation and
change. My focus is on change in organizations; more
specifically about transforming employee relations
environments in companies that have recently won union
organizing campaigns. Yet fundamentally its lessons are about
moving any group from a state of negative energy to one of
positive energy.

Physics teaches that it takes a considerable amount of energy
to change direction or momentum, much more than it takes to
simply continue going in the same direction. The same thing is
true with organizations.

In organizations this means it is much easier to stay mired in
negativity (complaining, second-guessing and undermining
others) than to change direction and become positive. In my
experience, when it comes to organizational change, the
physics equations may be too optimistic.

Once an organization has altered its course and achieved
some positive gains, a new momentum is established. This
creates momentum just as powerful as that which reinforced
the negative environment. The goal of this book is to teach
you some principles for creating this energy shift that is so
elusive for some organizations.

---

[1] Note: This book was originally published as *The Next 52 Weeks* in 2003.
This new edition has been completely revised and expanded (it's nearly

We often look for quick fixes and instant gratification. Give us something in a box that will solve all of our problems, but only if it will work by the end of the day. Most of the time the promise of the quick fix is a myth; it is almost always a myth in organizations. Certainly there are some changes that can have an immediate impact on the morale of a company (a leadership change or a new line of business, for example) but these changes do not, by themselves, create enough energy to change the momentum of an organization.

It is fashionable today (some would argue not fashionable enough) to fire the CEO when a company fails to reach its financial goals. The theory is that a new leader can breathe life into the organization and "turn it around." Often the new arrival does create a splash, both on Wall Street and in the company. But these changes are often short-lived. That is because more energy is needed to create lasting change; the momentum of negativity can be very difficult to counter.

Organizations are simply an amalgam of all the human relationships that exist between and among all the members of that community. Each interaction between each person is a brief example of what the larger organization represents, what it is. These interactions <u>are</u> the organization.

Big changes can alter the interactions among the members of a community, but that does not in and of itself change the organization. Instead, these interactions must become habit, a permanent alteration of the way members interact with one another. Only then can one say that the community has changed.

You are what you do every day. Organizations are what their community members do every day. Going on a crash diet might help you lose weight, but to maintain that weight loss you must change your daily habits of exercise and eating. Likewise, leadership changes, downsizing and change programs may create a period of improved performance in an organization (oftentimes even this does not occur). However, if the daily habits and interactions of community-members do not change, these organizations, like the individuals that define them, will slip back into bad habits.

This book, then, is not about a corporate change program or initiative to improve employee relations environments. Instead, it is about habits organization members can adopt, particularly habits in dealing with employee problems, that will eventually improve the overall employee relations environment in an organization. This is not a quick fix. It is not something you can only do for a while. It is definitely not easy.

The good news is that these new habits, by definition, create new relationships, new possibilities and new organizations. They create their own momentum. Only by changing these daily habits will there be enough momentum and energy created to transform a negative environment into a positive one. Change, seen this way, is not a program your company goes through; it is a series of new decisions individuals make that are different than the old ones.

You make decisions every day. You decide whether you will drive straight to work, or whether you will stop for gas or coffee. You decide whether you will say "good morning" to people in the hall, or go straight to your office and get to work. You decide whether you will attend a meeting, support a project or avoid talking about a subject you know should be discussed. Each one of these decisions has an impact on the world. Each one creates (or avoids creating) an interaction that defines your relationship with someone.

Not every person in an organization must change for the environment to change; many will not. In fact, trying to change other people is a fool's errand; the only person you can change is yourself. What you can do, however, is change the way you interact with others. These changed interactions, at least in that moment, create a change in both people. Over time, these changes in daily interactions among individuals will change the organization.

These interactions and habits are created by decisions that you control. I hope that you decide to read this book. I hope that you decide after reading the book to change some of your daily habits and interactions with the people around you. I hope that others in your immediate network also decide to change some of their habits, based on your example. My most sincere hope is that these changes in interactions can create the momentum and energy needed to transform your organization. So, what is your decision?

Phillip B. Wilson
July 2003

"A stitch in time saves nine."
English proverb

About five years ago I had a call with a prospective client about their preparations for the so-called Employee Free Choice Act. We were in the throes of the "Great Recession." President Obama had recently entered office. The Senate was on its way to a filibuster-proof 60 votes. Unions were ascendant. Employers were scared.

This call was like many calls we did at that time and in most ways it was unremarkable. But I will never forget one moment. I was making a point about the value of proactive employee relations practices. I mentioned that among the more important reasons to focus on employee relations before a problem was leverage. An ounce of prevention is worth a pound of cure.

Someone on the call mentioned that it reminded him of an article he had read about how the military was handling attacks by insurgents in Iraq. The articles talked about a major strategy shift that resulted in a dramatic decrease in deadly improvised explosive device attacks in Iraq. He said that the same lessons I was teaching were the lessons the military learned in battling insurgents. I was intrigued.

The more I read about this "left of boom" strategy shift, I understood that it fit perfectly with what we teach companies about creating a positive workplace. If you don't work hard at preventing employee relations problems you are likely to experience major problems in your company. That's the bad news.

The good news is that if you do work hard to prevent problems you earn "compound interest" on your employee relations investment. First, you avoid the major "boom" events (lawsuits, government complaints and even union campaigns). You also reduce the day-to-day annoyances that by themselves don't seem like a big deal, but over time become a huge drain on companies.

One of my professional frustrations over the years has been how much time I spend working "right of boom" – putting out labor relations fires. Not that this work isn't important or valuable. It is. But it is not nearly as satisfying as helping company leaders learn how to create satisfying direct relationships with coworkers. It's not flashy, but it is the most rewarding work we do.

The original version of this book was called *The Next 52 Weeks*, which referred to the fact that once a company wins a union election it has only one short year to avoid another. This book still helps a company do that. But a lot has changed since I wrote the first book.

As I write this preface to the new version of the book the NLRB and the DOL are working hard to dramatically re-write the rules for the express purpose of tilting (unions would say leveling) the playing field against companies in union elections. Unions will continue to pressure the government to make it easier for them to organize new members. They must do this in order to survive.

The cumulative effect of these new rules is to make it extremely difficult for a company to win a union election. While we continue to win union elections in this new environment it is getting harder and harder. Unions are extremely effective at using the many tools at their disposal (government agencies, traditional media, social media, and the like). They know that if they can get a toehold at a company it won't be long before they turn it into a stranglehold.

This new environment makes the lessons in this book that much more important. Companies must be in "campaign mode" 365 days a year. By "campaign mode" I don't mean holding employee meetings or educating employees about unions. While every company should be ready to do that, it is probably too late if you have to bring out your campaign in a box. What I am talking about is a positive employee relations campaign.

This book teaches the principles and practical activities of an "always on" positive employee relations campaign. It is designed to give you a clear, step-by-step plan for creating a positive workplace. If you follow this program you will create an environment where employees feel engaged and ready to give you the discretionary effort needed for any company to out-compete others. In many industries today it is this discretionary effort that spells the difference between success and going out of business.

Even if your company is never the target of union activity (in fact, even if your company is already unionized) this book will still be helpful to you. That is because the principles and activities you use to avoid a union are exactly the same as the principles and activities you employ to be an employer of choice.

The "left of boom" metaphor is powerful. It isn't just good strategic advice for winning on the battlefield or in the workplace. It is how you win the game of life. Living life "left of boom" means living in an intentional way, working on things that are important but not urgent. Doing what you should do before doing what you "must" do. Working with purpose, not just reacting to what comes at you in the moment.

Too many of us waste our lives putting out fires, working day after day right of the boom. I hope this book inspires you to abandon that place. I hope to see you left of boom.

Phillip B. Wilson
September 2014

Table of Contents

DISPUTE RESOLUTION AND PEER REVIEW   398

WHERE DO WE GO FROM HERE? LIVING LEFT OF BOOM   417

APPENDICIES AND END MATERIAL   424

Chapter 1

Left of Boom

"You can't armor your way out of this problem."
U.S. Army Brigadier General on IED attacks in Iraq, 2005

What You'll Learn In This Chapter

- ❏ Why most of your "proactive" measures aren't proactive at all and how to tell the difference between real and "fake" preventive measures;
- ❏ The five key tactics military strategists used when they realized they were losing against insurgent IED attacks – and how you can apply them in your business today;
- ❏ Six different "left of boom" activities you can use now that will give your company big leverage in its positive employee relations strategy; and
- ❏ Four "right of boom" strategies you should be ready to use in case you are targeted by union organizers.

You've seen the video.

A patrol of U.S. military vehicles rumbles along a mountainous road. Suddenly the road erupts. A bubble of earth and debris is hurled upward. The huge armored vehicle is tossed like a toy into a ditch, engulfed in a ball of flames.

The rest of the patrol screeches to a halt. Soldiers spill out in a desperate effort to try to catch the renegade

Figure 1.1 – IED Explosion

insurgent who triggered the road-side bomb (referred to by

the military as an "improvised explosive device" or "IED" for short).

The tug-of-war between U.S. forces in Iraq and Afghanistan and the insurgents bent on disrupting U.S. patrols with IEDs has been a constant game of "move, counter-move."

US Military Move	Insurgent Counter-Move
Defeat microwave trigger devices	Develop cell phone trigger devices
Jam cell phone trigger devices	Develop infrared and laser triggered devices
Use thermal detonation devices to pre-detonate infrared triggers	Remove infrared triggers from IED
Jam radio trigger devices	Begin using "dumbed down" pressure plate triggers
Increase armor on vehicles	Increase explosive power of IED devices

It became apparent early in the Iraqi conflict that this cat-and-mouse game could go on indefinitely. In the words of one general, "you can't armor your way out of this problem."

What does all this have to do with creating a positive employee relations strategy? Everything.

Military strategy is a useful model for dealing with thorny, complex, and high-stakes situations. It informs much of our work by teaching us ways to to develop business strategies to respond to attacks by outside "forces." For example, when faced with the growing success of IED attacks by insurgents in Iraq and Afghanistan, the military created the Joint Improvised Explosive Device Defeat Organization (JIEDDO in the typical military "shorthand").

In analyzing the problem, the JIEDDO created a way to describe the sequence of events leading up to and in the aftermath of an IED explosion. All of the events preceding the actual explosion are called "Left of Boom." The explosion itself of course is the "Boom." All the events post-explosion are "Right of Boom."[2]

Early strategies dealt with the explosion of the device and the immediate actions and responses to each incident, from "Boom" to "Right of Boom." The cat-and-mouse game described above focused on that small window in the timeline from just before "Boom" (when a convoy or patrol arrived near the location of the emplaced IED) and the immediate

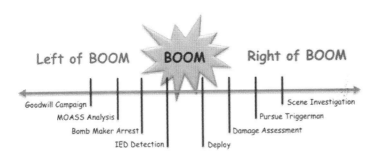

Figure 1.2 – IED Explosion Sequence of Events

aftermath, or "Right of Boom".
It quickly became apparent that in order to effectively defeat the enemy, they had to turn "Left of Boom," moving backwards in time from:

- who planted and/or triggered the bomb, to
- who recruited the person who planted the bomb, to
- who built the bomb, to

---

[2] Much of the information about "Left of Boom" and the struggle with fighting IED attacks comes from a series of articles in the Washington Post written by Rick Atkinson. I highly encourage you to order the articles, which are now available as an electronic download on Amazon. You can find a link directly to the articles here and on our webpage http://LRIonline.com/leftofboom.

- where did the bomb-making parts come from, etc.

In other words, "Left of Boom" focuses on disrupting the bomb chain long before it can be emplaced and detonated.

The military clearly understood the importance to the lives of American soldiers to focus on "Right of Boom" issues. Nevertheless, they came to the realization that the only way to diminish and eradicate the threat was to focus on attacking the network that produced the bombs and the bombers. "We should focus less on the bomb than on the bomb maker," stated Brigadier General Joseph Votel, the first JIEDDO Director, arguing that the effort had to move "Left of Boom."

It became increasingly clear to those thinking about "Left of Boom" that the bomb maker was the "disproportionately valuable" person in the terrorist chain because of his technical skill. Bomb makers build the devices and troubleshoot emplacements that fail when attempting to counter the military's counter measures. Thus, taking out skilled bomb makers remains vitally important to stopping the IED network from placing IEDs.

That network had to be attacked long before the bombs were in place if deterrence was to be effective. The strategies that worked in Iraq and Afghanistan include:

- **Investigation:** A large group of "crime scene investigators" conduct complete investigations of every bomb blast, including finger print analysis, study of the detonators, study of the circuitry used and the chemical makeup of weapons. The point of this research is not only to understand how the devices are being made but also to track down the bomb makers. These teams are responsible for numerous arrests and kills of bomb makers. They have tracked down the critical, "higher in the chain" bad guys instead of the less important insurgents who placed the IED devices.

- **Pattern recognition:** All data points possible are collected from each and every IED detonation into what is called "MOASS" or the Mother of all Spread Sheets. The military uses this spreadsheet to recognize patterns of where bombs are placed, what times they are placed, and how they are detonated, among other data. This creates a robust database to help predict and potentially interdict IEDs before they go off.
- **Disrupt the network:** The military monitors, arrests, interrogates, and turns over any members of the network to the Iraqi or Afghani governments for criminal prosecution. This allows them to know where to watch and how to interdict the insurgents placing the bombs. It also helps the military to stop and destroy delivery of key bomb making components.
- **Engage the "enablers":** The military has learned so much about how and where emplacements happen that they can target and engage community leaders in the areas most likely to produce bombs or insurgents who will trigger them. This reduces the capacity of the bombing network to deploy devices and increases the likelihood that insurgent "triggermen" or bomb makers will expose themselves to the military out of stress or frustration.
- **Reduce leverage points**: Winning "hearts and minds" in the community is not only critical to getting citizens to turn over insurgents to the U.S. military, but also encourages them to directly attack insurgents who are living near them.

By focusing more heavily on "Left of Boom" the military has made it much more difficult for the bomb-making networks to do their dirty work. But it has not stopped the attacks. This is a very important lesson about Left of Boom. No "magic pill" will stop the insurgent networks from doing damage. A holistic strategic approach is key.

"Right of Boom" is easy. Every fiber of human nature wants to respond to the "Boom." The problem with "Right of Boom" is that it allows the networks to become effective in the first place.

Hindsight is 20/20. During the initial invasion of Iraq, the U.S. military could have substantially reduced the impact of IED attacks today. Substantial amounts of bomb parts were buried – and in some cases even ignored - in the rush to take Baghdad. This material was later used to kill American soldiers.

The American military was not expecting an insurgency. Instead it prepared for a more traditional battle against an organized military force. Much of the planning failed to attack the real enemy. In many ways, the initial attack gave the "real" enemy heavy advantages over the U.S.

While it is hard to imagine a "successful" outcome for the insurgency, they have effectively disrupted U.S. military operations. If the U.S. forces had focused more heavily on "Left of Boom" strategies, particularly before the insurgency really got legs, the American military could have stopped the insurgency in its infancy. Instead, today it deals with a mature and deadly enemy.

One can take the comparison between negative employment events or union organizing and insurgent networks too far. After all, unions preposterously call consultants like me "corporate terrorists!" Nevertheless, from a strategic standpoint, there are similarities in the underlying strategies of a guerrilla insurgency and a union organizing campaign.

"Boom" In The Workplace

I define "Boom" in the business workplace as a significant negative event. This could mean a lawsuit, a regulatory complaint, a fight or other disruption. We will focus primarily on a union organizing drive as the "Boom" event.

The analogy with military forces and IEDs breaks down with all but the most sophisticated employers at one crucial point. The military is a single organization with deep and wide experience dealing with IEDs. Every individual encounter is a learning experience. The lessons learned and strategies devised are dispersed across the network by the JIEDDO. Every military convoy or patrol benefits from them. As General Votel put it, "I've got the greatest testing ground in the world in Iraq."

Businesses rarely have similar opportunities to share experiences. Look at it this way: each business is like an individual military convoy or patrol of a different army. The experiences and difficulties faced by that patrol stay within the patrol, and are not spread to all other military units (i.e. businesses) across the country. Until a "Boom" event occurs within a company, its defenses–or lack thereof–are based more on theory than rooted in experience.

Sometimes a company has multiple locations or facilities spread across a wide geographical area. In these cases, it is possible that the effect of a "Boom" event at one location might be transferred across the company, but there are no guarantees that it will. Because lives are not at stake (as in the military), such experiences are often handled within a facility, and local managers may attempt to hide or diminish the scale of the problem, hoping to protect their reputation and job. This is a reality of the "politics" of business.

There are two key lessons here.

First, companies that grow from negative experiences foster a "learning organization."[3] If upper management nurtures an environment where middle-managers and front-line supervisors and employees are encouraged to bring mistakes and failures to light in a manner that protects each individual and promotes learning across the company, the company is protected from losing the value of lessons learned.

Second, when you find a body of knowledge developed from hundreds or thousands of similar experiences, you should do all you can to harness that resource. This is how to move beyond theory or limited experience and to tap into the deep and wide experiences of others. This is one of the advantages our consulting firm enjoys. LRI has focused on the "Boom" of union organizing events for over 35 years. We have studied over 10,000 "Boom" events (union organizing campaigns) over that time. Our methodologies, consulting services and tools are tested and have been constantly refined over those 10,000 organizing campaigns.

Workplace "Boom" events can cause significant damage to a company. There are legal costs and consulting fees. These events often lead "Right of the Boom" to reduced productivity, quality problems, and customer service issues. Added up this can result in loss of business and – in today's highly competitive marketplace – sometimes even business failure.

Furthermore, these "Boom" events can be incredibly disruptive to the lives of the people that work inside that company. It's not uncommon for people to experience a significant emotional impact, physical health impacts, and in extreme cases even violence (whether physical or

---

[3] The term "learning organization" was coined by professor Peter Senge. You can learn more in his book: Peter M. Senge, *The Fifth Discipline: The Art & Practice of The Learning Organization* (Crown Business, 2010).

psychological) due to the stress that occurs during union organizing events.

Because "Boom" events are so significant to a company and its employees, it is useful to think about them the same way that the military thinks about the IED attacks. Union organizers can be compared to the insurgent networks that attempt to disrupt the U.S. military in Iraq.

Union organizers often work to disrupt and create fear and a division between employees and their employer. If they cannot convince employees to organize internally, they will often engage in corporate campaign tactics to destroy a target company or cause such significant damage to that company that it will give in to union demands. These events often appear to come out of nowhere and are purposefully intended to increase conflict and emotional stress in the workplace.

"Left Of Boom" In The Workplace

How do you disrupt the network that leads to the "Boom" events in your workplace? Understanding the idea of "Left of Boom" is important, but its application in your company's employee relations strategy is what really matters. Just like the initial military response to IED attacks, it is very common for companies to place most of their attention and investments "Right of Boom." As the military also learned, your return on investment is likely to be much greater if you focus "Left of the Boom."

The cornerstone of a "Left of Boom" strategy is creating a positive workplace. Negative employment events, especially those involving union organizing, usually begin in an employment environment where there is a lack of affiliation with the company. In order for one of these boom events to get any traction, there must be a fertile environment.

Much like the environment in Iraq is conducive to the insurgency, a negative work environment is conducive to union organizing events. Thus, the crucial element of a "Left of Boom" strategy is to eradicate the issues that give rise to the negative workplace environment in the first place.

To start, identify the activities or events that create the proper conditions for boom events. A big part of the Left of Boom strategy in Iraq was to win the hearts and minds of the communities. There are numerous public works projects and other partnerships with local schools and religious leaders that instill a positive impression of the U.S. military, and also create a community that is more willing and able to stand up for itself and to reject insurgent elements within.

A similar situation occurs inside companies. There are always going to be negative pockets of employees in any organization. The trick is to make sure that those groups remain isolated and, to some extent, are even rejected by the rest of the organization. It should be uncomfortable and segregating to be a negative voice in your work environment. The point isn't to be mean-spirited to that individual or group, quite the opposite. The point is simply to highlight that their experience of the employer is uncommon. Most employees in the organization should see the company as kind and supportive of co-workers.

Key "Left Of Boom" Strategies

There are a number of practical strategies and tactics you should employ to create the proper work environment. These strategies are outlined in detail throughout the remainder of this book. But at a high level the six critical strategies are:
1. Assess Your Vulnerabilities
2. Effective Employee Research
3. Positive Employee Relations Training for Supervisors
4. Enriched Employee Communication
5. Hiring and Onboarding Process

6. Create a "Net Promoter" Culture

The book is divided into 6 Sections, covering each of the 6 key strategies. In each section we will go into detail about "left of boom" tactics you can start implementing today to succeed at each core area.

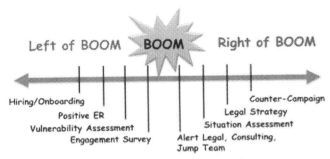

Figure 1.3 – "Left of Boom" Strategies

What You Can Expect From Left of Boom

Left of Boom provides some helpful strategies for those interested in changing their employee relations environment. It teaches you how to change your focus from "right of boom" to "left of boom." It offers hope to those organizations that feel that their employee relations situation is hopeless. There are practical tools to use as a starting point in your change effort – a sketch to follow as you begin to paint your own picture.

This book is not a comprehensive guide on the subject of organizational change. There are some suggestions at the end for additional reading that can help you add color and depth to your palette. Your organization's environment is unique, and your change program will reflect that uniqueness. Yet I can tell you without reservation that you can successfully transform your employee relations environment. If you decide to try, I accomplished my goal in writing this book.

Left of Boom describes a program to attack the weaknesses most prevalent in who have recently been attacked by a union. So, is this an anti-union book? No. And I am not anti-union (no matter how many times I've been called a "union buster"). Many companies have a productive collective bargaining relationship with their employees, and prefer to operate that way. Still, even these companies can profit from the lessons described in this book.

I do feel, however, that a company committed to operating union-free, one that strives to create a workplace where employees do not feel the need for third party intervention, is a much better place to work than one that is not. Furthermore, companies that lose union elections usually deserve it.

What about companies that have never been threatened by a union and are already doing a good job in these areas? Left of Boom still offers a way to check the pulse of your company. I encourage all companies I work with, whether petitioned for a union election or not, to "think like an organizer" – the same way the American military had to think like an insurgent to develop its "Left of Boom" strategies. This method of thinking trains you to attack weaknesses as they arise. It is a logical, outcome-oriented method of continuous improvement that can dramatically improve your HR management system.

These strategies are just the beginning of a comprehensive "Left of Boom" mindset. Your program will be unique to your own organization, but this book provides a good road map for how to begin. Make sure that you are focusing at least half of your attention, if not more, on the "Left of Boom" strategies. They will have two important impacts on your company: First, it will reduce the likelihood of the "Boom" in the first place. Second, whatever "Right of Boom" strategies you employ will be much more effective if you have laid the groundwork by having a strong "Left of Boom" framework already in place.

Take Action

- [ ] Make a list of recent "Right of Boom" counter-strategies your organization has been making. What were the "Boom" events that spurred those actions?
- [ ] Identify the events and/or employee concerns that lead to the "Boom" events.
- [ ] Think of 3 "Left of Boom" activities that could have prevented one of the "Boom" events listed above.

SECTION I: VULNERABILITY ASSESSMENT

Today companies are under huge competitive pressure just to survive. Every part of the company, from the production areas to the C-suite, must deliver more with less every day.

Organizations and their people are under constant stress. Systems under stress either adapt or break. The company and its employees are constantly looking for ways to adapt the system to the new stress. Ideally, a system that adapts will find a "new normal" where the company and its people learn to provide their product or service better, faster and cheaper.

But sometimes these adaptations fail and the system never gets to the new normal – instead, the system breaks. This is when people within the system start looking outside for ways to fix what is broken. For employees, this sometimes means looking to a union.

Often companies don't pay attention to the signs of a system at the breaking point. This isn't surprising. Remember that managers are also being pushed to the limit. After they implement one "fix" they are on to the next crisis. These managers are not trying to break the system or its people, they are simply trying to do their difficult jobs as best they can. This is why every organization needs to have a robust risk management system in place to identify danger signs before they become "boom events" in the organization.

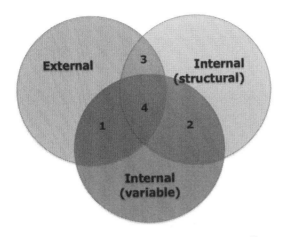

1. Higher risk of "outside-in", but few "self-inflicted" wounds
2. Higher risk of a "home grown" campaign, lower risk of "outside-in"
3. Higher risk of external campaign, may not gain traction internally
4. Most vulnerable target for union organizing

Figure I – Risk Vulnerability

The diagram above gives a quick outline of how we look at risk in an organization. Chapter 5 explains Figure 1 in detail, but the basic point is that employee relations risk can come from many places. The threat can be from inside or outside. The vulnerability may or may not be something the organization can control. It could be a people problem, a system problem or even a market problem.

For this reason our firm uses a number of tools to analyze risk, such as structured interviews with managers, employee engagement research (which we cover in Section II) and employee focus groups. We also look at external data on union organizing activity. These are all data points that provide a picture of overall vulnerability in an organization.

In this section of the book you will learn about how unions think about organizing companies, what motivates employees to seek out union representation, and how to assess risk in your own organization. Try to answer these two questions while you read about our approach to vulnerability assessment:

- What data points are readily available to me in my organization now? You probably already have a lot of data you can assess if you just look for it.
- Are there any of the key internal or external factors we look at that are "blind spots" in your company? List these and, if you can, put them in a rough order of priority.

When you finish the next few chapters you should have a good handle on how to assess risk in your organization. This will set the stage for the rest of the book, where you will find plenty of strategies to shore up any weaknesses you uncover in your own risk assessment.

Chapter 2

Making Unions Irrelevant

*"Only those who risk going too far will
ever know how far they can go."*
Anonymous

What You'll Learn In This Chapter
- ❏ The three common characteristics of companies recently petitioned by a union;
- ❏ What a union means to the management of an organization;
- ❏ Why union-free status is a poor indicator of an organization's employee relations skills;
- ❏ How to determine if your company is "at-risk;"
- ❏ How union "pre-emption" can help your organization achieve or maintain union-free status; and
- ❏ Why you should avoid being overdrawn in your "Employee Relations Bank Account."

Characteristics of Companies Attacked by Unions

When the military changed its IED response strategy from right to left of boom, a key task was identifying what made them vulnerable to attacks in the first place. These vulnerabilities ranged from the very specific (like what routes or what equipment they used) to the very general (what religious or tribal leaders were targeting them, and why). They were constantly changing and at first the task of getting ahead of these factors was overwhelming.

However, over time the military began to chip away, and while it remained a game of "cat and mouse," the more proactive the military got the more difficult it was for insurgents to launch major attacks.

The bulk of our work is with companies after they have successfully defended themselves against a union organizing attempt (a boom event in an organization). Like the military units in Iraq, these companies face enormous and complex challenges. They often have serious business challenges that caused in part because they do such a poor job managing their employee relationships. They normally share three common characteristics:

- Employees lack trust or confidence in top management's ability to solve their problems, an issue worsened by the six week election campaign in which every decision made by management was examined under a microscope and picked apart by union organizers;
- Management expended enormous effort communicating its position on unions, creating a void in communication after the campaign was over; and
- Expectations were created during the campaign and employees are waiting to see them fulfilled. These expectations are rarely explicit, and they are often unreasonable. Fair or not, management will be held to these expectations as employees judge whether they made a good decision in the voting booth.

After going through a union election campaign, most companies are poorly prepared for actually winning the election itself. The natural reaction after winning is to celebrate the victory. An election is a stressful, complex process that requires considerable time and resources from management. It is understandable, given the huge expense and enormous loss of productivity that normally accompanies most campaigns, that management just wants to close the chapter and move on. However, this reaction is very counterproductive; often this is the exact reaction union organizers count on.

If your company does not manage these three reactions properly, you are falling into a trap. Organizers rarely look at an organizing drive as a "one-shot" deal. Today unions are known to file second and even third petitions regularly. Any good organizer (no matter the results of the first election) can capitalize on the traits listed above, creating excellent campaign issues. The steps you take in the next six months will determine whether you will be vulnerable to another petition next year.

You Don't Want a Union, Right?

Most HR professionals, and almost all operations people (even officers of very large companies) answer this question in the affirmative without even thinking about it. About the only people I've met who really question this proposition are CFOs, usually for all the wrong reasons. Finance people are programmed to look only at how something hits the books or affects the bottom line – which never accounts for the financial impacts associated with an unhappy workforce.

I've sat through many meetings where the top finance officer argues for quite some time that "this union thing" won't hurt us and fighting it will just be expensive. Depending on the culture of that management team, the CFO might be right. If the company doesn't plan on correcting the issues that created an atmosphere ripe for organizing activity in the first place, the odds are that fighting it will be an expensive, and ultimately lost, cause.

So why don't you want a union? The answers to this question will often depend on who you are. Good supervisors don't like unions because their jobs change from managers to contract administrators. (Bad supervisors, by definition, really couldn't care less). In the worst cases supervisors will spend the vast majority of their time dealing with minor administration issues instead of managing production. If they try to run things the old way, or if they get into a battle with the union or one of its officers, they will usually get the added pleasure of defending numerous grievances filed against them.

Operations managers don't want a union for the reasons listed above. They become the ultimate contract administrator and have to resolve all the grievances filed. They spend an excessive amount of their time defending managerial actions of their supervisory team, often in front of outside parties who have no clue about the operation.

In addition, depending on the company, operations managers get to negotiate a contract every few years, with the possibility of work stoppages. In larger companies, they get to do this with the labor relations experts or lawyers shipped in to make sure they do a good job. Every major operational decision will include a significant discussion about how to get the union to sign off, and many good ideas will be simply tossed aside because of fears regarding implementation.

Human resources professionals have the most to lose when their workplace becomes unionized. Their jobs change dramatically, or they're fired and a "labor" person is brought in. In addition to relearning the worst parts of their jobs – record keeping, benefits administration, hiring administration – there are the added headaches of contract negotiations, arbitrations and contract administration.

Furthermore, almost all of the positive employee relations opportunities are lost, because they are seen as a threat by the union (which has a vested interest in employees' distrust of management). Companies and unions can successfully work together, but the vast majority of the time things become less cooperative and more adversarial.

Officers of companies that become unionized have to learn a new way of thinking about their businesses. Sometimes these people are also the operations managers (and even the human resources professionals) so they get all the headaches listed above and typically don't have enough hours in the day to worry about anything else. In larger companies, a unionized location adds an additional layer of bureaucracy on all operational and many financial decisions. Unionized locations are more rigid and often less productive than non-unionized ones.

Acquiring a union at one location makes your company much more vulnerable to organizing at other locations. In fact, most unions today include neutrality and card-check recognition at non-union locations among their highest priority in contract negotiations at unionized plants. Additionally, there is the obvious problem of potential work stoppages at unionized locations.

Financially, there are hundreds of additional expenses from legal fees and costs of in-house labor expertise, to time lost in contract administration and the inability to deal fluidly with labor expense issues. (Temporary, part-time and overtime are life-and-death issues in unionized operations.) If you screw up a contract, you are usually stuck with it for three years and then left with an enormous problem correcting past mistakes. There's a reason why unionized operations are typically valued at a significant discount in comparison to non-union ones.

Is There a Difference Between Union-free Companies and Unionized Ones?
In a broad sense, there is little difference between unionized companies and those labeled "union-free." You can have two identical companies making an identical product or offering an identical service and employing the same type of people, yet one may have a bargaining obligation and the other one may not.

It is incorrect to automatically assume that because a company has a bargaining obligation it is doing anything "wrong" or it is "worse" than a company without a union. In fact, the opposite is sometimes true. There are thousands of companies out there that, although they don't have a legal bargaining obligation, have working conditions much worse than unionized companies. Unions of course would claim that this is because the companies are not unionized (also an overstatement).

Many deluded CEOs and company owners believe that their union-free status is evidence that they are doing things right. Even worse is the owner who believes that because his employees voted in favor of the company in a representation election, he no longer has a union problem. This is a mistake made by managers of companies across the country. They believe that, because they are union-free, the company must be a great place to work. Union organizing drives are a symptom of a sick company and winning a union election, like getting an angioplasty, is not a cure. It protects you for a while, but if there is not a significant change in lifestyle, the patient may end up dead anyway.

It is instructive, then, to compare companies petitioned for representation against their will with companies that have employees who have been approached by union organizers and turned them away. The former group of companies I refer to as "at-risk," meaning that, but for the grace of God, they probably would have a bargaining obligation. A tremendous number of companies in America fit into this category

Companies Who Get Organized Usually Deserve It
Like the heart patient who refuses to follow his prescribed diet, at-risk companies that fail to react to and correct the symptoms of illness in their workforce are increasingly likely to have an attack.

Many business owners believe that they have an inalienable right to run their company the way they see fit and that no union is going to be able to take that away from them. But companies that refuse to change their management style to respond to the problems evident in their workforce deserve to be unionized. Like physical health, if you refuse out of stubbornness, principle or even fear to respond to the symptoms, you should expect to pay the consequences.

Union organizers will scream from the highest mountain that employees have a right to organize. They are right. But they never mention the equal and opposite right to refrain from organizing. These people also refuse to acknowledge that this right is not the right of unions, but of employees. If employees don't want to join a union, they don't have to. Period.

By the same token, operating union-free is not a right. You can be virulently anti-union. You can hire union-busters and labor lawyers until you don't have any money left (not an uncommon occurrence), but if your employees want a union, they will get one. You can litigate and negotiate and commit all the unfair labor practices known to man, but if your employees really want a union, you can't stop it unless you close down your company. That is the labor law version of a heart attack. You may somehow and miraculously get resuscitated, but basically you're dead.

Symptoms of "At-Risk" Companies

There are as many ideas on how to properly manage human resources as there are human resource professionals. Yet, there are some common symptoms endemic to at-risk companies. Of course, for each symptom there is a countervailing characteristic of "healthy" companies. The table below summarizes the most common symptoms and characteristics:

Symptom of "At-Risk" Company	Characteristic of Healthy Company
Feeling that management fails to keep hourly employees informed	Good communication of business issues; consistent feedback on job performance

Poor complaint procedure – feeling that input is ignored	Complaint and suggestion procedure in place; appeal process; regular feedback
Unfair application of policies and procedures	Clearly communicated and fairly applied policies and procedures
Unfair promotion or advancement procedures	Clear, objective requirements for advancementtraining and development available to prepare for advancement
Feeling that terminations are handled unfairly	Unbiased review process for all terminations; appeal process
Poor working environment or conditions	Clean, comfortable and safe work environment
Uncertainty about future with the company	Confidence in company's health and personal growth opportunities
Lack of training and development programs	Variety of training opportunities; consistent dialogue on personal development
Pay and/or benefits below market levels – poorly communicated compensation and benefit plans	Pay and benefits at or above market levels; well communicated compensation and benefit policies; clearly communicated and consistently applied salary administration
Poor recruiting pre-employment screening and new hire orientationprocess	Strong hiring and screening process; high effort during first several months of employment to ensure new hires are the right "fit"
Poorly trained or incompetent front-line supervisors	Effort made to promote individuals with best supervisory skills, not best technical skills; ongoing training and development of front-line supervisors

While no chart of this nature can capture all the weaknesses of "at-risk" organizations, these are the first things an organizer will look for when determining whether or not a company is a good target. They are, consequently, the first things you should look at when deciding where to begin your work to remain union-free.

What If We Already Have a Union?

This book is not only for companies who are without a bargaining obligation at the present time. All the principles discussed here can be applied in a unionized environment, so long as a few key points are remembered.

First, many of the things suggested would be subject to a bargaining obligation and, therefore, should not be implemented without first offering to bargain with the union. Depending on your relationship with your union, this may mean you cannot accomplish everything you want. Even if your bargaining relationship is less than productive, there are still many areas where you can make improvements without bargaining. In particular, your pre-employment, orientation and supervisory development programs can normally be adjusted without bargaining.

Second, you also need to consider your ultimate goal. If it is to one day create a work environment where employees will conclude that they no longer need union representation, you obviously want to avoid creating the impression that the union is driving the positive changes in the workplace (particularly if they are not). On the other hand, if your goal is to create a better bargaining relationship, you will want to join with the union in implementing these changes.

Obviously these are strategic issues well beyond the scope of this text. The key point here is that unionized and non-union operations are encouraged to consider implementing as many of the applicable aspects of this program as possible. The mere fact that a bargaining obligation exists does not mean that a company cannot transform itself into an employee relations leader.

What's the Secret?

People often ask, "What is the secret to maintaining union-free status?" The best reply, as taught by my mentor Dick Wessels, "there are no silver bullets in labor law." If there is any "secret" at all, it is that you must be vigilant in wanting to make your workplace as good a place to work as possible. It requires constant effort, and small mistakes can have enormous impact.

There are two theories on avoiding third party intervention. The first is to eliminate its source, or "to cut the head off the dragon." This approach is attractive to clients because it is the quick fix. You've heard of the situation where that horribly disgruntled employee finally leaves, usually involuntarily, and it's like a cloud has been lifted from the workplace. The supposed success of this approach (by itself), like dragons, is a myth.

Client Story: Why "Cutting the Head Off the Dragon" is Not Enough

> A longtime client recently called us in to work on his case. The company fought three organizing campaigns back to back, and after winning the third, we were asked to help turn things around. The last campaign, as one might imagine, was horrible. Soon after we began working with the company, we witnessed one of the most incredible displays of insubordination from an employee ever seen/experienced. (He was also quite outspoken in favor of the union.) This employee accosted the owner of the plant and nearly assaulted him.
>
> A week or two later during a conference call, we learned that not only was the employee still with the company, but he did not even suffer disciplinary action for the incident. Why? He was the number one union supporter and had already filed many unfair labor practice charges over the prior campaigns. We asked why, if they were going to let this guy run the plant, they even hired us at all. After hearing about legal fees and how unfair the NLRB is

on discharge cases (both entirely true) I had heard enough. "Either fire him, or fire us," I said.

The client saw this as the reason for our success. We did not. Firing an employee whom you have just cause to fire is not a great act of courage – it is just common sense. The fear of unfair labor practice charges being filed during union campaigns, when they are filed in virtually every discharge situation no matter how egregious, is a weak excuse to fail to do the right thing. This employee's union sympathy was totally irrelevant. He was one of nearly a hundred union supporters, and not even the most vocal. However, he was the only employee who was disrespectful and openly hostile to all management. This employee believed he was untouchable – and his co-workers knew it. So he spent his workday making every other employee in the company miserable. He was a cancer.

Yet firing this employee was only a small first step. The action created an environment in which the company could get the benefit of the doubt – but only that. Consistent, measured and public acts over the course of the next months were needed to turn this workforce around. Solving the problems involved supervisory training, implementation of a variety of positive programs for employees, and a bunch of hard work.

Ultimately, these employees determined that it was time to give the company a chance. Does this mean a union is now an impossibility there? Absolutely not. Did terminating this one employee "win" the case? No way. Consistent attention to the employees of this company will keep the company union-free forever. Failure to continue the lessons learned will lead to election number four – and near-certain defeat.

The second theory is called "substitution" by unions, or "preemption." This approach recognizes that in most workplaces where third-party intervention is a risk, the "dragon" is more like the Hydra from ancient mythology – you cut off its head and it just keeps coming back. This is the usual situation and a quick fix won't work. Although things might get better for a while, the root causes of the problem do not go away with the fired employee. So after a little while a new dragon head appears, usually more fierce than the last.

Third-party intervention, whether by unions, government agencies or other employee representatives, are "boom events" and are a response to something that has gone wrong. Unfortunately, there's no magic elixir that will clean up a toxic workplace. Sure, a supervisor or manager here or there may need to go, but the problems in these workplaces are almost always deeper than that.

In order to effectively eliminate the need and/or threat of third-party intervention, it is important to remember why employees seek it in the first place. Employees turn to third parties when they feel:
- a problem or issue is too big to handle on their own;
- the third party will get them more or get them a better outcome than they can on their own; or
- the third party somehow adds more credibility to their problem or issue.

Any strategy to eliminate the threat of third-party intervention must attack each of these three motivations.

The key is to focus your third party preemption strategies on the three areas described above – helping employees deal with all problems (especially the "big" ones); convincing employees that they can get as much or more for themselves without turning to third parties; and helping them believe that there is no additional credibility gained by turning to a third party. This framework will help clean up the underlying problems that lead to interventions and, if or when they do occur, make those interventions less costly.

We often see managers get extremely frustrated when they begin the transformation into an employee relations leader. They feel like their hard work is totally unappreciated. There is nothing more frustrating than to have made a commitment in your own mind to really want to solicit employee opinion, only to hear a collective yawn in response. A commitment such as this requires incredible patience. Employees in a company that has consistently failed to listen have been trained not to talk. They must be retrained, and this process takes time. Trust, which is what all this comes down to in the end, is something that is earned over time.

An example that we find compelling is Steven Covey's "emotional bank account." Covey believes that we should look at our personal relationships like mini bank accounts, in which emotional deposits and withdrawals are made. If you act like a jerk to someone, you've made a withdrawal. If you are nice, you've made a deposit. Companies are the same way – consider it the Employee Relations Bank Account. Those that have consistently failed in their employee relations practices are probably overdrawn in their accounts with their employees. It will take a significant number of deposits before these businesses will begin to see results.

So, the secret is to commit to change and to stick to your plan, even if it looks like nobody else is on board. Experience shows that these suggested tactics are the best way to manage your employee relations. You will get resistance – as any change, no matter how beneficial in the end, is usually met with resistance at first. The key is to meet it head-on, stay vigilant and know that one day the opposition will turn into cooperative effort aimed toward mutual goals and a better way to get the job done.

Take Action

- [ ] Which characteristics of at-risk companies do you recognize in your own company?
- [ ] What are your employee relations goals for this year? How about 5 years from now?
- [ ] Does your organization focus most on "preemption" or "cutting the head off the dragon?" Is it working?

Chapter 3

Learning to Think Like an Organizer - How Unions Organize Employees

"What else can you expect with peace running wild all over the place? You know what the trouble is with peace? No organization."
Bertolt Brecht, Mother Courage and Her Children

What You'll Learn In This Chapter
□ How union organizing campaigns get started;
□ Summary of the NLRB election process;
□ Some of the common tactics used by organizers to persuade potential voters;
□ The early warning signs of union organizing activity; and
□ The key campaign themes used by unions today.

For companies that may undergo a union organizing effort, one key is to teach managers to think like organizers. If you appreciate how unions attack companies, you can better defend against those attacks. More important, if you have already identified and improved the areas organizers focus on to gain support, organizers will have a tough time finding the issues needed to get a campaign to take hold. If the ground is barren, the organizer will look elsewhere to plant.

There are three things you need to do in order to start "thinking like an organizer." First, you must thoroughly understand how unions organize workers. Second, you should be aware of the early warning signs of union organizing. Third, you must learn the themes and tactics used by today's organizers.

How Unions Organize Employees
Union organizing is not a mystery. Contrary to what many practitioners preach, unions do have a product to sell. It is

called "a better future." The better they do the job of convincing potential members that they can deliver this product, the more likely they are to win a union-organizing election. Like any other election campaign, unions organize employees using typical grassroots campaign strategies. They visit homes. They pass out campaign literature. They make speeches and hold rallies. Sometimes they even advertise. Sure, unions will also engage in economic pressure tactics against an employer (see The Jagged Edge at the end of this chapter), but the only way unions have any hope of winning is by convincing a majority of employees in an appropriate unit that they will have a better future organized than not.

We had the pleasure of listening to a speech given by Richard Bensinger a several years ago. Bensinger was the very first head of organizing for the AFL-CIO. He left that post after some undisclosed conflicts with the AFL-CIO leadership. Although he never made the admission, my feeling while listening to him speak was that he was just too honest with the leadership to remain politically capable of doing his job. It probably did not take long for Bensinger to burn a lot of bridges when he started naming the heads of unions who were more interested in waiting to collect a pension than expanding their membership. He seemed to hold union leaders to organizing standards they were not prepared to attain. Nevertheless, he also appeared to be a man of great integrity and vision.

Bensinger is currently very disappointed in the labor movement, particularly with regard to organizing. His comments, we feel, are equally applicable to management. Bensinger believes that the labor law is unfairly tilted toward management, and has some compelling arguments in his favor. But, he claims that unions put too much blame on things like the labor law.

Bensinger argues that unions can continue to lobby for card-check recognition and other rules to ease organizing, but until unions create a mass appeal to the idea of being organized, they will never succeed. While he supports ideas like card-check recognition and streamlined voting procedures, Bensinger also says that if the union doesn't have a solid majority, it should walk away. Although we approach the issue from opposite ends of the spectrum, we couldn't agree with the conclusion more.

Companies can also complain about the law favoring unions (there are certainly some compelling arguments on this side as well) and may lobby as hard as they want against changes that make organizing easier. But if they don't ensure that their employees see no need for third party representation, all the lobbying and rules changes are useless.

One thing is certain. No matter which way the campaign gets started, a union can only be successful if there are a substantial number of employees who feel that union representation is in their best interest. Without that basic element, none of the tactics can ultimately succeed. By the same token, the union's worst-run organizing campaign will succeed where the employees of a company see no other way to protect their futures.

How Do Organizing Campaigns Get Started?

There are three primary ways an organizing campaign gets started. First, and most common, is when an employee (or group of employees) gets fed up and contacts the union. This is an "inside-out" campaign.

The second type of campaign is one where the union targets a company, usually as part of an industry or community campaign strategy. The union will try to contact employees at target companies and attempt to start organizing activity even if there was no initial call for help. Sometimes they will "Salt" an employer, sending a union organizer in to apply for a job with the intent that. If hired the Salt will start an organizing campaign.

The third type of organizing campaign is the corporate campaign. This campaign is directed at top management and even corporate board members. It is intended to embarrass a company, usually one that is in the public limelight, into recognizing the union. This is the type of campaign being run against Wal-Mart. Campaigns that start under methods one and two can also use corporate campaign tactics. Other corporate campaigns are intended to create financial problems for an unorganized competitor or to create competitive advantages for unionized companies in the same industry.

Information-Gathering – the Union's "Secret" Weapon
When a union is first approached to organize a company (if "called in" by employees) or when the union is deciding to organize a company from the outside, they will engage in an information-collecting process. This process must be fully understood if you are serious about maintaining your union-free status. Union organizers want to know as much as possible about a target company before beginning a campaign. They will study every aspect of the business in an effort to define campaign issues, learn weaknesses of the company, and customize general themes to the particular facts of the target.

This information-collecting process is described at length in a textbook for union organizers titled *A Troublemakers Handbook*. It contains an interview with Richard Leonard, an organizer for the Oil, Chemical and Atomic Workers Union, who explains how he begins gathering information for an effective campaign. Leonard looks at sources such as a company's 10-K and annual financial reports to get financial data. He researches articles from newspapers and magazines. He uses search services to find out who the major shareholders and company insiders are, and to determine if there are any major institutional investors.

Leonard also conducts group interviews with employees whenever possible. He states, "the thing that empowers workers is knowledge. What we do is based on the notion that the workers know as much if not more about the company than management does, at least at that location. If you can collect this knowledge, it can work miracles. We've seen it happen over and over again."[4]

Union organizers create big research libraries during major organizing drives. I've seen them. They're chock full of company information, and they're impressive. Organizers can sit down with an hourly employee, flip open a slick binder full of newspaper articles touting the company and financial reports showing numbers most hourly workers can't even comprehend, and that employee quickly becomes very upset. Organizers include copies of employee handbook statements that are favorable to the union (especially statements on "at-will" employment and termination). They will show contracts at other workplaces where employees make more money. Their agenda is very much a sales process, and organizers are very good at selling the program.

After spending time talking with employees and gathering information, union organizers are able to target the campaign to the specific issues relevant to that particular work force. They know that the attendance policy isn't enforced fairly across departments or that the supervisor on second shift is a real jerk. They "prove" how much money the company is making (whether true or not) and tell prospective members they need to get their share. Organizers package the sales pitch to account for these known problems. This propaganda is very difficult to counter.

Therefore, when thinking like an organizer, your first job is to gather this same information. The company, of course, is in a

---

[4] Dan LaBotz, *A Troublemaker's Handbook*, (Labor Notes, 1991) p. 132.

much better position to collect it. The problem is that most companies never look at these things through the eyes of an organizer. The process of gathering this information is enlightening and puts your company in a position of strength when it comes to responding to organizing. If you don't gather this information, you are wide open to an invasion when the organizer comes knocking.

Sometimes our clients engage us to "mystery shop" their company using a real former union organizer. Our consultant will investigate the company and build an attack plan just like a union might do if it was targeting that employer. This intervention employs all the same tactics and strategies an aggressive union might use. In the end our client gets a very accurate report of what a union organizer would uncover if he or she were targeting the company. Our clients are often quite surprised at what they look like through the eyes of an organizer.

Recognizing the Early Warning Signs

The purpose of thinking like an organizer is to be prepared for organizing before it occurs. Once your company has integrated the concepts outlined in this book into your employee relations plan, most organizing activity will fall on deaf ears. Yet, while the purpose of this book is to protect your company from organizing activity altogether, there is no way to eliminate the possibility of card-signing activity.

Unions are increasingly sophisticated in their handling of "pre-petition" campaigning, and many companies are taken completely by surprise when a petition is filed. They shouldn't be. Many companies look back after a petition (hindsight is 20/20 after all) and remember an incident and say, "How could we be so blind? We should have known right then that we were being organized." There are many signs that organizing activity is occurring in a workplace. You just have to pay attention to them.

Watching Behavior Change as an Early Warning Signal for Organizing Activity

The labor relations climate is changing rapidly. The NLRB recently finalized new rules to "streamline" the union election process. They also plan to implement even more rules to shrink the period employers have to communicate to employees during a union organizing event. For this reason, early detection of organizing activity (basically the last point before "boom" on the organizing timeline) is more critical than ever.

In this new labor law environment where time is everything, training managers and supervisors to recognize the signs of behavior change in the workplace is critical. This is normally the first early sign of union activity (and is always the first sign of something awry in the workplace). It is also **the part that almost everyone gets wrong**. The traditional way "early warning" is taught betrays a huge misunderstanding about the best way to train front line supervisors to create an early warning system for organizing activity. You cannot get this wrong. Early warning is critical to your success.

Although most companies and labor professionals know that supervisors are important, **most focus training resources on the wrong topics and provide limited resources to the topics where they should focus**. This problem is compounded in our current "ambush election" environment.

A front line manager's job is a very difficult juggling act. They have one foot in the day-to-day operations, and the other in management. Many are promoted directly out of the hourly ranks and tend to relate better to their employees than they do to management. A weak or new supervisor will commonly respond, "I don't know why those guys make decisions like this. They don't really understand how things work, and I can't really do anything about it. I just have to do what I'm told."

Through lack of ability, experience or training, frontline supervisors often fall into traps and make mistakes. When faced with the daily pressures of getting products out the door, maintaining high quality levels, responding to customer issues, and handling paperwork and reporting requirements, there is a tendency to gloss over mistakes and avoid learning opportunities.

The primary reason that people pay lip service to supervisor training is because it is difficult to implement effective training that provides learning experiences that are quantifiable, memorable and actionable, while not interfering with normal work processes

So what does this mean to your early warning system? How is it possible to add yet another layer of skill sets to your supervisors' repertoire without overwhelming them and decreasing their overall effectiveness?

The key is to reduce the scope of what front line supervisors are asked to do. As far as union organizing is concerned, most companies try to make miniature labor law experts of these already over-taxed managers! This strategy is difficult to do well. Labor law is incredibly complex. As rapidly as labor law changes even labor lawyers have a tough time advising clients. Do not misunderstand this. I'm not saying to avoid your labor attorney – quite the opposite, you'll need your labor attorney on speed-dial. But limit the scope of your training, no matter who does it.

I've done legal training for first level leaders hundreds of times. I've seen supervisors go through training on all the TIPS and FOE rules related to employee union communication, and the nuances of labor law. I've watched overburdened managers just shrink under the weight of labor law training, even when it is made as simple and entertaining as possible. It's complicated stuff. For somebody who's not a lawyer, asking them to become comfortable talking about these issues when they're worried that they'll get themselves or their company in trouble, is asking a lot.

The NLRB is constantly moving the goal-posts based on its political make-up and various factual situations. Because labor law can be so fluid, don't try to train supervisors to learn a bunch of labor law. This can even hold true for your upper management and HR administrators. What is the proper mindset when considering how to best utilize these front line supervisors in proper union organizing defense? I suggest a concept called Tripwire Team™ Training.

The idea of creating a "tripwire" is to train supervisors to recognize the sometimes subtle behavioral signs of union organizing, and then have them "push the silent alarm button," so that the Jump Team can then enter the picture and ascertain the proper response. This training works because it is based on real-life situations developed from the former union organizers on our team. Once they get a picture of what is going on "behind the curtain," they begin to notice behaviors and vulnerabilities that they would ignore otherwise.

What are the advantages of the tripwire approach? First, it's easy to do. The training focuses on how organizers attack companies and what goes on behind the scenes. It includes a simulation of exactly what's happening when a union organizer picks out and begins meeting with employees. The focus is heavily weighted on employee behavior. This type of training teaches supervisors what types of behaviors are going to change inside their plant or facility when organizing activity hits.

An additional value of this approach is that beyond simply predicting union activity, focusing on behavioral issues provides early warning signs of other kinds of potential problems in the work place – from substance abuse and alcoholism, to harassment or bullying, to personality conflicts between employees.

Why does this work? There are certain behaviors that change when these types of events are going on behind the scenes. If you can train supervisors and managers to be skilled at recognizing the behavior change, you can get early warning of all of these potential events.

This type of training is different than the standard "early warning signs" drill. This isn't stumbling across notices of employees meeting off property, or finding authorization cards in the bathroom, or getting strange requests from employees. Those are indeed "signs," but they are typically later-stage signs. The early tip-off comes from observing behavior, not "things." The idea is to understand what happens during organizing – the behind-the-scenes agendas involved – and then translating that into how it would present itself in workplace behavior.

Here's an example. Suppose a union meeting occurs one night, run according to a typical organizer playbook. Employees are asked to do various things by the organizer – including, to keep things quiet and to assume the worst about their management team. The employees who attended will behave differently the next day.

Employees sometimes fear that if management learns of their organizing activity they will be disciplined or terminated (which of course is illegal and should never be considered). Employees who may have earlier had good relationships with a manager may now change their attitude or stop communicating. This is not just a sign of organizing activity, but also of other potential problems (a fight among employees, possible discrimination or harassment, alcohol or drug problems, etc.) These changes should be thoroughly investigated when they occur.

Another behavior supervisors should notice is the social relationships among coworkers. For example, employees who lead organizing campaigns, those who want the "protection" they think a union provides, are often low performers not considered leaders in the workforce. (Of course, there are exceptions to the rule, and an employee has to possess some leadership capacity to get a campaign going.) If employees with this profile suddenly take a leadership role or gain a following among employees who did not spend much time with them before, it is a sign of organizing activity.

If supervisors are properly trained to pay attention when "something doesn't feel right" about how employees are behaving, the tripwire is created. The supervisor's job is simply to notify the company of these incidents as they happen. If it appears that the unusual behaviors are more widespread and/or consistent over a period of time, it's the company's turn to drill down to get at the issues behind the behavior.

There are 3 critical advantages to implementing the Tripwire Team™ concept. First, supervisors are more likely to sound the alarm because:

- they have no fear of messing up due to fear of legal liability, and
- they haven't had to "cross the line" to management's side in the eyes of their employees. You are much more likely to receive notice of activity under this Plan.

Second, you know that issues get handled by the most skilled people available. The other problem with training supervisors to "handle" incidents with employees is that you may never learn about these incidents. An over-confident supervisor will simply assume the issue is taken care of – even if it was handled poorly – and never give you the opportunity to know about the activity until it is too late.

Third, you can focus your training investment more productively. If you limit your labor relations training investment on the simple task of creating a Tripwire Team™, the rest of your training resources can then go into training them to be great supervisors. Talk to them about creating a positive work environment, teach them coaching skills, support them in being good managers, and don't worry so much about making them good at handling labor issues. The investment that you make in creating good positive leaders far outweighs anything that you're going to get in terms of labor law training.

What Happens Just Before "Boom"?

The idea behind the Tripwire concept is that you should notice the behavior changes in the workplace long before a union organizing campaign gets traction. But what if you miss the signs? There are a few warning signs that aren't really "early" but still might give you a jump on a union campaign that is about to explode.

Here are some of what we call the "late warning signs" of union activity:
1. Union authorization cards or fliers.
2. Strangers meeting with employees on or near company property.
3. Rumors of cardsigning, meetings or other union activities.
4. Open talk about unions, pro-union slogans or pro-union graffiti.
5. Employees compiling contact information about co-workers, or contact lists "walking off"
6. Increased complaints or "grievances"
7. Unusual interest in company policies and procedures
8. Union activity in the community

Next to each warning sign, we outline how each sign should be interpreted.

- Union Authorization Cards – Fliers: As outlined in the first chapter, union authorization cards are the last step before a union files a petition If you see authorization cards or leaflets, you have an organizing campaign on your hands. Contact your labor attorney immediately and get your counter-organizing campaign started.

- Strangers Meeting with Employees Near the Company: Organizers don't usually get this public unless they are very close to getting enough cards to file a petition or are having difficulty meeting with people outside of work. Unions don't want management to learn about the activity until they are ready to file their petition.

- Rumors of Cardsigning, Meetings or Other Union Activity: As the union attempts to expand support outside of its core group of supporters, it will inevitably have to approach people without being able to predict where they stand on the issue. If union workers approach a strong company supporter, this will often be communicated to a supervisor. Sometimes an observant (or lucky) supervisor will overhear a conversation. Of course, if you've conducted Tripwire training you are much more likely to spot these signs. This sign requires immediate response.

- Open Talk About Unions, Pro-Union Slogans as Graffiti: This sign does not necessarily mean that organizing activity is occurring. In every large work force there always seems to be a few people who, in response to any work problem, will cry, "If we had a union here you wouldn't be able to get away with that." Same thing goes for graffiti. However, if these signs are occurring more frequently than normal, you should certainly start looking for other early warning signs.

- Employees Compiling Contact Information on Co-workers: The union's preferred method of early campaigning is phone calls and home visits away from the workplace. In order to do this, however, organizers have to collect phone numbers and addresses. They will enlist inside organizers for this information. Most companies have policies against this sort of activity, as well they should. If you catch someone engaging in this subversive activity, that employee should be disciplined under the policy and you should start looking for some of the other warning signs. Do not try to find out directly from the individual whether he or she was compiling the information for union organizing purposes – this creates potential unfair labor practice liability and could prevent you from enforcing your policy.

- Increased Complaints or "Grievances" About "Past Practice": Complaints certainly do not always mean organizing activity is occurring, but an unusual increase in the number or frequency of complaints often corresponds with organizing activity. You should pay particular attention to the way the complaints are worded. If words like "grievance," "past practice," "arbitration" or other terms commonly found in labor contracts are being used, the likelihood is that someone with a union background is encouraging the complaints.

- Unusual Interest in Company Policy, Handbooks: An unusual increase in the number of requests for employee handbooks or copies of policies can also be a signal of organizing activity. Union organizers want to have copies of these documents and will ask employees for copies of their employee handbook or policy manuals.

- Union Activity in the Community: Another important signal that should alert you to be on the lookout for organizing activity is an increase in organizing in your community, especially at a competitor or business in close proximity to your location. Unions will often focus on a particular industry and if they are organizing one business in an area, they will also try to generate interest at other businesses in the area.

Today's Key Issues and Campaign Themes

Another important part of thinking like an organizer is to know and understand the themes and language organizers use to persuade employees to join a union. There are a number of common themes used in almost all campaigns today. It is important to be able to respond to these issues and, more important, to educate your employees regarding them.

One major theme today is that of wage inequality. Unions always promise wage and benefit increases as part of their sales pitch to employees. In addition to making these promises, which employees may or may not believe, unions also make a broader social argument about distribution of wealth. The "occupy movement" is the most recent example of this narrative, with its "we are the 99%" messaging. Union organizers point to statistics showing the increased gap between the highest paid and lowest paid members of the workforce and claim that unions are the only way to reduce income disparities and build up the middle class.

Unions also highlight the large compensation packages of corporate leaders and point to corporate profits to make their claim. The AFL-CIO sponsors a popular Web page called "CEO Pay Watch" (http://www.aflcio.org) that tracks the compensation of several major CEOs. Especially in the post "great-recession" economy of today, this hits home with many employees.

A second important theme today is workplace democracy. Unions promise to give employees a voice in their workplace. Union organizers make employees believe that, with a union, they will be able to change the things they don't like about their workplace. This theme is compelling and promises to give power to those who may feel powerless.

Another theme used in campaigns today is that of dignity and justice. A now-famous industry campaign by the Service Employees Union is "Justice for Janitors." It focuses on organizing housekeeping, maintenance and janitorial departments in companies across the country. Unions convince employees who may feel treated unfairly or discriminated against that the union can prevent this treatment. And this ploy works. The table below shows how union win rates increase when dignity and fairness issues are a major issue.

1986-87 NLRB Elections

UNION TACTIC	Sample Proportion or mean	Proportion or mean for wins	Percentage win rate*
70% or more employees surveyed one-on-one	.53	.57	.46 (.39)
Bargaining committee created before election	.15	.23	.64 (.39)
Solidarity days used	.12	.15	.53 (.41)
Union held rallies	.03	.04	.50 (.42)
Union held job actions	.02	.05	.10 (.41)
Community-labor coalitions used	.16	.19	.50 (.41)
Union used media	.11	.14	.52 (.41)
Dignity, fairness primary issues	.27	.36	.56 (.37)
Total number rank-and-file tactics used	2.12	2.69	NA

Richard Leonard explains the strategy:

> "In all such newsletters or other communications – such as articles in local newspapers that you clip and mail – it's important for the union to present itself as commanding the high ground. This means that the company is allowed ownership of the goals of profit and personal ambition, greed, etc., while the union appropriates the goals of quality, customer satisfaction, productivity, fairness, equitable social cost accounting, etc."[5]

Employers who wish to remain union-free need to be aware of these common themes and make sure that they don't allow the union to "appropriate the goals" of fairness and dignity (which in reality they have no claim to in the first place). When employees are approached by a union organizer with these issues, they should have an immediate reaction of, "I don't need a union for that – my company already does it." If you accomplish this, you will never have an organizing problem.

The Jagged Edge – What's New In Organizing

Unions are desperately trying to organize new members. Union membership has suffered a steep decline over the last several decades. Unions now represent 6.7 percent of private-sector workers, the lowest level in history. There are many causes for this decline. Global economic forces, public skepticism about unions, and enlightened management practices are among the most important.

This decline has resulted in a lot of soul searching among unions. It has also resulted in a fair amount of innovation. Adopting lessons learned from their success in political

---

[5] Dan LaBotz, *A Troublemaker's Handbook*, (Labor Notes, 1991) p. 135.

campaigns (where they have been much more successful than in organizing campaigns), unions have certainly improved their win rates, even if that has not translated into large numbers or new members.

Unions are winning a larger percentage of organizing elections than ever. Unions are not filing as many petitions as in years past, but they appear to be picking their targets better. This is illustrated in the chart below:

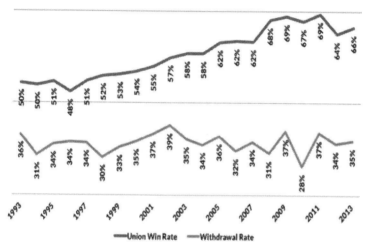

Figure 3.1 – Union Win Rates 1993-2013

A significant amount of attention is being paid to organizing at the very highest ranks of various AFL-CIO unions. The focus on organizing has even led to a schism in organized labor. In the summer of 2005, several large unions such as the Service Employees International Union, the Teamsters, UNITE-HERE, the United Food and Commercial Workers, the Laborers, the Carpenters, and the United Farmworkers of America left the AFL-CIO and formed their own labor federation, Change to Win. The split was at least partially because of personality differences between the labor leaders, but the Change to Win leaders, most notably SEIU President Andy Stern, felt that the AFL-CIO leaders were not devoting sufficient resources to union organizing. While the long-term future of Change to Win is unclear, there is no doubt that these unions strongly believe that labor should focus on organizing and will continue to press for more union organizing against employers.

A terrific amount of work still needs to be done in order to weed out some of the old-school thinking in unions across the country, but there is certainly more being said and done about organizing now than in recent memory. The AFL-CIO has also asked that its member unions pledge a minimum of 10% of assets to organizing activities.

Unions are leveraging community-based contacts to assist with organizing efforts. A variety of new and bold techniques are gaining popularity. A few are listed below, with a brief description of how each operates:

- Corporate Campaigns – Unions are taking on large targets and using national resources to attack them. They are using corporate campaign tactics previously used in strike situations to organize large corporate employers. Unions now pressure corporate board members and executives, personalize the campaigns, and employ legal guerrilla warfare tactics and other strategies against them. Some of the best current examples of this tactic are the sweatshop campaigns against Wal-Mart and other big box retailers. Also, more direct campaigns against health care giants can be found by looking at Kaiser Permanente, Catholic Healthcare and Genesis.[6]

- Political and Religious Leaders – Unions today do not hesitate to enlist the support of political and religious

---

[6] For an excellent discussion see *Devil at my Doorstep*, David Bego (2009). You can order this book directly from LRI.

leaders in organizing campaigns. In several recent cases, local priests and ministers have been enlisted to convince employees to join a union. Organizing meetings are held in churches and churches distribute handouts listing biblical quotations "encouraging" organizing activities. These are especially effective because it makes it seem as if the employer opposing unionization is not only anti-union, but also anti-church, which is a public relations nightmare.

- "Virtual" Organizing – Several recent campaigns have occurred largely over the Internet. Borders Books, Microsoft and Intel have all fought (and continue to fight) Internet-based campaigns intended to increase support for unions. The AFL-CIO is using its Web page expertly in trying to organize new workers, and many international unions (Steelworkers, Autoworkers, Teamsters and Service Employees to name just a few) are doing the same.

- Collective Bargaining as a Civil Right - this is a prevalent theme in leftist literature today and is increasingly common rhetoric in contemporary political discourse and in organizing campaigns. Using the same themes and arguments of civil rights leaders of the 1960s, labor leaders hope to usher in a new era of rights founded on the freedom to organize and bargain collectively. The United Auto Workers have made this a key argument in their recent drive to organize workers at foreign auto manufacturers in the South.

- Class Warfare – One of the more popular themes for union organizers today is the gap between rich and poor in the United States. The most recent version of this is Labor's alliance with the "Occupy Wall Street movement." Other examples include CEO Paywatch, discussed earlier. It paints an ugly picture of corporate greed. Equal pay is another powerful issue intended to motivate women, who today make up the majority of wage earners in the American workforce.

- Alliances with Alt-labor Groups - Unions are also leveraging relationships with left wing groups in the United States and around the world (Occupy Wall Street, Fight for 15, Warehouse Workers United, Jobs with Justice and the Restaurant Opportunity Center are a few of the best known, but there are many others). Unions will use these groups like immigrant centers, student activist groups, environmental groups, social justice organizations and others to add scale and voice to a protest. They will also try to apply foreign pressure to companies owned overseas, especially in Europe where unions have much more power than they do here. Whenever possible they will attack a corporate target on multiple issues including environmental or human rights issues.

These are a few of the themes and tactics targeted companies must be prepared to respond to over the coming years. Unions are desperate to increase their memberships and remain very powerful organizations. Unions have proven again and again that, when pushed, they can bring political, social and economic power to bear to accomplish their goals. For an employer to remain union-free over the long haul, it is critical to remember these facts and to employ strategies that respond to the unions' strength.

Take Action

- ☐ What are the weaknesses in your company? Investigate and counteract the areas union organizers are most likely to focus on.
- ☐ Would your supervisors recognize behavioral changes in employees if it occurred? Do you ask supervisors to learn a lot of labor law? Reduce the scope of what you ask frontline managers to do if necessary, in order to allow them room to notice changes in behavior.
- ☐ Are you aware of the most commonly used union campaign strategies in your community and industry? If not, make it a priority.

Chapter 4

Motivations - Why Employees Choose to Be Union-Free

"Here choose I. Joy be the consequence!"
William Shakespeare, The Merchant of Venice

What You'll Learn In This Chapter
- ❑ The three categories of union-free motivation: relevance, pragmatism and fear;
- ❑ Identifying the primary union-free motivation of your current group of employees;
- ❑ How the primary motivation impacts your employee relations efforts; and
- ❑ Modifying your strategy based on the primary union-free motivation of your employees.

If Employees Want a Union, They'll Get One.
There are many freedoms taken for granted in our country and many more privileges assumed. Unions claim that the right to organize a union, for example, is a civil right on an equal level with the right to be free from racial or sexual discrimination. On the other hand, many employers feel they have a right to operate their business as they see fit – without a union.

We don't know how many times we have heard a client, after he or she first learns of organizing activity, calmly declare, "We won't be having a union here." It is as if to say that by willing it away, the union will be gone. If only the solution were that simple. The fact is that, legally, if a majority of employees in any company want a union and are willing to go through the proper procedure, they will get one. Period.

As ridiculous as the recent civil rights rhetoric from the house of labor might be, one thing is certain -- a protected right exists for employees to organize a union. Unlike other civil rights (i.e., rights based on characteristics for which an individual has no choice like race, gender or national origin), employees also have a right to refrain from organizing activity. Therefore, labor's call for the supremacy of the right to organize is misguided -- it ignores the right of others (the majority, in fact) to refrain from organizing. Nevertheless, the employer who wishes to remain union-free must recognize the nature of the rights granted to employees under the NLRA.

Many employers, especially smaller companies that may have begun as family businesses or closely held organizations, refuse to understand the concept that employees have the right to bargain collectively over wages, hours and working conditions. The fact that a person can build a successful business without any interference whatsoever and then, after one simple vote, suddenly have to negotiate with an outside third party seems un-American. Some company owners go so far as to close down their businesses to avoid giving up control over these issues.

The simple fact remains that an employer who plans to remain in business and remain union-free can only do so with the consent of the individuals employed by the organization. While this concept is often difficult for business owners to grasp, it is fundamental to an understanding of how to remain union-free. If you understand that the decision to operate union-free is not yours alone, but ultimately resides in the hands of the individuals who work for you, your strategy will begin to gain clarity.

Relevance, Pragmatism and Fear

It is imperative to gain the support of your employees. The majority of them must believe that they prefer working directly with you rather than through an outside bargaining agent. Employees will reach this conclusion for any number of reasons. This nearly infinite number of motivations can be separated, however, into three broad categories: relevance, pragmatism and fear. These categories are summarized below, ranging from the most preferable motivation to the least preferable:

3 Categories of Union-Free Motivation

Relevance – These employees like their current work environment, are loyal to the current leadership, and are internally motivated to continue representing themselves as individuals in the workplace. It is virtually impossible to convince this group to seek unionization as an alternative.

Pragmatism – While employees in this environment may not love their current employer, they have examined the facts and do not want to pay for representation they can provide for themselves or feel will be ineffective. These employees choose the devil they know versus the one they don't.

Fear – These employees are the easiest to organize. They choose to remain unorganized due to either implicit or, worse, explicit threats regarding their job security, the company's security or the outcome of negotiations. Groups of employees with this motivation have little trust of management and are difficult to turn around.

It is important for you to recognize that a workforce may contain groups of employees with each of these motivations (or even individuals with more than one motivation) i.e., some may generally feel that a union is not relevant to them, while others may not consider unionization because they fear conflict in the workplace.

How Union-free Motivation Affects Your Plan

Whatever the myriad reasons your employees have for remaining union-free, there is normally one overriding motivation. As an employer you must understand this motivation. It drives any attempt to re-work your employee relations strategy. Let's look at the three categories of motivations in greater detail in order to identify how different motivations will alter your approach to re-tooling your employee relations program.

Fear

Fear is the least effective motivation. Unscrupulous or simply unsophisticated employers use this approach during the organizing campaign process, but it is also used by employers who simply have not experienced organizing problems before. Unions complain about these employer tactics and blame them for the loss of union density in recent years – even though unions frequently use fear and intimidation techniques during their organizing activities.

Experience teaches, however, that employers who rely on fear as a primary motivational tool are the most likely to lose an organizing campaign. This occurs for two reasons. First, unions are very effective at turning fear of employer tactics into reasons for choosing a union. An employer who fires employees or threatens to close down an operation during an organizing campaign is a sitting duck when it comes to organizing success for unions. Not only do these tactics create a huge number of issues from which employees feel they need protection, but they also create potential unfair labor practice liability. These charges, if proven egregious enough, can lead to a legal order to bargain with the union.

Second, fear can only motivate individuals for limited periods before employees become numb to it. Eventually, good employees will leave an employer who relies on fear. They will seek out employment in environments that are less stressful.

Employers who rely on fear are not employers of choice and will eventually be left with lower-skilled and unmotivated employees (those who may feel they are unemployable, for example) while competitors gain higher-caliber workers. This scenario is not a recipe for long-term business success. As today's focus on work/family balance suggests, maintaining a healthy work environment is a key method of attracting talent. In today's increasingly knowledge-based economy, the company with the most talent wins.

Pragmatism

This motivation isn't as big a problem as fear. In fact, when I see a company whose union-free strategy is driven by fear (especially when that strategy has failed and the employees are openly seeking a union), I will often recommend they turn to pragmatism as the primary communication model. Nevertheless, in the long run this strategy is also unsustainable.

Pragmatism motivates employees to remain union-free by means of logic. Explaining the disadvantages of collective bargaining, the risks associated with strikes or recounting examples of employees who were failed by their union are effective strategies. These appeals can be very persuasive with workers – very few employees who look at the facts objectively will decide that unionization is desirable.

Pragmatic appeals, however, particularly after an extended period of time, begin to lose their effectiveness and eventually fail. An employer who relies only on pointing out the negatives of unions, while failing to respond to internal problems, does not earn the trust of its employees. Unions can return the favor, reminding employees of their grievances and complaints against their employer. If these grievances and complaints occur over an extended period while the company has made empty promises to resolve them, the union's pragmatism can be very persuasive.

The "give us another chance" campaign is just not that persuasive. An employer who fails to respond to employee concerns in effect says, "We don't care what you think." Employees tend to respond in kind.

The High Road

The Service Employees International Union (SEIU) issued a manual for its health care organizers titled "The High Road: A Winning Strategy for Managing Conflict and Communicating Effectively in Hospital Worker Organizing Campaigns." The manual is based on a two-year study of experimental approaches to organizing hospital units. The study included opinion polls and focus groups of hospital workers. The study reached four conclusions:

- Decisions made by hospital workers to join a union are primarily made for pragmatic reasons;
- Hospital workers' concerns about conflict outweigh their desire for a voice at their hospital;
- The most effective strategy for unions, even in hospitals where employer opposition is intense, is to stay on the high road with a positive campaign; and
- The methods that organizers use to manage conflicts in an organizing campaign can dramatically influence the outcome.

The lessons the SEIU learned provide some important lessons for management as well.

First, the tried and true tactic that organizations use when attacked by unions is fear. Companies often base a campaign on the alarming issues of strikes, violence, trials and a number of other "hot button" issues. These issues can turn fence-sitters into company supporters or, at least, reduce their support for the union. Even when not relying on these concerns, companies will focus on the conflict injected into the workplace by the presence of the union, and the wedge it drives between employees and management. The SEIU found that the vast majority of the time employers have plenty of evidence to point out such a conflict.

Second, the decision to vote for or against unionization is not visceral, but pragmatic. This is a critical lesson. Instilling fear only works to the extent that the target is affected in a way that enforces your position. The SEIU found that employees weighed fear of unionization against the perceived advantages of the union. By downplaying this fear and refusing to inject additional anxiety into the campaign, the SEIU learned that employees are more likely to weigh the alternatives fairly. The SEIU also learned that by taking the high road they defuse some of the fear injected by employers, thereby exposing it for the tactical ploy it often is.

Stressing the possibility of confrontations and conflict during the campaign, the SEIU found, can be effective for management, but has its costs. The SEIU learned that by taking the high road (moving from fear to pragmatism) they could defuse the conflict often present during a union campaign. This teaches organizers to respond to conflict by explaining that it is just an unfortunate tactic used by employers and it will go away once the election is won. By appealing to the pragmatic side and helping to defuse conflict (not adding to it, and not giving management excuses to escalate it), the union gains the upper hand during the campaign. Unions, like employers, would ultimately like to shift from the pragmatic motivation to one of relevance.

Relevance

This strategy is by far the most effective and sustainable of the three. Employees who honestly feel that their work environment is fulfilling and their jobs are challenging, rewarding and important will not seek unionization and will reject the notion out of hand when it is proposed. They simply cannot imagine what a union could contribute to their work environment. This work environment is "inoculated" in a sense, because it is not fertile ground for organizing activity.

Operating Union Free is Not an Accident

Before deciding on a direction to take with an employee relations strategy, you must not only know what issues your employees face, but also what works to motivate them. If your employees are primarily motivated by fear, the first step is building trust between management and co-workers. If pragmatism is the prime motivator, the first step is moving past this calculated support for the company and on to internal motivation. This motivation will manifest itself in support for the company. If relevance is the primary motivation of your employees (in which case there is probably little current fear of union activity), then the key is to maintain those aspects of the employment environment that create this internal motivation.

This sounds good, but how does it work in practice? Let's say we have a company that has identified a perception (real or imagined) that supervisors are "playing favorites." If your employees are motivated by pragmatism or relevance, you might conduct small group meetings in order to identify which supervisors are biased or which policies are being administered unfairly. Armed with this information, you may either retrain supervisors, revise policies or educate employees about application of those policies (depending, of course, on whether the perception is real or imagined).

If fear is the prime motivator, however, the strategy changes. In this circumstance, small group sessions tend to be ineffective. Employees motivated by fear are unlikely to confide in managers or supervisors who may not act in the best interests of employees. Therefore, anonymous surveys (or focus groups conducted by outside consultants) become a valuable method for identifying supervisors or policies that may be problematic. These sessions should occur in the context of broader training in the areas of approachability and candor, and must be conducted with the participation of top management and line level supervisors. In this way trust can begin to develop among all levels of employees.

Depending on the history of the company, the process of identifying and managing these issues can take anywhere from a few months to several years. Moreover, certain issues may be "fear" issues while others may be "pragmatic" ones, requiring different approaches. The important thing is to identify the issues and develop a strategy that targets the motivation of all employees instead of applying a "one-size fits all" solution.

Moving From Fear to Relevance

Your goal should be to move the primary agent behind issues from fear to relevance. This process is a continuum, and certain issues may always have fear as the underlying motivation. The goal is to move as many issues as possible from fear to pragmatism and then from pragmatism to relevance. This means there is an educational process that must take place when solving any issue.

Implementing this educational process with employees first involves understanding and believing that the employer does have their best interests at heart. While they will not always agree with the employer, employees should never feel that the employer does not care about their concerns. The next step is to educate employees about how and why decisions are made. This is a dialogue, and employees are given the opportunity to contribute ideas and provide input as to the successful operation of the company.

During this phase, employees can learn firsthand the pros and cons of various strategies, like why a particular investment was made versus another. Employee involvement makes them more likely to choose the pragmatic decision of sticking with their employer rather than turning to any outside third party. Finally, after establishing a history of solving problems together (particularly when the employer is perceived to value and actively collaborate with employees) the pragmatic motivation turns into one of relevance.

Client Story: Strategy Driven By Employee Motivation

One of the first things I try to assess with a new client is where he or she stands on the fear-pragmatism-relevance continuum. Recently we began working with a manufacturer who had four plants – one in the Southwest, one in the West, one in the Southeast and a new one in the Midwest. Our firm conducted surveys at each location.

The four plants each had distinct personalities. The manufacturer's Southwest location was organized by the steelworkers and the working relationships there were quite hostile. This plant was a workplace primarily motivated by fear. The Midwest plant and the plant in the West were both "middle of the pack" with a good amount of uncertainty about job security issues. The plant in the Southeast was one of the highest rated I'd ever seen.

The first order of business after every survey is communicating the results. Next the client develops action steps based on that location's issues and "personality." According to the survey results, the Southwest plant employees exhibited extreme distrust of management. Taking public action and communicating the results in focus group sessions with our consultants would demonstrate the company's commitment to this plant.

These sessions were sometimes heated, but each group expressed surprise that management actually invested time and effort to communicate the results. Some employees even said they would have answered a few of the questions differently if they believed management intended to seriously consider the results. After exploring each issue in depth, it turned out that much of the conflict was based on misperception. Few employees could come up with concrete examples to back up poor scoring on certain statements. These sessions, while not an ultimate solution, provided an effective starting point for building bridges between management and its unionized employees.

The Western and Midwest plants required a different approach. While there was not open hostility toward management, these employees still faced significant issues that needed to be discussed. For example, they expressed concern about the direction local management was taking. At these locations a corporate human resources representative presented the survey results.

I helped them put together a communication package that the representative used to discuss the results and identify issues that the company would focus on in the coming months. To contend with these issues, specific action plans were outlined and teams were created to respond to the issues raised. Local management at each plant was given the key role of ensuring that these teams were given the opportunity to succeed. The process implemented in these plants constituted a more pragmatic approach.

The Southeast location had very few issues and required little process implementation. Local management was dispatched to communicate the survey results and the areas where improvement should be made. While these meetings were (predictably) very positive, local management made clear that the company was not resting on these accomplishments but would take action to improve in every area it could.

Many businesses rely on fear as a primary union-free motivation. Depending on the type of industry and its geographic location, this strategy may work in the short term. However, this strategy is without a doubt the least sustainable and also the least productive in the long term. Relying on an employment environment driven by fear is precarious. Given the wrong set of circumstances, these companies can quickly become targets of unions and will often become organized.

More important, in today's labor market these companies are not employers of choice. All things being equal, companies that rule by fear will have higher turnover and be less competitive than competitors who stress an open and collaborative work environment. From a business perspective, employee relations is an area where the right thing to do is also the smart thing to do.

Employees motivated to remain union-free by pragmatism are a step further in the right direction. These employees have decided, perhaps through enlightened self-interest, that they do not want a union. The disadvantage of relying on this motivation is that it can be turned against a company, as shown by the SEIU's significant improvement in organizing health care units through pragmatism. Although much preferable to fear, pragmatism is not a cure-all.

In order to guarantee union-free status, a company must make unions irrelevant to their employees. Creating a work environment where unions are seen as irrelevant is hard work. It is not enough to simply explain the disadvantages of unions. Employees must feel in their core that their company is a great place to work. The thought of unionization never crosses these employees' minds. If forced to confront the idea, the notion is comical to them. An employer who accomplishes this difficult task creates an employee relations environment that is collaborative, productive and generally, more profitable.

Take Action

☐ Are your employees primarily motivated by relevance, pragmatism or fear? Modify your strategy to fit their motivation.

☐ Do your employees feel that they can speak honestly with their first level leaders?

☐ Do you have leaders who rely on fear or pragmatism when they talk about unions? Talk to them about the importance relevance.

Chapter 5

Third-Party Intervention, Vulnerability and Your Union-Free Strategy

"The art of being wise is the art of knowing what to overlook."
William James

What You'll Learn In This Chapter

☐ What can go wrong with "traditional" vulnerability assessments;

☐ How the Hawthorne, Salem and Halo effects damage vulnerability assessment protocols;

☐ The 3 main areas of vulnerability every organization must assess;

☐ What items should be part of a successful employment practices audit;

☐ How to establish the external vulnerability for your area; and

☐ What impact your company's size has on its vulnerability.

Nothing is more depressing than seeing the president or owner of a business receive an NLRB petition for the first time. Their initial reaction is often one of shock. They find it difficult to believe that employees whom they consider family would betray them and their business. These employers are usually at a loss to explain what issues, if any, exist in their work force. When they begin to look, they find that the process of identifying the origins of the organizing campaign is both difficult and revealing.

Ultimately, employers faced with petitions learn that they ignored telltale signs of discontent among employees. Now, they must act quickly. The learning curve is steep and expensive. There are many costs associated with fighting an NLRB organizing campaign. These are often coupled with demoralizing battles against regulatory agencies and the court system. Further, the constraints of this legal environment often prevent employers from acting on their first impulse – fixing the problem.

Instituting proactive measures to improve the employment environment is the natural reaction of most employers when they are notified of employee discontent. However, positive changes in terms or conditions of employment are many times considered bribes and are thus illegal. Likewise, team-based responses to employment issues are regularly disallowed in this environment. In sum, the employer's hands are tied once the NLRB petition is filed.

Employers embroiled in this mess typically wish for one thing: that they had known of their employees' unhappiness prior to their turning to the union. They want to turn back the clock.

The bad news is that you can't turn back the clock – once "boom" has happened you can't put the bomb back in its case. This is why vulnerability assessment – identifying issues far left of the boom event – is the critical foundation of any positive employee relations strategy.

Unfortunately, a symptom prevalent in these companies is that employees feel constrained in some way from discussing these problems with management, or worse, they have expressed their problems and been ignored.

No system exists that can tell you with complete accuracy if your company will be attacked by a union or another outside party. Human beings simply do not act as rationally as management consultants or company owners often would wish. At any time, and under a variety of almost infinite circumstances, employees can turn to outside third parties who are waiting and watching for the opportunity to intervene. The idea behind vulnerability assessment is to help identify whether or not an outside third party would find "fertile ground" for intervention at a particular company.

The "Embarrassing Truth" About Vulnerability Assessment

You can't quite put your finger on it, but you know you're not feeling right. And it seems to be getting worse. It's late, so you head to the emergency room. A nurse weighs you, sticks a thermometer in your mouth, and takes your blood pressure. After an interminable wait, an intern comes in, looks over your vitals, asks you a few questions, prescribes an antibiotic and sends you home to ride it out. "You should be fine in a few days," he says. You're not so sure.

After a few days, you don't feel better, so you get an appointment with your family physician. He orders blood work and an MRI, shaking his head at the slipshod treatment you received in the ER. Once the test results are in he gives you an accurate diagnosis of the real problem and prescribes the proper treatment to speed your recovery.

Would that ER visit frustrate you? It would frustrate anyone. But visits like that happen at companies around the country when they hire consultants and law firms to conduct "vulnerability assessments" of their organizations. Wouldn't you want your vulnerability assessment process to be more like an MRI? This chapter will show you how.

The traditional vulnerability assessment process has always bothered me. Too much voodoo and not enough science. I have seen the vulnerability assessment processes of many consulting firms and law firms across the country. Often I see them after we are hired to help a company who, like the patient above, got a "clean bill of health" from a prior assessment. The process used by these firms is just like the one I used for clients in both my law and consulting practice, the same process our consultants used until recently. They treated symptoms but rarely addressed root causes.

Every vulnerability assessment process I've seen is primarily driven by the "gut feeling" of managers or consultants. They are often inaccurate. Frustrated by the simplistic nature of how vulnerability assessments are conducted, I've looked high and low for how to improve the process. This is what I've found.

The "Traditional" Vulnerability Assessment Process
Let's take a look at how vulnerability assessment is typically conducted today.

First it is important to understand that there are two types of vulnerability. There is <u>external</u> vulnerability and <u>internal</u> vulnerability.

External vulnerability is based on factors like geography, industry type, union density in the immediate area, state labor laws and other political factors. This external factor is often completely ignored in many vulnerability assessment

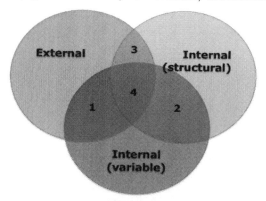

1. Higher risk of "outside-in", but few "self-inflicted" wounds
2. Higher risk of a "home grown" campaign, lower risk of "outside-in"
3. Higher risk of external campaign, may not gain traction internally
4. Most vulnerable target for union organizing

Figure 5.1 – Is Your Company Vulnerable to an Organizing Attack?

protocols – and it is vital. It's like trying to treat someone suffering from sleep problems, without asking about their work schedule, their family situation or where they live.

Internal vulnerability can be further broken down into two components, structural and variable. Structural internal vulnerability is based on factors within the company that are hard or impossible to change. The type of work being done (factory work or work in the elements) or the physical work environment are examples. The company has little control over these factors. Other factors such as relationships with supervisors, communications, policies, and even the people performing the work are variable factors. The company has more control over these factors.

The interplay between structural and variable internal vulnerability factors can sometimes explain why two plants within the same company doing similar work under similar conditions can have very different vulnerability profiles. This is especially true if you have bad leaders at one location and good ones at another. But it can also be cultural. What works in the "rust belt" may not work in the South (and vice versa). These various internal factors combine to create the employee relations environment inside each company location and even within each company department. Figure 2 illustrates how these various factors combine to create the vulnerability profile of an organization.

This brings up an important point about the overall vulnerability of any operation. Even though each of the three areas of vulnerability interplay with each other, they also work independently. Many companies have no control over where they are located, either because of customer requirements or they have too much invested to move – their external vulnerability may mean that they will face organizing efforts regularly irrespective of how well they are doing internally. This means that if you have a problem with one factor (i.e. you are located in a "bad neighborhood") then you have to be extra vigilant about the other vulnerability factors.

Assessing Internal Vulnerability

The internal factors are normally the most significant for employers. Even in areas where there is very little external vulnerability, an organization with high internal vulnerability is still at high risk for an organizing campaign. At the same time, a company that has been externally targeted by a union remains relatively safe if the internal vulnerability factors are absent. This is the focus of much of my writing around creating a positive employee relations environment.

The problem with the way vulnerability assessment is normally handled today is that it boils down to one overly simplistic question: does he like us or not? This is compounded by the fact that the person answering the question may be the least able to answer the question objectively (I've never had a supervisor say, "well, this guy wants a union because I act like a jerk.")

Other companies make the mistake of thinking they are conducting vulnerability assessment when they aren't. Some companies think that if they conduct an employee opinion survey and look for the "low engagement" locations that they know where they have internal vulnerability. That's not vulnerability assessment. Don't get me wrong: I'm a huge proponent of survey research (Section II of this book comprehensively covers the subject). However, survey research is a tool for issue identification. Knowing the issues is important and can help you prioritize action planning, but as we will soon see, just because you fix issues that employees complain about does not necessarily mean you are less vulnerable. You have to assess vulnerability separately from engagement.

There are two typical formats of vulnerability assessment interventions: manager interviews and focus groups. The most common intervention is a manager interview process. A consultant or attorney comes into an organization and interviews company managers and supervisors. The interviews go something like this:

Consultant/Attorney: "So, do you think Joe wants to have a union?"
Supervisor: "Nah, I don't think he wants a union."
Consultant/Attorney: "Why's that?"
Supervisor: "Oh, he hangs out with people who hardly ever complain, and a couple of years ago his aunt was in the hospital and we gave him time off he didn't have coming."
Consultant/Attorney: "Oh, I see." (Consultant or attorney marks employee as pro-company.)

That script may sound exaggerated, but it's not. Most of these interviews have little more substance than that conversation. At the end of the day, each of these interactions are really just a supervisor's rough guess as to whether they think an employee is pro-company or anti-company.

The second intervention format is a "focus group" session held directly with employees. These are often conducted by consultants and many times should be considered "persuader" activity.[7] In addition these meetings with employees can also create potential unfair labor practice issues, especially if they

---

[7] "Persuader activity" refers to activities by attorneys or consultants that must be reported to the Department of Labor under the Labor Management Reporting and Disclosure Act. Most law firms – and many consultants – do not engage in persuasion because they do not wish to report their activities publicly. For more information on these rules (and how they may change) please contact my office to request a copy of my confidential white paper on the subject. This paper is not available on our website due to its sensitive nature.

are being conducted around the time of union organizing activity.[8]

Consultants who use the focus group process will claim it is superior to manager interviews, since you are actually speaking directly with employees. There is a lot of truth to that. At least you are talking to the people who you want to evaluate, and often employees will open up to the consultant when they won't open up to someone inside the company. Our firm conducts focus group sessions (usually alongside the MDI process I describe below). They can be very effective ways to do issue identification and, more important, connect directly with employees. But even though you are speaking directly to employees and they may tell you some complaints, it is unlawful to ask them whether they support a union or not.

Because of this legal problem, the "focus group" protocol shares some of the problems with manager interviews. Instead of relying on a manager's rough guess, the consultant makes his or her own rough guess based on the reactions and behaviors of people in a meeting. Most of the time the consultant only sees these employees once (they don't have a relationship with them like their supervisor does, who can base their best guess on observed behaviors over time).

Additionally, anything the consultant does to identify an individual employee is likely to raise legal issues. Many employees remain fearful and quiet (and others just say what they think the consultant wants to hear), which means the consultant must make a guess based on substantially less information than a manager or supervisor might have. If

---

[8] It is unlawful to make promises (or impliedly promise) that things will improve if employees don't support a union. Since most of these focus group sessions turn into "gripe sessions" it is very common for a union to complain that the purpose of the meetings was unlawful. See chapter 9 for a discussion of the law in this area.

employees don't open up, the company risks no return on its investment in the consultant.

The Critical Flaws of the "Traditional" Methods

There are four problems with using either of these two protocols alone. First, they are <u>too subjective</u>. Simply asking somebody to make a conclusion whether an employee is "for us or against us" (or deciding for yourself based on something they say in a focus group meeting) is much too speculative. Supervisors (and consultants) have varying levels of skill and ability to reach a conclusion about such a subjective question.

Second, they <u>don't focus on observable behavior</u>. Consultants and managers often have very little observable behavior on which to base their assessment of union sentiment. It's not like there are multiple opportunities a day to observe whether somebody is pro-union or not. Instead consultants and supervisors use observations about whether an employee is happy or agreeable as a proxy for whether they want a union. The problem is the assumptions are often wrong.

For example, there are many people who love their work and are aligned with the company who nevertheless are dissatisfied with processes, procedures and even people they work with. Some employees are looking for constant improvement and may grumble regularly about the fact that a process isn't working properly or a manager isn't doing their job correctly. A supervisor or consultant may view that person as negative, even though that person might see a union as the worst possible thing that could happen.

The third problem with the "popularity contest" method of vulnerability assessment is that it doesn't actually deal with the <u>fundamental motivations that cause somebody to want to join a union</u>. Whether you like the company or not is just one of several possible reasons that an employee would join a union – and it's not even a very important motivation. As we will soon see, there are other, deeper motivations that are much better predictors of whether someone is going to look at a union as a good solution to their problems. Simply asking about feelings toward the company just scratches the surface about what might motivate that individual to want a union.

Fourth, these interventions rely on only one data point. Instead of getting multiple observations about a variety of behaviors they rely only on an assessment of this one point. In most cases it is a conclusion based on other behaviors that aren't clearly identified or systematically examined across the workforce. This substantially reduces the statistical reliability of the traditional model.

There are myriad reasons individuals give when they say they want a union. But those issues can generally be boiled down into a handful of fundamental needs. Traditional vulnerability assessments do not analyze these underlying motivations. Instead they create a laundry list of problems that employees expect the company to fix. Unfortunately, the company has no idea where to focus energy and resources, or even whether fixing any of those issues will actually deal with the underlying motivations.

Can Vulnerability Assessment Actually Make You MORE Vulnerable?

In addition to these basic problems of the process itself, ironically the traditional method of conducting vulnerability assessment can actually leave the organization more vulnerable than when it started. There are several reasons for this. The first is the Hawthorne Effect. In our situation the Hawthorne Effect simply refers to the idea that when a consultant or attorney intervenes in an organization, that intervention in and of itself can create an observable change in the organization.

The Hawthorne Effect isn't always a bad thing. The original research concluded that monitoring a particular behavior led to an observed improvement just because people were paying attention to it. This improvement may be short-lived.

However, the traditional vulnerability assessment approach sometimes results in a "reverse Hawthorne Effect" by creating unrealistic expectations that things will change based on the interviews. This is particularly true of "focus group" interventions in companies that don't do them on a regular basis. Consultants regularly have to "manage expectations" and tell employees that they can't say that anything will actually change even while they are listening to complaints. It can leave employees very frustrated.

The second problem is what I call the Salem Effect. The consultant or attorney asks directly whether people want to have a union or not, all while telling managers it is illegal for them to do so. This creates the sense of a "witch hunt" that can make supervisors uncomfortable. They often feel like they are snitching on their co-workers. In extreme cases, a supervisor may feel so aligned with his or her employees that they will actively lie during the interview process to protect their co-workers. If the Salem Effect is in play your data set is highly unreliable.

"Haloing" is a third problem. Organizing events are highly emotional. Managers often fear they could be fired for problems uncovered during a campaign. A supervisor who suspects that the data could be used against him or her may answer questions wearing "rose colored glasses" to protect co-workers or themselves. Haloing also creates an unreliable data set. It is also especially difficult to uncover if you're only asking about one observation per employee. The dataset is so limited there is no way to test whether you're getting accurate data.

Finally you have the "squeaky wheel" problem. When a consultant or attorney hears about the same problem multiple times, they often conclude that this is what is motivating the union activity. But once again this confuses the issue presented with the underlying motivation to seek out a union. The traditional vulnerability assessment model is good at seeking out complaints, but poor at comprehensively identifying the underlying reasons employees might be motivated to join a union. It gives you little sense of how various issues might relate to one another, or the priority to give to particular issues.

Ironically, learning about all these complaints creates unrealistic expectations that things will improve, and can actually reduce engagement instead of improving it. Consultants and attorneys often do little to manage these expectations. They present the list of complaints and say, "fix this and you aren't vulnerable any more." If only it were that simple.

What A Solid Internal Vulnerability Assessment Process Must Do

How would a strong and valid vulnerability process differ? A solid vulnerability assessment process must rely on objective information. Instead of asking a supervisor to rate employees on subjective and non-observable factors, a strong vulnerability process asks them to rate individuals on behavior that they observe on a regular basis. It should be based on behavior the supervisor observed recently (preferably multiple times), not anecdotal observations that happened months or years ago.

The ratings should be verifiable. Instead of relying on anecdotal stories, you should be able to verify what the supervisor reports. For example, if one of the observations relates to work quality, you should go back and look at actual data to determine whether a particular employee who was rated high on work quality is in fact strong in that area.

The process should be <u>research-based</u> instead of relying on "gut feel." Many consultants and attorneys who conduct traditional vulnerability assessments will tell you that a lot of their process relies on a "magic" in the room during the interview process. They will readily admit that they rely heavily on their ability to "read between the lines" by looking at a supervisor's nonverbal behavior when they are making their assessment.

While there certainly are times that relying on nonverbal cues can help an interviewer generate more accurate data, a process that relies heavily on these "between the lines" observations is fraught with error. In many cases this explanation is merely an excuse to deflect the fact that their process is completely unscientific and based almost entirely on a "gut feel." How much more reliable would it be if the process was based on solid psychological research that is both peer-reviewed and proven?

A preferable vulnerability assessment process will also rely on <u>multiple data points</u> or observations, not just one. If you rely simply on one data point or one observation (i.e. "does Joe want a union?"), you substantially limit the usefulness of the tool and the reliability of your conclusions. The bottom line is that it is much too easy for a supervisor to provide inaccurate information when they are asked to provide only one rating per employee. Ironically it gives them too much time to think too hard about their answer – this is when they halo or try to figure out the "right" answer. Asking for multiple observations per employee makes the interview much more of a "data collection" process and increases the reliability of the data.

Rating people on only whether they like or don't like the company or on whether they have complaints or not only gives you one way to compare employees against each other. Instead, if you can compare employees based on such factors as their work production, their work quality, and their work balance, you have more ways to both compare and contrast employees against each other and more opportunities to determine whether or not a supervisor is providing accurate data.

A preferable vulnerability assessment process will look at fundamental motivations. There are 4 fundamental reasons that employees seek help outside their organization: the need for affiliation, power, achievement, and/or the need to feel in control of their work. Employees in the same organization can seek out a union for any of these reasons, and different employees are motivated by different fundamental needs.

The complaints an employee initially presents to their supervisor, human resources manager or outside organizer are rarely the key reason they are requesting help. Union organizers know this, and they alter their sales pitch depending on the needs that they think an individual employee may have. A good vulnerability assessment process will identify and map these fundamental needs in the workforce.

Chasing after employee complaints creates a big problem, because often a specific complaint is not the real reason an employee wants a union. Consider the following example. Let's say an employee's complaint (what we call their presenting issue) is that they don't agree with the way that overtime is being awarded. That presenting issue could be driven by more than one fundamental motivation for wanting a union. One individual might want to change the overtime process because they feel like they are not recognized for their hard work and effort. This employee may feel that they should be rewarded for their effort by being able to get more overtime. Another individual may feel they should have a voice or power over how overtime decisions are made. These are two very different motivations.

In the example above, even if you fix the overtime issue you have only dealt with a symptom, not the actual problem. This is what I call the "whack-a-mole" problem, and it is very frustrating for managers until they understand this concept of underlying motivation. Like the game of "whack-a-mole" every issue a manager "solves" without actually dealing with the underlying motivation merely sends the employee looking for another example of how their fundamental need is not being met. The issue isn't the issue.

A company that spends its efforts trying to resolve all these presenting issues will miss the point. In our example above, if you "fix" the overtime issue without dealing the each employee's need for either achievement or power, you really haven't fixed anthing. Both employees will still have an underlying motivation to seek out union representation and will come up with new issues they think a union can solve.

For this reason, it is vitally important that any vulnerability assessment process (and the resulting action plans) focus not only on the presenting problems, but also on the underlying fundamental motivation.

In addition to looking at these motivations, it is important for the instrument to look at multiple dimensions. As described in the example above, an employee might be motivated by achievement, power or some other fundamental factor. It is important to look at all of the needs that, if not met internally, employees will look outside the organization (like to a union) to address or satisfy.

Additionally, any vulnerability assessment process should leave the system better than before. Conducting vulnerability interviews should not make the organization more vulnerable to union organizing. As mentioned earlier, the typical interview process can create a lot of suspicion and worry among supervisors, which often spills into the rest of the workforce. Depending on the trust level of employees or supervisors in an organization, this can tip an organization into additional organizing activity. Care should be taken in any intervention, especially in an organization where there is a concern that employees are considering unionization, to ensure that the process you use to collect the data is sensitive to this vulnerability.

LRI's MDI Vulnerability Assessment Process[SM9]

Is there a vulnerability assessment tool that performs in the preferred way described above? Fortunately there is now. The MDI Vulnerability Assessment Process[SM] counters all of the problems with the traditional assessment process by taking advantage of current psychological research and implementing the best practices. The MDI™ (Multi Dimension

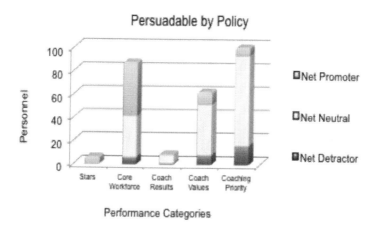

Figure 5.2 – Are your employees most persuadable by promises of power, policy change, or recognition?

---

[9] The MDI™ technology is a trademark and the MDI Vulnerability Assessment Process℠ is a sevicemark of Labor Relations Institute.

Interview) technology evaluates multiple behavioral dimensions through a course of structured supervisory interviews along with additional data collected through a comprehensive HR audit. It looks like a variety of fundamental needs that predict vulnerability to organizing activity.

MDI looks at the need for <u>affiliation</u>, or the need to belong to a group. One of the promises that organizers make to employees is that they will belong to a "brotherhood" and that this brotherhood will provide them protection. They often sell that there is "strength in numbers" and an employee with a strong need for affiliation (one who does not feel a strong affiliation with their company) could be easily swayed to join a union to fulfill that need.

Some people have a high need for <u>power</u>. They are motivated to join a union because they feel powerless inside their organization. This is a common promise made by union organizers. Somebody with a high need for power who does not feel like it is being fulfilled within the organization would be susceptible to an organizer's promise that if the union won the election, they would have a "seat at the bargaining table" and be able to force the company to listen to and adopt their ideas. The organizer may offer positions of power (a union steward position, bargaining committee position, grievance committee, etc.) to employees as part of their sales pitch to those motivated by power.

Other employees have a high need for <u>achievement</u>. They need to feel recognized for their work or their contributions. Employees that have a high need for achievement that is not being met inside the organization would be susceptible to promises by union organizers that relate to getting recognized for their work. It's not uncommon for organizers to tell employees that the company doesn't respect them and is not acknowledging their efforts. They'll say that with a union the company would be forced to recognize employees for their hard work and to reward them for it.

Another way to motivate employees to join a union is if they feel their workload is imbalanced. This could be either the work demand or the control that they have over their work. These factors are very task-oriented. The dynamic of work demand and work control is one of balance – you can have too much or too little of either factor. Union organizers often promise employees that they will fix these work imbalances. For example, sometimes they will promise to increase the number of employees to reduce the demands on current workers. Where a group of employees feels the work is much too demanding this promise can sway them to seek out unionization.

We look at each of these dimensions and compare against the "net promoter" score of employees in each group. A net promoter is an employee whose regularly observed behavior shows that they promote the organization. This is much different then simply asking whether they like or don't like the company. Rather, MDI relies on employees' observable behavior.

The observable behaviors of net promoters might be the actual comments that they make. But it can also be whether they refer the company to others or whether they have recommended co-workers to work there. Our engagement survey research shows that net promoter status is very predictive of overall engagement with the company. Therefore MDI looks at each of the various fundamental motivations through the prism of the number of promoters and detractors across each of those dimensions.

Finally, MDI looks at the informal leaders in the organization. These are individuals who are highly influential (whether for good reasons or negative reasons). These individuals are key movers in any union organizing effort. They are very important for the company and are also critical for the union. If the informal leaders are pro-company, even an organization with a large number of detractors is still not that likely to become unionized. The informal leaders will sway employees who are on the fence about the organization. Conversely an organization that is relatively neutral can still swing to the union if the informal leaders in the organization are detractors. Therefore MDI looks carefully at the informal leaders independent of the rest of the organization.

MDI collects <u>over 20 separate data points per employee</u>. This creates a comprehensive data set with thousands of observations. That amount of data gives our consultants a rich database from which to analyze not just fundamental motivations across the organization, but also the reliability of the data collected. Collecting data across so many points makes sure each dimension is measured through multiple statements. This substantially decreases the ability of a supervisor to "halo" employees. It gives us the ability to statistically evaluate "skew" in the dataset. In addition, we use Likert-scale measurements so we can compare similar rating scales across all of the dimensions.

Because we collect the data through structured interviews, MDI does not rely solely on anecdotal stories. We normally collect many of the same data points that get collected under the traditional process of vulnerability assessment, but these simply provide context to the statistical data collected through the MDI process.

The LRI MDI process reports across all of the multiple dimensions mentioned. For this reason you can identify not just overall vulnerability, but you can also analyze specific vulnerability to particular messages. For instance, using the example above, an organization that has gone through the MDI process can identify not just its overall vulnerability to union organizing, but also whether a message that relates to power would be more motivating to employees than one that relates to achievement.

The MDI instrument reveals specific areas for action. You will know whether particular departments are more or less vulnerable to organizing than others. You can also see whether certain demographic groups are more susceptible to union organizing. You will know where your positive employee relations efforts are working and where you should focus resources to get the biggest return on your investment in creating a positive workplace.

MDI also identifies informal leaders in the organization. It separates these leaders into pro-company and anti-company groups. Those groups can be further refined by their departments. This gives the company great opportunities to improve engagement. You can identify those employees who need to be fully engaged and aware of the company's message. You also know who would be likely to listen to a union organizer's promises and be able to persuade coworkers to do the same. Identifying this critical group is your company's most important opportunity, and segmenting them through an objective process gives you a lot of confidence that this core group has been identified properly.

Finally, MDI helps the organization improve its action planning, selection and performance management process. The process shows you where your current process succeeds and where it can improve. You can easily identify coaching priorities and areas in the company where an investment in training or selection is likely to pay the highest dividends. This gives the company additional actionable information that they can use to identify how to best target resources in their organization to help support those who are not performing at a high level and to help celebrate those who are. You are no longer chasing complaints. You are dealing with root causes of frustration or satisfaction. This gives your positive employee relations investments a lot of leverage.

The LRI MDI vulnerability process is much less susceptible to Hawthorne and halo problems. Since you're asking supervisors structured interview questions about observations that they can easily make, the interview process is actually seen much more as a training intervention than an assessment process. It is not uncommon for our consultants to be told by supervisors that going through the interview process is helpful because it focuses them on observations that they should be making on a regular basis as part of their job.

Most clients are surprised that the interview process never asks anything about unions. It doesn't have to. The focus isn't on union sympathy (which is a symptom of a broken employee relations system). Instead the focus is on the causes of employee engagement. If you take care of these basic needs, employees will see no need to seek help outside the organization.

The MDI process clearly identifies where the company should invest time and money. Instead of asking supervisors directly about whether their employees want to have a union or not (which as we've seen is unreliable at best) MDI looks for observed behavior and underlying motivation, telling you exaclty where to focus to improve engagement.

Because of the way MDI collects the data, it's easy to identify halo effect or other problems with the data. There are so many points of data that there are plenty of observations to run reliable statistical validity tests. If we find any problems we know exactly how they're impacting the report. Supervisors can be too optimistic or too pessimistic – with a solid data set like we collect, statistical tests prove whether our conclusions are reliable or not. This is a benefit that no normal vulnerable assessment process provides.

Some supervisors do question at the outset why they are being asked to rate individual employees. But once they get into the interview process, they understand that the point of the interview is to learn the various things that the company is doing that can motivate or de-motivate employees. The assessment asks what the company can do to improve the employee relations climate, versus whether particular employees may create problems for the company.

This is a major switch in perspective for vulnerability assessment processes. In addition to helping to relax the supervisors, which allows them to provide the most unbiased and accurate data possible, it also sends more positive signals down the company grapevine about what is going on, so that the MDI process doesn't contribute to heightened vulnerability the way some assessment processes can.

MDI is like an MRI for your business. When you want a thorough diagnosis to create an effective treatment – something that goes beyond just displaying symptoms – you want a full-spectrum perspective using the most current technology available. MDI identifies root causes rather than symptoms. The recommended action plans will then help you focus on the "wellness" of your company, not just avoiding symptoms. Rather than simply bringing down the fever, you will be building up a positive employee relations environment that not only mitigates risk, but enhances productivity. Your company's quality of life will improve, by every bottom-line measure.

Other Internal Vulnerability Factors: Regulatory Compliance

The more a company complies with labor and employment law standards, the less likely it is to be vulnerable to intervention from government agencies and employment lawsuits.

Regulatory non-compliance issues can also be a catalyst to union organizing campaigns. Sometimes failure to follow regulatory rules helps to start an organizing effort. Ignoring wage and hour or safety rules can lead employees to turn outside the organization to solve their problems. During a campaign (especially a corporate campaign) union organizers will often point to these concerns as a way to embarrass a company and hopefully pressure it into agreeing to demands for things like recognition, neutrality or card check.[10]

The following table summarizes a few of the major employment statutes and coverage requirements. You should consult the coverage of all laws (not just those listed here), both federal and state, for all locations in which you have employees.

---

[10] "Neutrality" is an agreement between and employer and union that the company will be "neutral" during an organizing effort (in other words not exercise its Section 8(c) free speech rights to discourage employees from seeking union representation). "Card check" refers to an agreement that the employer will recognize a union if shown proof that a majority of employees have signed authorization cards designating the union as bargaining agent. These agreements almost always happen under some threat of economic force by the union against the employer.

Law	Who is covered?	Summary
Civil Rights Act of 1964 (Title VII)	Employees with 15 or more employees	Bars employment discrimination based on race, color, religion, sex, pregnancy or national origin
Americans with Disabilities Act	Employers with 15 or more employees	Bars discrimination against individuals with disabilities and requires public areas to be usable and accessible to disabled persons
Age Discrimination in Employment Act	Employers with 20 or more employees	Bars discrimination against persons aged 40 or older
Fair Labor Standards Act	All employers	Establishes minimum wage, overtime and child labor laws
Family and Medical Leave Act	Employers with 50 or more employees	Requires unpaid, job-protected leave up to 12 weeks per year
Occupational Safety and Health Act	All employers	Requires safety and health standards to avoid illness, harm or death
National Labor Relations Act	Employers meeting certain "interstate commerce" - covers most employers	Governs union organizing and collective bargaining

There are, of course, many other statutes, standards and theories under which an employer can be sued. This list only covers a few of the "highlights" that are often the most common sources of employee litigation. It is critical to conduct regular audits of your company to identify potential liabilities under these or other statutes.

If you have any questions about the requirements of the laws in your state, or how to comply with the listed federal laws, it is important to discuss these with your labor counsel before you have a problem. Once you receive notification of a complaint, you are operating right of boom and it is too late.

A variety of different issues are analyzed when determining a company's regulatory compliance. A thorough review of the employee handbook and any other policies and procedures is a good starting point. There are some policies you want to pay special attention to. A few of these are:

Discrimination Policy	ADA Compliance
Harassment Policy	Family Medical Leave Act
Safety Programs	Overtime Compliance/Exempt Status
Hiring Practices	Independent Contractor Designation
Employment Testing	Dispute Resolution Programs
Social Media Policy	Employee Access/Solicitation
Confidentiality Policy	Civil Treatment Policy

There are a number of other laws and regulations that employees can rely on for third party intervention. This list is not meant to be exhaustive, but does include some of the more likely areas where third party intervention often occurs.

If you have never conducted a thorough HR audit before you should consider having an expert walk you through it the first time.[11] Reviewing these areas and determining your firm's compliance will significantly reduce the likelihood of facing regulatory action or lawsuits based on unlawful employment practices.

Assessing External Vulnerability

There are thousands of companies with high internal vulnerability and low regulatory compliance that are never approached by unions. This often is due to the fact that unions are inactive in their region, or there are no unions proximately located that could economically organize the group of employees. External vulnerability research helps to identify

---

[11] If you would like a "done for you" option where you can ride shotgun while an expert conducts your audit feel free to contact us at 800-888-9115 and we can put together a proposal that fits your situation. Another alternative is to use the Laurdan HR audit program called ELLA, available through SHRM. This program walks you step by step through the audit process. It is a lot more work, but allows you to rely on internal resources.

whether poor performance in other areas are likely to result in an attack by a union.

Organizing costs money and time. Unions will normally base their targeting decision on where they think they can get the best return on this investment. Many LRI consultants used to organize for unions. They helped unions choose company locations to target. We also know from experience in thousands of union election campaigns what factors make a company easier to organize.

This experience teaches us some core assumptions about how unions target companies. They prefer:

- Organizing in a location where they have a strong local presence (strong union locals, number of members they can mobilize, allied union locals, etc.) that can be mobilized without huge resource investment;
- Areas where they already have strong relationships with local allied groups, politicians, media, etc.;
- Locations where they can easily access targeted work groups and employees;
- Places where anticipated dues income is high and "servicing costs" (the cost to support a particular location through bargaining and contract administration) are low.

Generally, unions will avoid locations where at least 3 of these assumptions aren't met.

Method
Knowing these assumptions, external threat assessment is straightforward. When comparing locations, you can test–based on available data–whether a union would consider that target more or less desirable by applying these assumptions. Each location must be evaluated based on its specific geographic location and the business conducted there.

For example, a small retail store with just a few employees is unlikely to get attention from a union across town. On the other hand, a distribution center in a large metro area might be targeted from a union many miles away depending on if other factors are acceptable.

When mapping labor vulnerability around a particular location we recommend two types of analysis. In some locations an overview of the area is all you need to make a determination of vulnerability. A "metro area" analysis (sometimes called a "zone area" in large cities where looking at the city as a whole is likely to mask potential threats) provides this overview.

In some cases the metro/zone research suggests that the risk of external campaign activity is high. In that case, a deeper analysis is in order. We provide a comprehensive look at a location when the metro area research indicates that a "detail report" will help us make more focused decisions.

Metro Area Reports: A typical metro area (or a zone area in a very large city) looks at:
- Which unions of interest are located in that zone or metro area? Where are they located specifically? Have they shown interest in organizing other targets in your industry?
- Do unions of interest file many petitions? When they do file do they take the company all the way to an election?
- Where have they filed petitions in the last 5 years? Have they filed against companies in your industry or employers your size?
- Are any particular locals more active than others in the zone or metro area? Does proximity to the union's office seem to be a factor in organizing?

- How many union members are located in the metro area or zone? How does that compare to national and state union density?
- How many union elections have happened in the last 10 years? Where did they occur? Are elections or union victories on the rise?
- What information can be found about key locals from their websites or recent news stories?
- Has there been any activity from social justice organizations or worker centers in the zone or metro area? When did it occur? Who was involved?

Detail Reports: A typical detail report takes the research above and looks at additional factors like:

- Are unions of interest well-funded based on their most recent financial reports? Do they have paid organizers on staff?
- Do unions of interest have labor contracts with any companies in your industry or employers of your size in the area?
- Does the internal union political situation in the key unions impact the potential risk of attack? Are the key locals politically stable or not? Would an attack on your facility help or hurt someone politically?
- When do the contracts close to your facility expire? Would a dispute there potentially impact ingress or egress at your facility? Are any of those contracted facilities in the retail or logistics business?
- What other potential allied groups are in the area (labor councils, community justice organizations, environmental groups, religious organizations, etc.)? Have they worked with unions recently?
- Who are the key political leaders in the community and the state? Are they more or less likely to align with labor or community groups? Will they have any

positive or negative influence over potential regulators?

- Have there been any similar campaign events in the last 5 years? What groups aligned at that time? What was the outcome?

Once the data is collected for each metro area or zone (and deep dives are conducted where needed) you can then evaluate these external threats, prioritize resource allocation, and take action on what you learn.

How to use the external assessment

Since external threats are just part of the puzzle, the next step is to apply that data to what you already know about internal vulnerability at potential target locations. Typically, an organization has 3 or 4 tiers of vulnerability across internal and external threats. Once you map those locations across each tier, clusters of high, medium and low priority locations normally emerge. That allows you to prioritize actions based on tiers.

High vulnerability locations normally receive direct intervention by corporate resources or outside consultants (these locations would be great candidates for our MDI™ process, for example). But there are a number of actions you can take at medium and low vulnerability locations based on what you learn in the external threat assessment.

For example, once you've identified key union locals of interest you will want to regularly monitor what is happening there. The same is true with contracted employers – you may choose to network with some of these to keep tabs on developments there that could potentially impact your organization. You may also want to network in the community with groups and political leaders who might be able to counteract efforts by unions or their allied groups.

Keeping things up to date

These external threat assessments are snapshots of a moment in time, and things can change rapidly. There are two things an organization should do to make sure they are acting with the best possible information. The first is an "Eye in the Sky" report. The second is a semi-annual "Refresh" report.

The Eye in the Sky report is a weekly snapshot of labor activity around each physical location you are monitoring. This report looks simply at petition and election activity near each location.

Region Four

1 HIGH ALERT PETITION has been reported by LRI Online since Jul 6, 2009.
1 District is affected: District 11

Location and Search Radius	All Petitions This Report	Six-Month Petitions Activity Feb-2009 through Jul-2009	Six-Month Election Win Rate Feb-2009 through Jul-2009
Region: Region Four Radius: 20 miles (34 Locations)	2 ▲	8 8 14 23 13 2 Feb Mar Apr May Jun Jul	Union 78% Company 22% Total Elections: 41

Region One

NO HIGH ALERT PETITIONS have been reported by LRI Online since Jul 6, 2009 in this region.

Location and Search Radius	All Petitions This Report	Six-Month Petitions Activity Feb-2009 through Jul-2009	Six-Month Election Win Rate Feb-2009 through Jul-2009
Region: Region One Radius: 20 miles (30 Locations)	0 ▼	19 9 11 4 9 0 Feb Mar Apr May Jun Jul	Union 83% Company 17% Total Elections: 24

Region Three

NO HIGH ALERT PETITIONS have been reported by LRI Online since Jul 6, 2009 in this region.

Location and Search Radius	All Petitions This Report	Six-Month Petitions Activity Feb-2009 through Jul-2009	Six-Month Election Win Rate Feb-2009 through Jul-2009
Region: Region Three Radius: 20 miles (37 Locations)	0	1 4 1 2 3 0 Feb Mar Apr May Jun Jul	Union 62% Company 38% Total Elections: 8

Region Two

NO HIGH ALERT PETITIONS have been reported by LRI Online since Jul 6, 2009 in this region.

Location and Search Radius	All Petitions This Report	Six-Month Petitions Activity Feb-2009 through Jul-2009	Six-Month Election Win Rate Feb-2009 through Jul-2009
Region: Region Two Radius: 20 miles (32 Locations)	0	4 5 8 2 2 0 Feb Mar Apr May Jun Jul	Union 71% Company 29% Total Elections: 17

Figure 5.4 – Eye in the Sky Report

These reports have two purposes. First, you want to know quickly if an employer close to one of your locations is experiencing an organizing event. It is not uncommon for campaigns to spread from one location to another, so early warning of a campaign close by gives you a chance to counter that activity. Second, you can spot trends that might indicate that a Refresh report would be worthwhile.

A Refresh report looks at anything that has happened since the last report period and quickly indicates whether it makes sense to do any additional research on the zone or metro area. If another report is indicated, these new developments are added to the original report along with any modifications based on the new information.

External threat assessment is an important component of any comprehensive labor risk assessment. When unions evaluate potential organizing targets these external factors can be as important – and sometimes more important – than internal factors. Unions are likely to be more aggressive in a favorable regulatory environment. Therefore, I recommend all clients include external threat assessment as part of any decision on how to allocate employee relations resources, and to regularly update those assessments as conditions change.

Where to get the data

Just like with auditing your internal situation, there are two primary ways to audit your external vulnerability: you can do it yourself or have an expert do it for you. Most HR leaders we talk to are unaware of the resources available today to track union activity. A lot of this information is available for free directly from government websites. For more comprehensive research our company, the Labor Relations Institute, tracks all petition activity, strike activity, election results, union local information and even news articles on every union in the

United States. Our libraries go back to 1990 and are updated every day.[12]

Some of our clients conduct regular searches of these online libraries for activity around their locations. To make this easy we provide the ability to research activity by zip code radius (our databases can also be easily exported into spreadsheets where the data can be readily analyzed). This gives any company an easy way to get a snapshot of what is happening around a particular location.

Reviewing local publications, websites, Twitter feeds, etc. of union locals is another great source of information. If you are monitoring a union's website (especially something like a Facebook page where individuals may reveal their identity), be careful if talk turns to employees of your company. Monitoring conversations of your employees – even in a public space online – would likely be seen as unlawful surveillance.

Company Size

All things equal, larger groups of employees are more attractive targets to unions because they represent greater potential income from union dues. Unions are more likely to expend great resources on units of over 100 employees than on very small units.

At the same time, there are often diminishing returns in attempting to organize an employer with thousands of employees, due to the huge investment of resources required to accomplish this goal. Larger employers are often much more sophisticated and capable of spending great amounts of resources to fight an organizing campaign. In addition, a limited number of targets (in 2008 there were only around

---

[12] For more information about LRI RightNow visit http://search.lrionline.com or contact us at 800-888-9115.

11,000 employers with 1,000 or more employees – many of whom are already organized) are at the very large end of the spectrum.

This does not mean small employers have nothing to fear. Many companies are not aware of the fact that union win rates also improve in smaller companies. In fact, many companies are surprised to know that the median unit size in union elections has been less than 25 employees for years. In 2012, half of all union elections occurred in units of 23 or fewer employees. There are also a lot of companies to target (over 4.5 million in 2008) with less than 10 employees.

If you were to look solely at the numbers (I caution against that below) your probability of a petition based on company size, using 2012 petition data and 2008 census data (the most recent statistics available) looks like this:

Company Size	Percent chance of petition in 10 years
Under 10 employees	.11%
10-20 employees	.93%
21-99 employees	1.07%
100-999 employees	2.51%
1000 or more employees	3.61%

One conclusion stands out immediately. If you have more than 100 employees at a location, you have a much higher risk of a petition over the next 10 years than a very small company. And it gets worse: these numbers understate the risk of a petition.

The first way they understate risk is because unions will only target non-represented firms. The actual pool of target companies shrinks based on the number of unionized firms in your area. In heavily unionized areas of the country, the pool of possible targets your size may be quite small.

Second, they do not account for any of the other factors we've discussed. While it is true that the likelihood an "average" company will be targeted in any one year is small, that only tells part of the story. You also must look at the other factors we've discussed. Where is that company located? What industry is it in? Are there unionized competitors nearby? Is the company doing anything internally to shoot itself in the foot?

Once you start looking at these factors you begin to see that the statistics aren't all that helpful. There is no such thing as an "average" company. Each company has its own unique profile. And while company size can certainly increase or decrease the likelihood of getting targeted, it does not tell you much about a company's overall vulnerability.

External research for site selection
In addition to researching external threats to existing locations, we also help companies determine the relative labor vulnerability of potential "greenfield" or "brownfield" development opportunities. Using the same data and research tools, you can compare several locations and identify which would be best from a labor vulnerability standpoint.

Site selection research is quite interesting and sometimes surprising. This is because a lot of the "rules of thumb" really don't apply when you dig deep into the data. For example, many companies simply assume that, all things being equal, it is always better to be located in a right to work state than a forced dues state when considering labor vulnerability. But this isn't always the case.

States aren't monoliths. You don't locate a plant or distribution center in a "state." You locate them in a city or community inside a state. And those communities can have very different labor vulnerability profiles even within the same state.

For example, Nevada is a right to work state and, in most cases, locating there would create less vulnerability than locating in Ohio, which is a forced dues state in the rust-belt where unions are more prevalent. But would you believe that an employer in Nevada is nearly 3 times more likely to be attacked by a union than one in rust-belt Ohio? It's true.

And if you are locating a new casino, hotel or restaurant in Las Vegas and plan to operate it non-union, you for sure have a target on your back (just ask Steve Wynn). In fact, the average casino is 320 times more likely to be petitioned by a union than the average retailer. Even more surprising, an employer with 20 or more employees is more likely to be petitioned by a union in anti-union South Carolina than in Wisconsin.

The bottom line is that a state with a very little labor activity overall may have a city where all the organizing for that state is focused. A location in that community might be more likely to be organized than one in a so-called more vulnerable state. Or a city that otherwise has a lot of union activity may be zero threat to a company in your particular industry because unions in the area you are considering just don't go after companies like yours. Therefore, it is really important to look at data down to the zip code for each area where your company is considering locating.

The labor vulnerability tail isn't likely to wag the real-estate dog in most site location decisions. But when you have two or more viable locations and operating union-free is a high priority, this type of research could tip the balance in favor of one location over another. Either way, it is an important factor to examine as you establish a company in a new community.

How Do I Take Action After My Vulnerability Assessment?

In a perfect world none of your company locations would have any employee relations problems. Unfortunately we don't live in a perfect world.

Vulnerability assessment is primarily a tool for approximating risk and allocating resources. The reason I say "approximating risk" is because even a company that scores well using the tools described here can still face a union petition or a government complaint. Nevertheless, a company that scores poorly on internal and external vulnerability factors is more likely to face (and lose) a union election.

The most precious resource any of us has is time. Even if you have only one location to worry about, you still need to allocate your time and attention to the areas where it will provide the most value. And that is what vulnerability assessment tools let you do: focus your limited time and other resources to the areas where they'll have the most leverage.

The best way to use your various assessment tools is to prioritize actions based on what you learn. This should be done first at the location level, and then at the department level.

Here is a typical example. Let's say you have 8 facilities and 2 of them are in the "red" zone for vulnerability. These two locations show high internal vulnerability (your research identified some poor supervisors who could use training) and are also externally vulnerable due to their locations. While all 8 facilities have some things to work on, you will probably want to focus most of your resources in those two locations.

Thus, your plan might look something like the following. You personally oversee the supervisory training and post-survey action planning at the red locations. You visit the other locations when you can, but probably only once or twice during the year. This does not mean that you ignore the other facilities, but since they are in better shape (and probably have better leaders in place) you may want to ask local leaders to conduct the same training and action planning you will be doing at the red locations.

Your specific plan for the red locations will be determined based on what you uncover in the vulnerability assessment. For example, you may determine that the problem supervisors are in two departments. They have poor communication skills and tend to order people around. Since the employees in these departments are motivated primarily by power (you found this out during the MDI process) you know that your training should focus not just on communication, but also on including employees in problem solving. You also look for other location leaders who do a good job of communicating and involving employees. You ask these folks to help mentor the problem supervisors when you aren't available.

If you allocate your resources in this way you make sure that you have the best possible chance to turn around the red locations. You are applying the best possible resource to the locations and departments that need it most.

Ultimately these tools are not about avoiding union petitions, but it is certainly one benefit of taking action on your vulnerability assessment. The most important benefit of these tools is it makes it easier to create a positive work environment. It tells you where to focus, gives you a road map of things to work on, and a "punch list" of priorities where your limited time provides the most value.

Take Action

☐ When was the last time your company conducted a vulnerability assessment? Which area needed the most attention?

☐ Of the 4 fundamental reasons employees look for help outside their organization: the need for affiliation, power, achievement, or the need to feel in control of their work, which would apply most to your employees?

SECTION II: EMPLOYEE ENGAGEMENT RESEARCH

LRI performs Employee Engagement Surveys for companies across the United States. It is an ideal tool to identify early whether you have an employee relations problem at a particular location or in a particular department. Surveys help map out a strategy for turning around a negative environment. The survey data also provides a great platform for discussing your company's employee engagement process.

Some people call these surveys "satisfaction surveys" (I used to refer to our survey research as satisfaction research, although I usually call it an engagement survey today). "Engagement" is the employee relations buzzword of the decade and it is worth a quick discussion here.

Satisfaction versus engagement is a topic that could be a book in itself and is generating a lot of emotion in Organization Development circles (well, as much emotion as PhD Organization Development consultants generate about anything). The debate boils down to this question: can you really measure engagement?

On one side of the aisle the argument is yes, not only can you measure engagement but that it is the only thing really worth measuring. On the other, people argue that engagement is really a behavior ("am I willing to go above and beyond what is expected of me") and that you can't really measure it at all. Instead, you measure other factors that can predict whether someone will give that extra effort.

I don't really choose a side in this debate because I think both schools of thought offer something. I do like asking some questions about satisfaction. Some of those are not behavioral (Do you like your job? Do you like your supervisor? Do you think the company is headed in the right direction?). Other measures are behavioral (When you are asked about work are your comments positive? When you have a problem at work do you discuss it with your supervisor? If you have an idea or suggestion do you feel comfortable bringing it up?).

Measuring both behavioral and non-behaviroal factors gives you a good baseline picture of how a group of employees feels about their job. They also predict whether that group of employees will provide discretionary effort. As I discuss later in chapter 12 on Approachable Leadership™ discretionary effort (also called Organizational Citizenship Behavior) is the best measure of engagement. But sometimes you want to get a "pulse" or snapshot of where how you're doing. Looking for examples of OCB can be one measure, but survey research is another great tool.

I also highly recommend measuring "net promoter" factors, which are behaviors that relate specifically to whether you are likely to promote the company to coworkers or outsiders. This could be considered both a measure of satisfaction (if you're not satisfied you won't say nice things) and engagement (going out of your way to say something nice about the company is a small example of discretionary effort).

So do I recommend measuring satisfaction or engagement? I answer the question, "Yes." In the end what you specifically measure is much less important than what you do with what you measure. That is why the action-planning component of employee research is most important.

The key components of effective employee engagement research include:

1. Make sure that you're asking net promoter questions (more on this in the next few chapters);
2. Make sure that you are segmenting your survey data and not treating the organization as a monolith – remember

there is no "average" employee and every person is unique;[13]

3. Respond to the issues based on the most important groups. Again, focus on the key segments of employees who are "on the fence" about the company (what we call the "mushy middle") before you focus on other groups. Focus on moving those in the "mushy middle" into promoters of the company; and

4. Take action. Do not get too caught up in the data and avoid the most important work, which is taking action on what you learn. A survey is only a snapshot of a moment in time and the organization moves constantly. Instead of trying to figure out how you got that particular snapshot, what is really important is using that snapshot as a platform for planning out where you want to be.

The chapters in this section will help you implement an effective employee survey (or if you don't want to get teased by the PhD's on LinkedIn you can just call it an engagement survey). This is truly the foundation of any employee relations transformation. It sets the baseline, directs the discussion and the action, and lets you know whether you are heading the right way (or the wrong way). If you get this part right it is hard to go wrong, but if you get this part wrong it is hard to get anything else right.

---

[13] See Chapter 5 on vulnerability assessment to learn more about the importance of evaluating individual motivations when it comes to understanding union vulnerability.

Chapter 6

Employee Engagement Surveys: Left of Boom Companies Do This – Do You?

"You could not step twice into the same river; for other waters are ever flowing on to you."
Heraclitus

What You'll Learn In This Chapter
- [ ] Why conducting an engagement survey on the heels of a union election is a good strategy;
- [ ] The three key strategic concepts that form the foundation of an effective survey program: fluctuation, segmentation, and action (the OODA loop);
- [ ] How to avoid survey fatigue; and
- [ ] The main tools for assessing employee engagement: Pulse Surveys, Employee Engagement Surveys, and Structured Interviews.

My Uncle Lester used to take my father to the horse races in Sallisaw as a kid. On the way there they'd look at the racing form and my uncle would let him pick a few horses to bet on. One of the things Dad remembers most about those trips is my uncle's betting advice. He told him, "the Bible says the *race is not to the swift, nor the battle to the strong...* but that's the way to bet."

The same advice applies to employee engagement. As we discussed in Chapter 5, fixing issues without understanding what motivates your employees won't necessarily reduce your vulnerability. Yet while fixing issues in the workplace does not guarantee success, that's the way to bet. After all, an organizer needs some issues to organize around if they are going to have success. Companies that systematically identify and respond to issues in the workplace are dramatically less likely to face an organizing event than those who don't.

Employee engagement is also a key element to employee satisfaction. I consistently see in our survey research that as engagement improves so do measures of satisfaction. The kinds of factors you want to measure include:

- Do we have a positive work environment? Do employees feel like we fix things when we find out they're broken?
- Do we follow good hiring practices? Are we bringing in people who are a good fit for the work and the culture?
- Are we effective at on-boarding employees? Do employees understand what is expected and are they trained to do their jobs well?
- Do our supervisors have the proper skills and abilities? Do they treat people with respect?
- Are we consistent with pay raises and promotions? Do employees have opportunities to develop their skills and talents?
- Do we have policies and procedures in place, and are they followed consistently?

When treated well, employees are satisfied and engaged. When treated poorly, they create unrest, increasing vulnerability. Because these factors are within our direct control, this is the place where focused and direct action can have a high payoff. This is the good news.

The bad news is since we do have direct control, employee satisfaction is where union organizers focus when building their case in favor of a union. Companies with a lot of issues are a "target rich environment" for a good organizer. Not all issues are created equal (in Chapter 10 I offer some strategies to help you figure out which issues to attack first). But generally speaking a workplace with fewer internal issues has a more satisfied and positive work force. Even if your organization has high external vulnerability, you will not be vulnerable overall.

Case in point. One client recently conducted employee engagement surveys in about a dozen locations in multiple states. When the results were tabulated, one of the facilities had abnormally low scores on several key factors (these would all be internal vulnerability factors). Before I could hold my management review conference call with the client, that facility was petitioned for union election! However, because the client was armed with the survey data they knew exactly where to focus attention. The union withdrew its petition days later.

Surveys on the Heels of Union Elections

Companies LRI has assisted through union elections are often reluctant to conduct engagement surveys. "Look, our employees already think we stink," they might say "We've been hearing it for over a month now. Why don't we just let this thing die down for a month or two – Lord knows we could focus a little more on our core business around here." These companies suffer from campaign myopia. In our experience, this is the perfect time to conduct a survey.

It is true that employees who have recently been through a campaign are normally more negative about management, particularly top management. The union has spent several weeks (more likely months) questioning every move made and characterizing all company moves as evil and motivated by greed. Companies that have suffered through this process, even if they ultimately win, are reluctant to give employees another opportunity to take a shot at them. This view is short-sighted and is a good way to get another petition a year later.

These companies fail to appreciate where they stand after an election. Companies attacked by unions typically have a poor history of communicating with their employees. During the weeks preceding the union election, many managers and supervisors spend more time talking to employees than they ever have before. This often becomes a reason that many "fence-sitters" vote for the company in the election – they have a new or improved relationship with their supervisor or manager and they believe things will change after the election. Companies often believe that this will happen too, as a natural side effect of the campaign.

But managers and supervisors often (and usually unintentionally) slip back into bad habits of the past. It is important in the first few months after an election to build new habits that will set the path for a better future.

You must also remember that there is a group of employees (sometimes almost half of the workforce) who wanted to have a union and are expecting management to return to its old ways. These employees, often prompted by the union organizers who helped them during the campaign, will continue to look for reasons to attack management. They'll be saying things like, "See, what did we tell you – business as usual." Or, "Well, you guys really screwed things up for us this year, but just wait until next time – we'll get that union in here then!"

In many ways, this negativity becomes a self-fulfilling prophesy. Even the employees who want to believe management will learn its lesson from the campaign need evidence. Otherwise, they will begin to believe that minority of the workforce who want management to fail.

Employers must act quickly after the election to give their employees a reason to believe things will be different. By taking a formal and public action on the heels of the campaign, management gives its supporters evidence that things will be different. The "fence-sitters" will give the company some time. The negative employees will, of course, begin knocking the company at every opportunity, but their audience will be limited at first.

Clearly things will be negative on this survey – employees do not invite unions into workplaces that have no problems. But the company has to start somewhere. Using this admitted "low point" in the company's history acts as motivation to improve and also places the bar at a level that should be easy to raise, giving you a "quick win." By completing the survey and quickly communicating the results, management takes leadership on the communication issue.

This is not to say that the survey is a "ploy" or just a way for the company to buy time. Any company using the survey in this way is kidding itself – failure to attack the issues that led to an organizing campaign will lead to another and, ultimately, a bargaining obligation. But acting quickly and publicly gives the company an opportunity to make significant progress on the issues that matter most to its employees.

Fluctuation, Segmentation, and the OODA Loop

The basics of engagement survey research are pretty straightforward. You ask employees to rate the work environment across a number of factors and measure where they are satisfied and where they see room to improve. Pretty simple, right? Unfortunately, there is much more to an effective engagement survey approach than meets the eye. Where most companies flounder is not having a good strategy up front. As Steven Covey famously taught, you should begin with the end in mind. What actions do we plan to take based on this data? How might we want to analyze or communicate the results? What questions do we anticipate, and can we set things up so those questions will be easy to answer?

There are three key strategic concepts that form the foundation of an effective engagement survey program. Those are fluctuation, segmentation, and action (the OODA loop).

The first key is the concept of fluctuation. As the Greek philosopher Heraclitus so wisely said in the quote that begins this chapter, you cannot step into the same river twice. All of life, especially the life of an organization, is constantly in flux. Employee engagement, and with it union vulnerability, are constantly changing over time. Most survey strategies ignore this fundamental fact.

Ignoring the concept of flux causes companies (and consultants) to make three big mistakes. First, they devote too many resources to analysis and too few resources to acting on the data (even if that data isn't fully understood). Since the river has already moved, why waste time trying to figure out exactly where the river was? Figure out which direction the river is flowing and identify any major obstacles ahead (Is there a giant tree in the river? Is the river dry up ahead? Are we headed for a waterfall?) Then get in and start paddling.

A second, related mistake is looking at the survey as having all the answers. Most people who are really into survey research (especially consultants) live in the data. That's what they're comfortable with. Yet this research is about people, and again the river is moving.

Think about it like this: survey research isn't a Google Map on "street view" – it's more like a map with a scale of one inch equals 25 miles. It probably gets you in the right neighborhood, but you still need to ask for directions when you get there. Survey research shows you the neighborhoods you should check out. It tells you where to ask for directions. But it's up to you to roll up your sleeves and have that discussion. The data can't do it for you.

Third, companies don't survey often enough. The river is moving. If you wait two years between surveys you may have missed that the river moved completely off the map. You can certainly survey too often and create survey fatigue (as we will see below, there are good strategies to counter this problem) and there are other ways to get a pulse other than a survey. But the vast majority of companies don't survey often enough. You need to stick your toe in the river every once in a while.

Another related concern is that while things are constantly moving inside the four walls of your business, they are also moving outside. These changes outside your building can impact how employees feel inside the building. Paying attention to changes in the labor market, competitive environment, and even what unions are doing in the area will alert you to issues that should be on your radar.

For example, while there is nothing you could do about the Great Recession, understanding how it plays on the psyche of your employees is important. Unions and non-union allied groups have used this situation to agitate over issues like job security and pay disparity. Knowing this, you might pay special attention to announcements related to pay, layoffs, consolidation, or executive bonuses. You might also decide to pulse check your workforce, even if it wasn't part of your original schedule.

Segmentation is the second key. The basic principle is this: every union campaign is won in what we call the "mushy middle." Likewise, your overall employee engagement is driven by this same group of uncommitted workers.

Political campaigns spend millions and millions of dollars trying to figure out how to move this mushy middle to their side. The way they do it is by segmentation. You can't get an independent voter (or even a lot of your party) to go your way by just saying, "Hey, I'm a Republican [or a Democrat] so vote for me!" People are concerned about their specific issues.

Expert pollsters help political campaigns figure out exactly what issues are likely to move what voters. With today's technology and media options they can literally send out campaign messages custom-tailored to an individual voter. And that is what you have to do as a company.

While this principle applies generally to the overall engagement of a group of workers, it is sometimes easier to understand if you put it in the context of a union organizing campaign. Conventional wisdom says that if the "average" employee at your company is unhappy, then your company is vulnerable to organizing, and vice versa. This is flawed thinking!

First, there is no "average" employee. What is critical to understand is who the unhappy people are. If they fit into one category, they may be insignificant to unionization efforts. If they fall into another, the organizer may have hit pay-dirt.

When organizers approach your company, they know that certain people are more important than others. They do not just blanket your employees with the same appeal. Union organizers go through an extensive training process, and even use software developed for the express purpose of segmenting your employees into specific groups.

Any employee population can typically be divided into five different buckets, or frames of mind. On one extreme are the people who love your company and love their job, and there is not much anyone can say to change their mind. On the other extreme are those who are outspokenly negative about your company. A lot of times these folks were mad at the world when you hired them and are very unlikely to change. But there are usually three groups in between these two extremes. These are the groups that union organizers seek to leverage, and consequently, so should you.

Next to the extreme positives there is a group that typically leans positive, but is not very vocal about it. If the pressure is on in a conversation among peers, they can be swayed negatively or at the least may reinforce negative comments made by others.

Next to the extreme negatives is a group that is just going through the motions – they really don't think much either way about their job, but they're sort of "checked out" and can easily be pulled into a negative discussion. Occasionally, when confronted with some of the positive aspects of their company or job, they can be swayed to the positive side.

Sandwiched in the middle is the group that wins or loses union elections (or tips an organization from high engagement to low engagement). They are basically "neutrals," and can be swayed one way or the other depending on who's got their attention at the time. This is the "mushy middle," the critical group to reach.

Smart union organizers gauge their potential for success by first eliciting a few of the extreme negatives to the union cause, and then having those employees approach some of these "mushies," especially someone who is influential at work. If these folks respond that they're comfortable with their company and don't believe they need a union, the organizer often will not waste further time at the company. If they respond favorably to the concept of a union, the organizer knows he's hit pay dirt.

The same thing is true with overall engagement. Imagine a group of your employees sitting around together in the break room discussing an issue at work. Some are in favor and others against. If you think your neutral or "mushies" would more often than not side with negative coworkers, you will have an engagement problem. If they would side with their positive coworkers your engagement scores will be high.

This segmentation idea has some huge implications for how to conduct and act on your employee engagement research. First, your research tools need to be designed to properly segment your employees into the 5 key vulnerability segments described above. Second, your tools need to assess which way each work group is leaning (pro-company, neutral or negative). Finally, you need to uncover the issues that are critical to the "mushie" middle segment, and focus improvement efforts on those issues.

This may seem like a lot of work, but it is actually much more efficient than the typical survey approach that just looks for any issue that polls below average. This approach lets you pay less attention to what is going on with the extreme groups (whether positive or negative). As you focus attention on the

Figure 6.1 – Employee Segmentation

key issues of the "mushies" in the middle, their attitudes will help move the negative leaning buffer group in the pro-company direction, and will reinforce the top two positive groups.

This is the highly-leveraged action application of the 80/20 rule. 80/20, or the Pareto Principle, says that 80% of the results in almost any undertaking are the outcome of 20% of the effort. Most businesses understand how the 80/20 rule operates in the sales arena – that 80% of their profit typically comes from 20% of their customer or sales efforts. The very best companies focus their energies on that critical 20%.

The 80/20 rule also applies to the arena of employee relations. This is why segmentation is so important. If you simply averaged out all of your employee engagement scores, lumping the extremes in with the middle groups, you would come out with a different set of issues that appear to be important to the so-called "average" employee. You lose leverage, probably working on issues that may be of concern to the insignificant majority of your employee population, rather than the significant few.

What is an OODA loop?

During the Korean War, Russians flew MIG-15 fighter planes and the Americans flew F-86's. If you were to do a side-by-side comparison of the two planes it would look something like this:

	MIG-15	F-86
Visibility	✔	
Climb	✔	
Turn	✔	
Control	Manual	Hydraulic

If you were about to be sent up into a dogfight which of the two planes would you pick? If you wanted to make it back alive you'd pick the F-86 (during the Korean war it won 9 out of 10 dogfights against the more powerful MIG-15). Based on the table though, most would probably pick the MIG-15, but that's because the table does not show the most important factor that predicts who wins a dogfight: the OODA loop.

A bit of background on the OODA loop. The concept was developed by a fighter pilot named John Boyd. Boyd wondered how the F-86 could perform so well despite its inferiority on paper. What he discovered became a driving force behind Air Force fighter plane design, fighter pilot training, and played a key role in the development of "maneuver warfare" (Norman Schwarzkopf's famous "left hook" in the first Gulf War).

The idea is that on the battlefield, or in an aerial dogfight, each opponent has a finite limit of factors that he can observe during the conflict. Each combatant orients himself based on whatever he observed most recently. Next, they decide on the most prudent course of action. Then they act. They immediately cycle back into observing the opponent's reaction, and start the loop again.

For example, in an air-to-air engagement, a pilot wants to know whether he is climbing or diving, his relative position to his opponent, whether or not he believes his opponent has seen him, his status of fuel and weapons, and the relative advantages or disadvantages of the opposing aircraft. He will then decide on a course of action, and a dogfight ensues.

Each pilot processes their own OODA loop, and the pilot who can process through the Observe-Orient-Decide-Act cycle faster than his opponent will almost always be victorious. The one advantage the F-86 had over the MIG-15 was maneuverability. Even though on paper it was the slower plane, in actual combat the plane went from Decide to Act faster than the MIG. And this made all the difference.

By the time the MIG pilot reacted to the actions of the F-86, the F-86 pilot was already re-orienting himself to the slower plane's actions and making new decisions. This continually forced the MIG pilots to react in a defensive mode. The only way the "slower" pilot can survive is to execute an action completely unexpected to his "faster" opponent, and capitalize on the possible momentary hesitation to get his OODA loop operating inside (or faster than) his opponent.

Again thinking about things from the perspective of a union organizing environment, the OODA loop concept holds significance for a company's defense to union activity. In a union organizing drive, you are in a battle against the union organizer for the hearts and minds of your employees. The OODA loop concept teaches that a properly executed vulnerability process gets you several steps ahead of the unions. The more information you have (on both internal and external issues) the faster you can make decisions that will change the landscape.

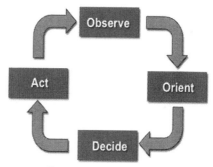

Figure 6.2 – OODA Loop

As an example, suppose you implemented a new policy that was not received very well by employees. This is the kind of thing a union organizer would use to agitate against the company, hoping to develop a groundswell of support for the union. Organizing does take time, however. If your assessment process uncovered the issue, and you acted quickly to address it, the organizer might find that the momentum he thought he had suddenly evaporated. Not only does he lose the benefit of the argument, he may even appear out of touch by trying to agitate around something employees no longer see as an issue.

These same principles apply even if no union organizer has ever darkened your doorstep. Any effective employee engagement process takes into account the fluctuation of issues over time (internal & external); focuses on identifying the issues pertinent to the "mushies" in the middle (there is no average employee); and allows speedy engagement of leveraged action (the OODA loop).

Qualities of an Effective Engagement Survey Plan

The tactics and tools used to properly create a satisfied workforce flow from the strategies we've described above. **First**, your tools must foster quick and ongoing observation of your company's current position, and provide the proper detail to allow you to effectively orient yourself to the current situation.

Second, your process must allow you to implement high-leverage actions on the 20% of issues that will have the highest payoff.

Third, move fast and trust your system to respond with new feedback. Ideally, you are constantly observing and orienting, making decisions and acting on them, and then starting the loop over again, fine-tuning as you go. The moment you leave the loop – stop assessing feedback and making continuous improvement actions – you leave the door open to slipping engagement scores and potential penetration by a union.

This plays out differently for every company. If you found that your "high-leverage" action issues pertained to a cluster of people within a particular department, or at a particular facility, you might test some actions with that group and measure the effectiveness. If it improves conditions in that limited scope, you can then roll out similar changes company wide.

Two benefits stem from using the "test and widen" concept.

Employees will see that their concerns matter to you and they will feel good that you are making an effort. They will also see that you're not just trying to placate them with any action, but that you are seeking out the actions that truly make a difference in their lives. By being faithful to continuous improvement (even starting small), you can stifle the critics.

Remember, vulnerability fluctuates constantly. Changes in the economy or local community, in your business market, or even within your company, all have the potential to cause a disruption to things that you thought were working smoothly. This is the law of unintended consequences. Get the law working in your favor by making sure your assessment process updates your employee relations assumptions on a regular, cyclical basis.

The main tools for assessing employee engagement (and therefore engagement and internal vulnerability) are Pulse Surveys (or what we call 80/20 Surveys), Employee Engagement Surveys, and Structured Interviews.

A Brief Word to People Who Hate Surveys

Many companies have used employee surveys in the past, with mixed results. Companies fail to benefit from surveys for several reasons. The biggest reason most companies don't benefit is they spend a lot of time analyzing and little time implementing (paralysis by analysis). Action planning is the most critical component of any survey strategy.

Additionally, most surveys don't account for segmentation, so even though the company takes action it doesn't recognize the points of high-leverage action. This can be frustrating since the actions you take don't really move the needle (many companies quit surveying after a while due to this problem). Finally, some companies take one survey, make a few adjustments, but don't measure the results with another survey. These companies stick their toe in the river once and think they know all they need to know about it.

Some folks are very gun shy about suggesting a survey process in their company because of failed attempts in the past. This is understandable. And you can dramatically improve an employee relations environment without ever conducting an employee survey. I don't recommend it, however, and here's why.

Trying to improve an employee relations environment without survey data is like trying to improve work quality without measuring defects. It can be done, but you will spend a lot of time wondering whether the actions you take are having a meaningful effect (or even worse, causing things to move in the wrong direction). It is also one element of proving the return on investment (ROI) of your survey process.

A formal employee survey is objective and comes directly from the employees. It is the only way I know to efficiently and accurately segment a population of employees. Other methods may provide useful feedback, but they do not allow for the employees to be effectively grouped. They also do not match issues to groups like proper surveys can.

Because you can acquire segmented results from a survey, you can focus your efforts (80/20 rule) rather than shotgunning across the company. This lets you focus your limited resources (you do have limited resources, right?) on the key issues, with the key groups of people, immediately. And, since surveys are "mathematically tabulated," the results can be turned into action steps quickly, keeping your OODA loop as tight as possible.

Surveys also provide a common platform for communication with your employees. You can reference the survey, describe action plans you've implemented as a result of the feedback, and keep the dialogue going about identified issues. Good, two-way communication is critical to a positive workplace environment, and surveys and survey results provide a great objective reference point to keep such communication ongoing.

There are two types of surveys, Pulse (or what we call 80/20) Surveys and Employee Engagement Surveys. The Employee Engagement Survey is the more detailed of the two. Our standard survey has 70 questions. Most employees complete this version in about 20 minutes.

There are three advantages to the more detailed Employee Engagement Survey. You receive refined feedback on a number of issues, letting you laser-focus high-leveraged actions. Second, you get a solid baseline to use in tracking changes. Finally, you can more easily segment groups because you have a large data set.

In the next chapter you will learn more details about how to break down survey data. But in addition to reporting out how each item scores on the survey, also look at groups of statements by category and a separate group of 15 proprietary Third Party Intervention Factors, that highlight issues most often used by union organizers during organizingcampaigns. In addition, consider using "net promoter" questions.

The Pulse or 80/20 Survey is short – usually somewhere between 3 and 15 questions on one page – and can be completed in about 5 minutes. This survey can be administered at a quick pre-shift meeting rather than having to break employees or take them off the floor to get the survey done. The Pulse Survey can also ask employees to self-rate their level of engagement, which provides a rough way to segment the population.

The Pulse Survey is obviously easier and less expensive to administer. I prefer quarterly surveys and some clients assess a sample of employees every month. This allows for regular tracking of any changes in vulnerability. It also provides up-to-date feedback for continuous process improvement.

While the Pulse Survey does not provide near as much data as the long-form Engagement Survey, it can be a powerful tool. As the name implies, the small survey is an application of the 80/20 principle. You ask the 20 percent of the statements that give you 80 percent of the value. Plus you are almost always dealing with "fresh" data. Combining the Pulse Survey with a larger Engagement Survey is a great foundation to creating a positive workplace.

Take Action

☐ List the top 5 issues employees have in your workplace. Conduct employee engagement surveys often to remain knowledgable of these concerns.

☐ Do you know who your "mushy middle" employees are? What campaign messages are most important for them to hear?

☐ Consider the fluctuation of issues over time – how will your river change? Train your system to respond quickly and efficiently to those changes by spending more time implementing and less time analyzing.

Chapter 7

How to Construct and Conduct Your Employee Engagement Survey

"Where an opinion is general, it is usually correct."
Jane Austen, Mansfield Park

What You'll Learn In This Chapter

- ☐ The types of engagement surveys you should consider;
- ☐ What you should know about "whole system" or appreciative inquiry methods;
- ☐ Key considerations when constructing your survey;
- ☐ How to tabulate your survey information;
- ☐ The best ways to communicate survey results to your employees; and
- ☐ Legal issues regarding the conduct of engagement surveys in a "post-campaign" environment.

You're convinced. You know you should conduct some type of survey process to discover the issues in your workplace. Where do you start?

As you learned in Chapter 5 the method you use for discovery should be driven by the primary motivation(s) of your workforce. There are situations where methods like focus groups or one-on-one interviews are ideal – those are covered at the end of this chapter. However, in most companies (especially companies who recently went through a union organizing event) an anonymous, forced-response survey is the most effective method of discovery. Getting the most out of these surveys is the focus of this chapter.

Let's review the three important reasons it is wise to start with an engagement survey:

1. Surveys provide a high-level road map for issue identification and action planning;
2. Surveys facilitate communication in companies that do not communicate well; and
3. Surveys provide a baseline from which a company can benchmark progress.

Effectively administered surveys provide critical information about your primary challenges and help to map out a logical path to solutions. You don't always act first on the issues employees complain about the most (chapter 10 on action planning covers how to apply the 80/20 principle to prioritize your "high impact, low difficulty" action items). Nevertheless, ranking the issues first is a logical first step toward designing a plan for attacking employee relations problems.

It is also critical, particularly in companies that have undergone union organizing attempts, to build solid communication habits. Asking for employee input and appropriately responding to that input when it is received is a great way to start that habit.

Further, in organizations where trust is a major issue, an anonymous survey process is a great vehicle to begin that discussion. By conducting an employee engagement survey and communicating the results of the survey, a company takes a great first step toward formalizing a communication process in its workforce. This establishes a "Communication Platform" for employee relations issues.

Finally, the survey results provide a snapshot of employee attitude at a moment in the life of your company. Starting from this point you can later identify, in an objective way, whether the company is making progress or backsliding. While administering a survey is not the only method for providing this benchmark, the information gained provides a background to interpret other data such as turnover statistics and numbers of grievances or complaints filed by employees. Survey information is a critical piece of the puzzle and, if used properly, can pinpoint areas for improvement.

Employee engagement surveys are not a "fail-safe" answer. They can be very problematic, which explains why some employers are reluctant to use them. There are a number of potential pitfalls to engagement surveys. Often employers are appalled at their results and hesitate to reveal them. However, companies must commit to communicating the results – good, bad or otherwise. Forget about a survey unless you are committed to communicating the results honestly. In fact, conducting an employee engagement survey without this commitment is worse than not conducting a survey at all.

Therefore, it is important to know ahead of time how you plan to communicate both the administration of the survey and the results once the data is collected. Additionally, since employee engagement surveys can take many different forms, it is important to pick a format that has a high likelihood of success in the unit you are surveying. The following information describes various survey formats and their respective strengths and weaknesses.

Anonymous Forced Response.
This is the "go-to" survey format for most clients, especially those who have recently suffered a union campaign. The anonymous forced response survey is usually a form containing various statements regarding work environment. For example, you might ask: "When I'm asked about work my comments are always positive." Respondents are forced to mark the degree to which they agree or disagree with the statements.

The anonymity of this survey is a great advantage. The survey can be administered in such a way that members of management don't ever see the actual surveys filled out by employees. This promise of anonymity helps some employees overcome the fear that their honest answers will have a negative effect on them at work. As a result, most employees feel that they can be more candid in this type of survey.

These surveys aren't perfect, as even anonymous surveys can have skewed results. For example, if a group of employees conspire to answer all questions negatively (or positively) the results obviously will be inaccurate. This problem is not unique to the anonymous forced response survey, but it can be more difficult to detect.

The good news is that in the thousands of surveys LRI has conducted, this type of "conspiracy" activity almost never happens (literally just a handful of times in 25 years). Even in these extremely rare occasions, this activity can be detected and still creates an opportunity to respond specifically to that group. In every group where it looked like "gaming" the survey might have occurred, the client quickly get to the root problem and turned that department around.

The primary disadvantage of the anonymous forced response survey is that the quality of the information gathered is limited by the quality of the questions asked. If questions are not framed properly, employees may not be able to communicate all the problems or concerns they face. In addition, you ideally want to ask several different questions concerning the same issue. Otherwise, there is a risk that the wording of a single question might skew responses toward the positive or negative. Approaching the anonymous forced response survey in this way will increase the size of the survey.

This is why I like adding open-ended questions to surveys. For example, ask: "What 3 things do you like least about working here?" This allows employees to voice issues not covered in the forced response section. It also gives space for employees to clarify or amplify what they answered on the rest of the survey.

Some employees may not respond to the open-ended questions, due to concerns about anonymity or they just don't feel like writing answers. Ideally, these concerns about anonymity will be handled during the administration of the survey. Nevertheless, these questions provide a good way to correct for any problems in crafting the forced-response questions.

Constructing Your Survey

The typical LRI survey asks seven statements in each category in a "Likert-type" scale (each statement is ranked from 1 to 7, 1 being most disagreement and 7 being most agreement).[14] In this way, you avoid the problem that the wording of one statement skews the survey results. The scores on these seven statements are then combined to get a category score. In order to give you an idea of the format, we have included a sample basic survey at the conclusion of this book. (See Appendix 1)

Statement wording should be carefully considered. Statements should not be vague or subject to varied interpretations. They should cover observable behavior as opposed to thoughts or motives.[15] Since the Likert-type scale is designed to capture degree of agreement or disagreement, it is better to word questions directly than to word them mildly positive or negative. For instance, "My immediate

---

[14] There is some debate in the academic literature regarding the validity of using various numbers of response categories in a Likert-type scale (i.e. 5, 7, 9 or more responses). Cf. PAUL KLINE, HANDBOOK OF PSYCHOLOGICAL TESTING 189 (2d ed. 2000) (7-point scale is most reliable) with LEWIS R. AIKEN, RATING SCALES & CHECKLISTS 238 (1996) (5- point scale best, although 7-point scale may be best where range of attitudes are small). We prefer the 7-item scale for employee attitude measurement.

[15] See Palmer Morrel-Samuels, "Getting the Truth Into Workplace Surveys," Harvard Business Review 111-118 (February 2002).

---

supervisor treats workers consistently" is better than "Managers usually treat workers well".

Asking questions about things you can observe is important for two reasons. First, it gives you a way to do a quick and dirty validity check on survey accuracy - you can independently verify results if they are observable. For example, if you ask a statement about pay raises being delivered on time, this is something you can observe independent of the survey results. If the answers don't jive with the reality then you need to dig hard to find out why.

Second, asking about things you can observe means that you'll be able to take action on the survey results. For example, asking whether your leader can "think outside the box" isn't really observable. Instead you might ask whether the leader "quickly responds to new information."

If you ask about things you can observe it gives you very actionable data. Leaders are much less likely to dispute the survey results, giving you a valuable place to start your action planning.

Survey designers can add even more reliability into the instrument by asking some of the statements in the positive and some in the negative (i.e. "My immediate supervisor treats workers consistently" and "My immediate supervisor does not treat workers consistently"). This prevents someone from skewing results by marking the same answer on every statement.[16] It can also help to ask a few items that can be independently verified.[17]

---

[16] See Kline, supra note 14, at 188-190 (2000).
[17] See Morrel-Samuels, supra note 15.

Identifying Sub-groups to Analyze

In Chapter 8 we cover analysis of survey results, but you have to begin your survey process with the end in mind. If you get this step wrong up front you may not be able to analyze the data the way you want when the survey is over.

The basic goal is to identify each group you want to look at separately from the company overall. For large, multi-site organizations you will obviously want to look at each site separately. However, within each site you need to figure out what other sub-groups you want to look at. These must be identified at some point in the survey administration or you won't be able to separate that group from the whole.

Most organizations select sub-groups according to Shift, Job Classifications, Department, Length of Service, etc. It is important to keep the number of suitable options as small as possible. There are two reasons. The first is anonymity. If you provide too many options an employee may figure out that only one person has more than 5 years of service and works third shift maintenance. That hurts the integrity of the process.

Second, you should only ask about categories you actually plan to act on. The biggest challenge most companies face with surveys is getting paralyzed with data. Keep it as simple as you can. In most cases asking by department is good enough. In very large organizations you may want to break down more than that, but this remains a situation where less is more.

You should have these options pre-printed on your survey form and when you administer, instruct participants to circle the sub-groups that apply. This is the ideal way to do it. Make sure each group who takes the survey is told which sub-groups apply to which positions so every participant knows what group they should mark. Also, make sure participants know to designate only one sub-group per category (only one department, only one shift).

Survey Administration Tips

There are a number of administration issues that can skew survey results. For example, where fear of management retaliation is a major issue (not uncommon in units who recently went through a union campaign), less candid results are obtained if a management employee administers or gathers the completed surveys. In some cases we recommend that an outside consultant or other "ombudsman" administer the surveys.

Another important factor is to administer the survey to groups of employees in as similar circumstances as possible. For instance, large time gaps between survey administration periods can alter results markedly. I recommend that companies conduct surveys in small blocks of time, no longer than a week.

It is also best to administer the survey during work time. Participation and thoughtfulness of responses improve when you conduct the survey during work hours (not on a break, after work, or even worse at home). This makes the cost of administration higher, but more importantly, it shows the value you place on the input and makes sure the survey is given priority.

Internet or Paper-Pencil Administration?

When I first started doing engagement surveys over two decades ago there was one option when it came to employee survey administration: paper and pencil. If you wanted to get really fancy you could use "Scantron" technology to speed up the data input, but for most small and mid-sized companies the investment didn't make sense.

Today Internet survey administration is not only a second option, but in many cases it is clearly the best option. If you use the Internet to administer your survey you can save a huge amount of money.

Not only are Internet surveys less expensive, but you can be dealing with your survey data the minute the last respondent completes the survey - paper-pencil surveys usually have at least a two-week lag before you can start working on the survey results.

That's the good news about Internet surveys. However, there are a couple of key considerations.

The first one is obvious: does your organization have the physical ability to administer surveys online? Many of my clients have a knee-jerk reaction to this question: no way. However, I have found that often with a little imagination it is pretty easy to administer online surveys in even in relatively low-tech manufacturing and health care facilities like nursing homes. All you really need is a couple of computers hooked up with Internet access in a reasonably quiet setting. Some clients even rent machines for a week or two for this purpose.

The second consideration is anonymity. We do a lot of surveys after anti union campaigns or in union avoidance situations where trust in the organization is low. People are less trusting of entering information into a computer than they are filling out a paper-pencil survey where they know they haven't included any identifying information. For this reason you must take extra care when administering the survey to reassure employees that nobody will be able to identify their answers.

There are many technical ways to handle this - the Internet survey tool I use has the ability to assign unique pass-codes to survey participants that are completely random. If you have a workforce where trust is not high, investing in this feature might be worthwhile.

Some people fear that using Internet surveys could mean fewer people participate in the survey. This shouldn't be an issue today.

Virtually everyone has access to a computer (and I'm not talking about Ph.D. computer programming here - if you can buy something on eBay you can fill out a survey online). I have found that participation rates on Internet surveys - even in manufacturing and trucking firms - are actually better than most pencil-paper surveys I administer.

My bottom line: if you can administer your way around trust issues, definitely use Internet administration. The cost and usability advantages are overwhelming, especially in larger organizations.

"Paint By Numbers" Survey Administration

Below I lay out a basic survey administration protocol that we offer to our clients as part of our basic survey process. You can modify this to meet the needs of your organization, but this basic outline will cover the vast majority of survey administration situations.

It is very important that whatever process you use to administer your suveys is followed as exactly as possible for each group you survey. You want to create the most consistent survey conditions as you can. Following these instructions will help to ensure that the results accurately reflect the attitudes of your workforce.

Step 1: Announce the Survey

About a week before actually administering the survey, announce that your company is going to conduct the survey. Use a memo along the lines of the following:

November 4, 2014

To: All Employees
From: Your Name
Subject: Employee Engagement Survey

I am pleased to announce that during the week of _____ we will be conducting an Employee Engagement Survey at all ____ locations. The purpose of the survey is to get your honest opinion about a wide variety of issues relative to your job here at ____.

The survey will be conducted by LRI Management Services, Inc., a company who conducts surveys like this for organizations throughout the United States.

The survey is completely confidential. The form does not ask for your name or any other type of personal identification. After all forms have been completed, they are sent to LRI Management Services for processing and evaluation.

LRI Management Services will prepare a comprehensive report that summarizes your collective responses. Shortly after they give us this report, we will share the results with you. Then, working with you, we will develop a plan to improve our weaknesses and build on our strengths to make ____ an even better place to work.

Step 2: Who Should Administer the Survey?

In most cases you will use someone from inside your company to actually administer or proctor the survey. This is usually someone from Human Resources. Other companies have the department manager proctor the survey. In an organization with high trust this is just fine.

In organizations with trust issues (like many companies who have undergone a union organizing event), participant responses may be more honest if an outside third party administers the survey. Sometimes they will request a consultant from our firm to handle survey administration. You can also have any other outside source (like a local minister, attorney, judge or any other person who the survey group would believe insures total anonymity of the responses). Some clients have a member of the survey group handle the administration and mailing, thereby assuring employees that management will never see their responses.

Please note that the only duty of the administrator is to read the instructions to the participants and collect and mail the completed forms to LRI or whoever is tabulating your survey results. The only reason to have an outside administrator is to provide the assurance of total confidentiality.

Step 3: Administrator's Instructions to Participants

If your survey will be conducted in two or more sessions, it is helpful if the instructions to participants are exactly the same or as close to exactly the same as possible. If you are using Internet administration this is handled for you – each survey participant gets the same instructions up front. But if you are administering the survey live, I suggest that you write out the instructions and have the survey administrator read the instructions to each group of participants.

The survey should be administered to each employee group with as little time between as possible to avoid the sharing of responses or changes in conditions which would impact the survey results. Here is an example of survey instructions:

Today, we are asking you to take a few minutes to participate in an opinion survey. The results of this survey will allow us to learn exactly what you as a group think and feel about a number of issues concerning your work environment, giving management the opportunity to consider your collective opinions when making decisions. Your responses to this survey are completely confidential. Please do not sign the survey form. After I give you a few instructions, please complete the survey and place your completed form in the envelope located ____. After everyone has completed the survey, I will seal the envelope and mail it to a company in Oklahoma for statistical analysis. This company will compile your responses and make a report detailing the collective responses of everyone who participates. After we receive this report, we will share the results with you. To begin, please read the first page of the form. Do not turn the page until I tell you.

[Allow enough time for everyone to read page 1 or if you prefer you can read page 1 aloud.]

Now, turn to page 2 of the survey form. At the top of the page you will see the name of our organization. Immediately following this line you will find two columns. On the left is a list of departments. Everyone find the department in which you work and circle it. If you have a question about your department, or feel you could fit into more than one designation, pick the one which most closely matches your job or in which you spend the most time. The second column lists three shifts. Circle the shift on which you work. Again, if you work on more than one shift, circle the one on which you've worked the most in the last few months.

Now, read the sample survey statement. Do not turn the page until everyone has finished reading.

[Allow enough time for everyone to read the sample survey statement.]

Does anyone have any questions about how to complete the survey form?

[Answer any questions.]

There are a couple of terms you need to be familiar with. When the survey refers to a supervisor, this means your immediate boss. When the survey refers to upper management, this means (all other managers that a supervisor reports to or another definition suited to your company's circumstances). When you finish the survey, please check to be sure you have identified your employee group and answered all 70 questions. Please do not fold the survey, as this delays processing of the results. Place your completed survey in the envelope located _____ and return to work. All right, begin.

Step 4: Send the Surveys for Tabulation

After all of the surveys have been completed, the administrator should seal the envelope containing the completed survey forms and mail it to LRI or whoever is tabulating your data. Sealing the envelope in front of the survey participants can reassure employees that their responses will remain confidential. Sometimes companies will have an hourly employee survey participant put the survey forms in the envelope and mail them. Again, the key is to make sure employees are certain that the survey forms are kept confidential.

Other Methods for Discovery: Large Group or "Whole-System" Meetings

An effective method of discovery, though used less often, is the whole-system meeting. These meetings, implemented most often in strategy or planning contexts, invite as many employees as possible into a large meeting room. These meetings are based on the "systems" philosophy of organizations that holds that any change to a system must engage that entire system to be effective. These meetings can be very powerful and, if done well, can result in immediate and long-lasting change in an organization.

The advantage of whole-system meetings is that they do engage the entire system. Usually mixed groups of employees and managers sit together and discuss a number of questions regarding where the company has been and where it is going. The groups are asked to report back to the whole system and key ideas are recorded. Often groups are asked to record their thoughts in pictures or on video. These meetings are very effective when conducted from an appreciative inquiry perspective (for more on appreciative inquiry, see the sidebar Appreciative Inquiry in this chapter).

Yet, I have found that there are two key disadvantages to whole-system methods. First, the meetings are open and are intended to go wherever the system wants; in fact strict management control signals that the company is not interested in employee opinion. Lack of control is unsettling for management groups that are not used to employee involvement.

In addition, the meetings can get out of control or become negative, particularly in a post-campaign environment. For this reason it is best that professionals experienced in facilitating whole-system meetings be in charge of the early meetings.

Appreciative Inquiry[18]

As mentioned earlier, there are numerous ways to engage in system discovery that don't involve surveys which ask critical questions of management. Some observers even argue that asking employees to think about or list the problems in an organization creates both the (often unrealistic) expectation that the problems will be solved and (more importantly) further ingrains the idea that the organization itself is a problem to be solved. These observers look at organizational life as more organic and fluid and less systematic. One of the most exciting areas of study to come from this perspective is that of Appreciative Inquiry.

Appreciative Inquiry was developed by Dr. David Cooperridder of Case Western Reserve University. This view holds that organizations are organic and constantly changing, much like the humans that make up the organization. Drawing on diverse fields like Gestalt psychology and medicine (studies of the Pygmalion effect, the Placebo effect and the effects of positive and negative self-talk on patient recovery rates) these researchers have concluded that the historic engineering-driven approach to organization development is in many ways based on a flawed model.

---

[18] For a broad survey of current thinking on the issue of Appreciative Inquiry and its application to organization development, see DAVID L. COOPERRIDER, ET. AL. APPRECIATIVE INQUIRY: RETHINKING HUMAN ORGANIZATION TOWARD A POSITIVE THEORY OF CHANGE (2000).

These researchers believe that the "culture" of an organization is simply a shorthand way to represent the thousands of conversations that occur each day between each member of the organization. The "vision" of the organization is really a shorthand way to represent the combined imagined futures of each of the individuals in the organization.

From this perspective, asking employees to criticize or problem solve their organization is counterproductive. It does not focus attention on where there is life in the system, but instead on where the system is failing. Instead of focusing on strength and possibility, the engineering mindset focuses on weakness and hopelessness.

Appreciative Inquiry asks the members of the system to concentrate on possibility and the things that give life to the system. Since the belief is that the conversations between group members are the culture, in this way the system is immediately energized and changed. By inquiring about what group members appreciate about their organization, they are implicitly invited to both celebrate and imagine how these aspects of the system can be brought to bear on its current challenges. Often, many "problems" are "solved" using this approach, without ever expressly seeking out the problems or the solutions.

Organizations like British Airways, Roadway Express, Verizon and Avon have successfully utilized the Appreciative approach in their organization development initiatives. The approach has significant possibilities for organizations that have recently experienced the negativity of a union organizing campaign. I have used the approach to design survey questions as well as when conducting live on-site interventions with large groups, small groups and teams. I have even effectively used this approach during union campaigns. There is an example of using Appreciative Inquiry to identify your key employee relations objectives in Chapter 8.

One-on-One or Small Group Interviews

As mentioned earlier, a forced response survey is only as effective as it is designed – if you fail to ask questions about a topic you won't get data on it. It is also nearly impossible to understand the emotion around an issue from a forced response survey. Small group interviews overcome this problem.

To conduct a survey using this method, a management representative or outside consultant conducts individual or small group interview sessions with a representative sample of employees. In smaller organizations everyone can be interviewed – which is ideal – but in most cases you just sample.

These interviews typically follow a structured format. Employees are asked to comment on various issues and discussion then ensues regarding peer reactions to those issues. Notes of the meeting are kept, and a record of the various responses to questions and issues is made, which summarizes the comments of the various groups surveyed.

The primary advantage of the focus group engagement survey is its free style. Employees are encouraged to talk about any or all issues affecting them. Employee input typically feeds on itself and often a variety of pertinent issues are raised in these discussions.

In conducting these sessions, employers will also receive opinions and input about many different aspects of the operation. A major advantage of the focus group method over a forced response survey is that if the forced response survey fails to ask a question about an important area, input on that issue may never come up during the survey. Topics like those will definitely come up during a focus group session.

However, there are disadvantages to the focus group method. A primary obstacle is finding a credible leader of the focus groups. A critical factor for success is to have a facilitator who can manage focus group sessions in a positive and productive way. Often these meetings raise contentious issues and can become highly charged and negative. This is not always a disadvantage, because employees must feel free to comment on issues.

A leader must be able to keep sessions productive and limit personal attacks (the goal is to always separate the person from the problem – although there are certainly cases where the person is the problem). The leader should be a capable facilitator who is interested in gaining insight into all sides of an issue. Obviously, a meeting facilitated by a manager who is dominant or viewed negatively is not conducive to an open meeting format.

You can overcome this challenge by using an outside consultant to facilitate these meetings. LRI clients have found that employees tend to open up and tell our consultants things they would never tell a manager or supervisor.

Another disadvantage of these meetings is they can be dominated by a few people or select issues. These events can skew survey results. An unskilled facilitator may allow only a few individuals (the "squeaky wheels") to dominate the discussion. This will limit what you learn, and make other employees feel like the meetings were a waste of time. In the same way, a particularly public or heated problem can dominate discussion and remove focus completely from other issues that are just as important.

A good facilitator can resolve these concerns in some respects, but these problems are inherent weaknesses in the focus group system. If employees are fired up about an issue, this opportunity will allow that issue to dominate their discussion. This situation makes it very difficult to get much discussion about other issues that, while they may be problems, are not as important at the time of the survey.

A final disadvantage of the focus group method is that it is not anonymous. Depending on the identity of the facilitator, employees may be very hesitant to openly discuss sensitive management issues.

One-on-one interviews can be an effective way to discover the level of employee engagement in your organization. These interviews can be used not only to learn employee opinion, but also to increase faith in a particular leader. One Navy Captain used the power of one-on-one interviews to turn a Navy destroyer from the worst ship in the Navy to the best in just a few short months.

Captain Mike Abrashoff used a simple four-question survey of his entire crew when he took over the USS Benfold.[19] Those questions were: Where did you come from? What do you like most about the Benfold? What do you like least? What would you change if you could?

Using just a box of 3x5 cards and these four questions (and a lot of hard work by everyone on the ship), Abrashoff was able to quickly revitalize a crew that had recently been rated the least battle-prepared destroyer in the navy. The title of his book, "It's Your Ship" was his mantra. When someone came to

---

[19] See Polly Labarre, "Grassroots Leadership: USS Benfold," 23 *Fast Company* 115-126 (1999); and Michael Abrashoff, *It's Your Ship: Management Techniques from the Best Damn Ship in the Navy* (Warner Books, 2002).

him with a problem he would start by asking them what they suggested – after all, it was their ship. There are many great lessons from this book and I highly recommend it.

There are, however, potential problems with one-on-one interviews. They can have some of the same disadvantages of small group sessions. Depending on the ability of the person conducting the interviews, employees may not feel comfortable opening up. These meetings can be intimidating for some employees. This can raise potential legal concerns.[20]

Once again, these issues may be resolved with a skilled facilitator. In some cases an outside consultant is most appropriate. However, like the experience with Mike Abrashoff shows, if a company leader really takes these meetings seriously they can have tremendous impact on both morale and the organization's effectiveness. However, a leader that looks at the meetings as a "chore" will fail to accomplish anything by going through the motions.

Supervisor Focus Groups

This method of survey is one level removed from surveying the opinions of line-level employees. In this method, focus group meetings are held with line-level supervisors and department managers. These meetings are different from the MDI process described earlier in Chapter 5. While MDI interviews often do unearth issues in the workplace, they are primarily designed to discover the core motivation of workers at a location. Supervisor focus groups are instead designed primarily for issue identification.

Supervisor focus groups are much like those for hourly employees. A facilitator, either a high-level company manager or an outside consultant, will ask a series of questions about the company and try to get the pulse of overall employee

---

[20] See infra. at 166.

opinion based on the opinions of supervisors who work most closely with the hourly employees.

The big advantage to this method is that it is the least disruptive to the work of hourly employees. Also, this process requires less time and reduces interruption of company operations.

Another advantage is that supervisor focus groups can prevent built-up expectations in the workforce (like the reverse-Hawthorne effect discussed in Chapter 5. Hourly employees sometimes unrealistically expect that, once they make their complaints, management will immediately act. You avoid this problem when you conduct supervisor focus groups since hourly employees are not directly asked about complaints..

However, supervisor focus groups are less effective in some respects. The method relies heavily on the capability of line-level supervisors, who are often the weak link in companies vulnerable to third party intervention. In addition you lose the advantages of talking to employees directly.

While employee focus groups can build unrealistic expectations, they also provide a great opportunity for management to "walk the talk" on employee engagement. Whenever possible we prefer to talk directly with employees. However, supervisor focus groups can be an effective way to get a quick "lay of the land."

One way to overcome the limitations of supervisor focus groups is to combine them with the MDI process discussed in Chapter 5. In that process, consultants conduct pattern interviews with individual supervisors. This gives the consultant an opportunity to evaluate whether a specific supervisor really knows his or her people well and to further evaluate the quality of the information gained in the focus group process.

The other advantage of combining the two interventions is that, in addition to issue identification, you also know a lot about how employees are motivated. This gives you a lot of useful information as you begin to map out plans to effectively act on what you learn in the focus group sessions.

Other Methods of Ascertaining Employee Opinion

There are other ways to learn employee opinion. Open door policies, suggestion procedures, and one-on-one conversations (management walking around) are other ways to find out how employees feel about their work. But we do not characterize these methods as effective ways of driving and evaluating company-wide engagement.

While these tools are important aspects to any employee relations program (they are all discussed later in the book), they don't provide an effective "set-point" for your employee relations activities. Furthermore, while they can help with early warning of issues, they don't deliver the information a company needs to design a third-party intervention strategy. Chapter 15 on proactive employee communications describes ways to take advantage of these other programs in your company.

<u>Take Action</u>

- ☐ List the different subgroups within your organization. Determine which will provide the most useful information for improving current challenges in your company.
- ☐ Which type of engagement survey would best fit your company: anonymous forced response, small group interviews, or supervisor focus groups? Would a combination of methods work best?
- ☐ Can you think of some ways to use an "appreciative" mindset in your company? Are there ways to get employees talking about things the organization does

well? What are some things you think the company does well?

Chapter 8

Analyzing and Reporting Survey Results

"Truth suffers from too much analysis."
Frank Herbert

What You'll Learn In This Chapter

- ❑ How to break down survey results in order to pinpoint exactly where problems are occurring (and where they are not);
- ❑ Four options for categorizing survey results: overall scores, response distribution, high-low rated statement, and reporting segmentation; and
- ❑ Why you should include open-ended statements in your survey and how to analyze them.

Tabulating Engagement Survey Results

One of the most important aspects of conducting an employee engagement survey is tabulating the results appropriately. Collecting groups of random comments without proper categorizing is a sure recipe for disorganization and, ultimately, failure. While you can easily get lost in the data (I'll provide some tips on this below) a scientific, statistical approach to the data is best.

Issues must be analyzed along logical employee work groups in order to clearly plan how to attack problems that are identified (and even which problems to attack). This is especially true today in a world of micro-units. Under the NLRB decision in *Specialty Healthcare*[21] union organizers are able to file petitions in extremely small groups of workers

---

[21] *Specialty Healthcare and Rehabilitation Center of Mobile*, 357 NLRB No. 83 (2011).

(some recent decisions have allowed units of just the women's shoe department of a department store, or just some of the bakers in a chain of bakery restaurants). This makes it even more important to look at issues at the department level.

No matter which method of gathering opinion is utilized, it is necessary to organize the data in a way that is useful for strategy and planning purposes. Normally you group comments into categories of opinion.

For example, comments regarding pay and benefits should be separated from comments regarding policies, and both of these should be separated from comments about supervision. The table below lists the categories of behavior we typically use to assess employee engagement surveys. Of course, categories can be added or subtracted based on the specific needs and issues of the company.

Work Conditions	Training
Job Satisfaction	Immediate Supervisor
Company Pride	Communications
Pay and Benefits	Work Relations
Advancement	Top Management

In addition to categorizing opinion according to question category, the results are also analyzed using the demographic selections discussed in Chapter 7. Examples of these selections might include:

Department	Length of Service
Shift	Hourly / Salaried
Supervisor	Plant Location
Job Classification	Product Line

When you break survey results down this way you can pinpoint exactly where problems are occurring (and where they are not). Failure to break results down into work group categories like these can often hide significant problems in the company. Again, remember there is no such thing as an "average" employee or "average" department. Some groups may be more positive, which could mask the scores of groups that are more negative. Presenting the data in this way provides the clearest picture for the company and creates opportunities to solve problems that may have remained hidden under other methods.

In addition you should segment these work groups as discussed in Chapter 6. In each department you will have some workers who are strong promoters of the organization, some who are on the fence, and others who are vocal detractors of the company. You should report survey results using these segments as well.

There can be problems with breaking down data too narrowly. If the size of the work unit is small, or if the number of breakdowns is too numerous, there is the real possibility that only a few employees will fit into any one category. This creates two major problems. First, it can reduce the reliability of data, due to the fact that employees may fear that management will be able to identify individual employees who made a comment. This may result in employees answering untruthfully to statements about their supervisor or management.

There are also legal issues raised by the National Labor Relations Board regarding surveys that identify the individual making comments. These are discussed in Chapter 9. As a result, it is vital to reach a good balance between enough data to make strong recommendations and too much data, which can negatively impact the results of the survey. For this reason we do not normally report results for sub-groups with fewer than 10 employees.

Care should also be taken in determining how opinion is evaluated among the categories and work groups because there are several different ways to look at issues. For example, one might look at the overall average score in a particular work group. Another angle is to look at the percentage of employees who rated statements across the various levels of engagement or dissatisfaction. Another way is to look simply at which statements rated the highest or lowest on the survey. Finally, you also want to look at the segmentation analysis. There are advantages and disadvantages to each type of rating, and our recommendation is that all of them should be used to best analyze issues in a company.

Overall Scores

Overall scores are good for gauging, in general terms, how a group feels about a particular statement or category. These overall scores are misleading at times because extremely high ratings can sometimes mask a significant negative opinion on a question or issue.

For example, a department consisting of three shifts may have very strong favorable opinions on first and second shifts but extremely negative opinions on third shift. While a significant problem exists on the third shift, it is not evident in the overall score. As a result, a company may be unaware of a significant employee relations issue.

Here are two examples of how LRI reports overall scores on survey reports. The first is a simple chart that compares the overall score for a category on this year's survey to the score from a prior year.

The second is a table that shows the overall scores for each category surveyed (each row of the table is a different

different category) separated by each department surveyed (each column is a different department). This is a way to get a quick scan across all the work groups surveyed.

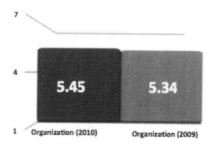

Figure 8.1
Sample Overall Category Score Report

Response Distribution

Category Comparisons by Group

	Organization	Organization (2009)	Department 1	Department 2	Department 3	Department 4
Total Respondents	137	35	20	23	72	21
Working Conditions	5.45	5.34	4.71	5.84	5.57	5.32
Job Satisfaction	5.49	5.12	5.08	5.76	5.51	5.53
Company Pride	5.23	4.63	4.64	5.41	5.26	5.46
Pay & Benefits	4.76	5.76	4.31	5.19	4.64	5.11
Advancement	4.73	4.32	4.38	5.32	4.57	4.93
Training	5.08	4.63	4.64	5.40	5.08	5.17
Supervision	5.49	5.32	5.17	5.83	5.50	5.39
Communication	5.07	5.76	4.34	5.50	5.07	5.30
Work Relations	4.94	5.13	4.44	5.50	4.83	5.18
Top Management	4.90	4.35	4.25	5.48	4.85	5.05
Overall Average	5.11	5.04	4.60	5.52	5.09	5.24

Figure 8.2 – Sample Group Category Comparisons Table

The advantage of this method is that a picture is formed of how employees feel on particular issues across the entire spectrum of responses. This method takes out the "averaging effect" of using overall scores. A disadvantage of this method is that it tends to create information overload. In other words, negative opinion is expressed to many questions. Without some sense of the overall score of a particular group, it becomes increasingly difficult to prioritize action areas.

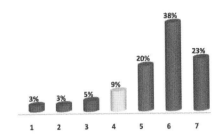

Figure 8.3 – Sample Response Distribution Chart

The charts below provides an example of how to report response distribution on survey results. This first is just a straight response distribution for a particular category. The second reports a response distribution for a particular statement on the survey.

High-Low Rated Statements
This is relatively straightforward. You simply rank order statements from high to low and look at the statements at each end of the spectrum. One key point here. As discussed earlier in the section on Appreciative Inquiry, it is vitally important to look not just at where an organization has challenges, but also to where it is achieving success.

Spend a lot of time during action planning looking at how to leverage the high rated statement areas against the challenges identified. For example, in an organization where communication is rated low, look for high-rated statements that have a communication component. For instance, if safety rated high I would want to know what the company does to effectively communicate around safety. That might be something you can apply to other areas. Often companies will be able to identify several "quick wins" just by focusing on doing more of what they already do well.

Below you can see an example of how to report high and low rated statements on our surveys.

10 High / Low Rated Statements

Overall Score	Statement	Category
6.25	11. My work area is safe and accidents are infrequent.	Working Conditions
6.20	3. I am proud to be an employee here.	Company Pride
6.20	1. Considering the work I do, my work area is orderly and clean.	Working Conditions
6.16	41. The company provides a safe working environment for employees.	Working Conditions
6.11	4. The benefits offered here are fair and reasonable when compared to similar jobs at other companies.	Pay & Benefits
6.09	32. I have no problem keeping up with my workload.	Job Satisfaction
6.07	18. I have a clear understanding of my job responsibilities.	Communication
6.05	52. If I had to do it over again, I would still go to work here.	Job Satisfaction
6.03	65. This organization has a great future.	Advancement
6.01	33. Our policies and procedures allow me to provide great service to our guests.	Company Pride

Overall Score	Statement	Category
4.85	45. People here get terminated only for good reasons.	Advancement
4.85	20. The management team does what they say they are going to do.	Top Management
4.83	8. Communications from top management are adequate for me to know what is going on in the organization.	Communication
4.81	58. I believe top management at my facility knows what employees think about most major issues.	Communication
4.77	59. There is very little friction between co-workers in my department.	Work Relations
4.74	30. My management team explains the reasons for their decisions.	Top Management
4.66	28. The channels of communication between employees and management are working satisfactorily.	Communication
4.52	66. Everyone here does their fair share of the work assigned to them.	Work Relations
4.12	25. Around here, "what" you know is more important than "who" you know.	Advancement
3.95	5. The most capable employees are always the ones selected for promotions.	Advancement

Strongly Disagree 1   7 Strongly Agree

Figure 8.4 – Sample High-Low Rated Statements

Reporting Segmentation

Next look at the segmentation of work groups. You can segment on a number of different items, but I like to do it based on our "net promoter" items. These are three items on the survey that we separate from the rest of the items. The three statements are:
- When I'm asked about work my comments are always positive;
- If I knew someone was looking for work I'd recommend they apply here; and

- If I had to do it over again I would still come to work here.

You then segment work groups based on the answers to those three statements. The answers to these statements are very predictive of overall engagement. Further, they also help you predict how someone looking for problems in your company (like a union organizer for example) is likely to perceive your company as a possible target. Here's an example of how to report segmentation on the three net promoter statements:

Analyzing Open-Ended Statements

Finally, many companies ask open-ended statements at the end of their survey. This is highly recommended. Here's a

Employee Engagement Index

	In-Group	Partially Affiliated	Neutral	Partially Disaffiliated	Out-Group
Grave	33%	51%	11%		
Swing	37%	45%	9%	4%	
Days	42%	46%	7%		
Overall	39%		9%	3%	
Goal	40%	30%	20%	10%	

Figure 8.5 – Employee Engagement Index

bonus tip in analyzing open-ended statements: pay special attention to the longer answers.

Longer answers tend to indicate the energy level around a particular issue. Someone who takes the time to write several paragraphs about something they dislike (or something they love – ask employees to rate what they like about work too) is probably spending a lot of time talking about that issue in other venues. As you consider action planning you should contemplate putting issues with long answers near the top of your pile of projects to examine.

There are a variety of different ways to report survey data. The key is to report it in a way that is easy to understand and helps you quickly identify opportunities for action. As I said at the outset, the important thing with analysis of data is to not get paralyzed by it.

Make the reporting work for you by focusing on identifying just a handful of the most important areas for action. Once those are identified, stop. Communicate the results and your plans (see the next chapter for tips on this) and then get to work acting on that handful of areas (chapter 10 covers this topic at length). Rinse, lather, repeat. Turning around an employee relations environment really can be that simple.

Take Action

- ☐ Determine what categories of opinion you would like the survey comments to be broken into, without making those groups too narrow.

- ☐ List five areas where your company is achieving success. It is just as important to know where you are excelling as well as where you are being challenged.

Chapter 9

Communicating Your Survey Results

"People fail to get along because they fear each other; they fear each other because they don't know each other; they don't know each other because they have not communicated with each other."
Martin Luther King Jr.

What You'll Learn In This Chapter
☐ How to determine what kind of setting is best for your organization when communicating survey results;
☐ How to utilize graphics when communicating survey results; and
☐ What legal issues to be aware of when planning an engagement survey.

Communicating Survey Results
The most important part of the engagement survey process is communicating the results. If you fail to communicate the survey results effectively, the survey can do more harm than good. There are a variety of methods for communicating survey results to a work group. We will discuss a few of those strategies here.

Involving Supervisors and Employees
Involve employees and supervisors in the survey communication process whenever you can. While there are situations where you may want to leave supervisors out of communication meetings (particularly where they are part of the problem), this is often not the best approach.

Even when you feel that employees may need some time alone, without their supervisor around, you can do both. Set it up where part of the meeting includes direct leaders while the other part gives employees a "skip step" opportunity with a leader at a level or two above their immediate manager.

There is a lot of benefit to including employees and supervisors in the communication meetings. This is especially true if you give them part of the agenda to deliver. There are several reasons you should consider having supervisors and employees involved in delivering survey results.

First, presenting the results forces people to really get engaged with the material. They won't just gloss over the report like they might if this was "just another meeting" to attend. If someone is going to present on the results, they will want to know them well enough to avoid looking dumb in front of their peers. This added pressure can really help get your supervisors or employees focused on the survey results.

Second, those who are tasked with survey communication also get more invested in follow up actions to the survey. Since a big part of the agenda relates to action planning the supervisors and employees involved in the communication process naturally tend to get more involved in the follow up. These individuals, who were there at the beginning of the process, will want to see it through to conclusion.

Third, employees tend to contribute more (and give their peers a break) when it comes to presenting material like this. They may have some good-natured fun about having a co-worker present material that is out of their normal daily routine, but they tend to be much more open and willing to contribute to the sessions when led by a peer or someone they work alongside every day.

Fourth, you can actually motivate your more negative team members to become part of the solution. One client recently assigned an employee widely considered to be the most negative employee in the entire company (not just at his plant, but he was a legend across all plants in the organization). It was a bold move, but it worked beautifully.

This employee didn't suddenly become a yes-man. But it was also the first time he ever felt like the company really wanted to know how he felt about things. Because of this, his feedback became much more constructive. He started volunteering to help with post-survey action planning. He became a big asset to the company (prior to this his managers would have removed a couple of letters from asset when discussing him).

Small Group Sessions
This is the most common – and I believe most desirable – method of communicating survey results for several reasons. The small group is more manageable in most companies. Between 10 and 20 employees in a group is about the size of most departments. It isn't too big, so the presenter can talk to each individual instead of a more anonymous crowd. This helps to prevent disruptions. But it is still a large enough group that people do not feel like they are being singled out.

The small group sessions should be delivered in a consistent manner. Companies typically have a formal 15-20 minute presentation about the engagement survey results and then about another 15-30 minute block of time for questions and answers. Depending on the results of the survey, more time may be necessary. A sample agenda for your survey communication meetings might look like this:

MEETING AGENDA
Recap of Survey Design
Present Survey Results
Comparisons with Last Year
Conclusions from Survey
Action Plan

Individual Meetings or Very Small Groups

For some businesses, especially small companies or ones in which large numbers of employees are not available at any particular time, this is the only effective method of delivering survey results in a meeting environment. The advantage of an intimate group is that the communication sessions can be custom tailored for the audience.

The disadvantage is that it takes a significantly larger commitment of time to deliver results in this fashion. It can also lead to concerns about whether everybody is getting the same information (which would be almost impossible).

Small group sessions can also be intimidating for the employees involved. Some workers might feel uncomfortable sitting alone with their supervisor discussing survey results – they may even think the supervisor knows how they responded to the survey. This scenario also raises concerns under the National Labor Relation Act, as discussed below. This is not our recommended method of delivering survey results. However, if it is the only alternative it is better to do individual meetings than to not meet at all.

Handouts Without a Meeting

This method is better suited for very large companies or companies where employee meetings are virtually impossible. These companies will create a handout that details many of the same things discussed during a communication meeting. The advantage of this method is that it ensures consistent communication across all groups of employees. The disadvantage is that it is impersonal and requires a significant amount of effort in crafting the document.

In addition, employers should be aware that such a document could be used as a tool during future organizing attempts or in litigation against the company. Complaints raised in the survey might be used to prove later that an employer failed to take action to mitigate, for example, discrimination complaints. Union supporters will use the negative scores as evidence the company should be organized. These are not, by the way, reasons to avoid communicating survey results – they instead are reasons to take extra care in communicating the results and reacting to complaints raised.

Large Group Meetings

The large group meeting format is often the only method available for some companies. The sessions are very similar to the small group sessions outlined above. The disadvantage of large group meetings is that they can be unwieldy and hard to control. Some employees are intimidated when speaking in very large groups.

In addition, particularly for companies that have recently undergone organizing activities, the possibility exists that overly negative employees will showboat or take over the meeting. These problems can ruin an otherwise excellent opportunity to begin the healing process in a company. For these reasons, meetings should be facilitated by an experienced individual. If these situations are present, it is best to hold smaller group sessions where the overly negative individuals can be isolated in one group.

Use of Graphics

Use of some type of graphic presentation when communicating survey results. A variety of different representations of statistical information are available. There are also a variety of different ways to use the information. You can see some sample survey communication slides in Appendix 2in the back of the book. This gives you several examples of graphical representations of statistical information we gather on surveys (some of these you've just seen in Chapter 8 on survey analysis and reporting).

While graphs and charts of this nature can be overused in a presentation, it is a good idea to use them as a jumping off point for a more in-depth discussion of the issues raised.

These graphics can be used in overhead slides, PowerPoint presentations and handouts to employees. Don't let the graphics become the presentation. Use the graphs and charts to supplement the key point being made: what can we do to create the best employee relations environment possible?

Legal Issues

There are a number of legal considerations when planning a engagement survey. These fall into one of two categories. First, there are a number of NLRB decisions regarding the use of engagement surveys. The second area of concern involves responding to complaints of discrimination or safety violations that come up on the survey. Failure to respond to these issues can lead to potential liability under Title VII of the Civil Rights Act of 1964 or the Occupational Safety and Health Act.

The NLRB has held in some circumstances that employee engagement surveys can violate the National Labor Relations Act ("the Act" or "NLRA" hereafter).

Section 8(a)(1) of the NLRA provides that "it shall be an unfair labor practice for an employer to interfere with, restrain or coerce employees in the exercise of rights guaranteed in section 7." This section (as interpreted through Board decisions) prohibits employers from soliciting grievances where a purpose of such solicitation is to induce employees to reject a union as their collective bargaining agent.[22]

Depending on the factual circumstances, the NLRB has held that some employee engagement surveys violate section 8(a)(1) as solicitations of grievances, while others do not.[23]

---

[22] See *Clark Equipment Company*, 278 NLRB 498, 516 (1986); *Ben Franklin Division of City Products Corporation*, 251 NLRB 1512, 1518 (1971).
[23] Cf. *Grove Valve and Regulator Company*, 262 NLRB 285 (1982) (satisfaction survey lawful where prior survey conducted in same unit absent union activity and questionnaire stated three times that survey does not imply changes in wages, benefits or work conditions) and *Leland Stanford*

The Board relies on a number of factors when determining whether a survey violates the prohibition on soliciting grievances, including the existence of union activity, the types of questions asked, the timing of the survey, whether participants are anonymous, whether the company has conducted surveys in the past, whether issues brought up in the survey are corrected.[24] Let's now look at two NLRB cases, one in which the NLRB said that the survey was legal and another where the NLRB objected.

In *Clark Equipment Company*, a union lost an election that was first held in February of 1978. The union objected to the first election and the NLRB, agreeing with the union objections, set aside the election and directed a second election. The second election was conducted in July of 1979, and the union lost again. Once again the union filed objections to the election. In May of 1980, while the NLRB considered the objections to the second election, the company announced and conducted a survey by distributing a questionnaire to all employees in its manufacturing operation.

Jr. University, 240 NLRB 1138 (1978) (survey lawful where, although administered in pre-election context, no active campaigning occurred during the period before or after the survey and no election was scheduled or imminent) and *Clark Equipment*, 278 NLRB 498 (1986) (survey lawful where conducted 11 months after election and during time where there was no special union activity) with *Mid-State Distributing Company*, 276 NLRB 1511 (1985) (survey unlawful where no surveys were ever conducted prior to union organizing activity, and where employees were told during meetings that the problems that came up during the survey would be addressed by the company) and *Ben Franklin*, 251 NLRB 1512 (1971) (satisfaction survey unlawful where first formal survey conducted during midst of very active organizing campaign and where employer quickly made changes in wages, benefits and work conditions in response to survey) and *Tom Wood Pontiac, Inc.*, 179 NLRB 581 (1969), enfd. 447 F.2d 383 (7th Cir. 1971) (survey unlawful where conducted one week after stipulated election agreement and survey organizer repeatedly discussed correcting issues that came out of survey).
[24] See e.g. *Clark Equipment Company*, 278 NLRB 498, 516 (1986); *Ben Franklin*, 251 NLRB 1512, 1518 (1971).

The survey questionnaire was not the first survey conducted by the employer, who had earlier surveyed randomly selected groups of employees and on a separate occasion surveyed its supervisors. However, these earlier surveys were substantially different than the survey distributed in 1980.

The new survey asked about policies and procedures, if the company was a good place to work and whether or not employee complaints received attention. It also contained an open-ended question that asked what employees would change about the company. The employer asserted that the survey was confidential, but employees were asked to reveal their department, work shift, sex and length of employment. The union filed an unfair labor practice charge alleging that the survey violated section 8(a)(1) of the Act.

The NLRB ruled that the survey did not violate the Act. The Board found that the survey, conducted 11 months after the second election and at a time when no "special union activity" was under way, did not unlawfully solicit grievances.[25] They ruled the survey lawful in spite of the conclusion that the survey could identify individual employee opinions on questions that could readily disclose employees' union sentiments.[26]

In *Ben Franklin*, the employer opened a distribution center in 1978 and union activity began almost immediately after the facility opened. In April of 1979, the union filed a petition to represent the employees of the facility, with an election scheduled for July 13. On June 6, the employer announced an employee engagement survey and asked employees to complete a survey form. One employee asked whether the surveys were being conducted because of the union activity

---

[25] *Clark Equipment*, 278 NLRB at 517.
[26] Id.

and was told no and that surveys were common. The employer testified that, while informal surveys of a sampling of employees were common at other facilities, they decided to conduct a more formal survey using a questionnaire at this facility.

Follow-up meetings were conducted later in June, where the survey results were communicated to employees. The employer representative explained that the survey showed that communication between employees and supervisors needed improvement, and that there were questions about benefits and wages. Employees were told during the meeting that the company would train the supervisors and that they would receive feedback about wages in July. True to their word, in early July the company announced pay increases to go into effect over the next year. Insurance plans were also explained.

The Board held that the conduct of the engagement survey violated section 8(a)(1) of the Act. Among the critical factors noted in the decision were that the survey did not follow the same pattern as other surveys, the survey occurred during the middle of a very active organizing effort and that the employer made improvements in wages and work conditions as a result of the survey.[27]

Holding individual or very small group meetings with employees can, under certain circumstances, also run afoul of the Act's protections. A number of NLRB decisions have found that, when an employee meeting occurs at a time, place or with personnel such that the employee may feel threatened or intimidated, the employer has engaged in unlawful interrogation under the Act.[28] The NLRB will examine all the

---

[27] *Ben Franklin*, 251 NLRB at 1519.
[28] See e.g. *Huntsville Mfg. Co.* 211 NLRB 54 (1974), *enforcement denied*, 514 F.2d 723 (5th Cir. 1972) (threat interfered with election even though only

surrounding circumstances when determining whether an employer's meeting was conducted in such a manner as to be threatening to the employee.[29]

In order to avoid problems with individual meetings, we suggest that employer's begin these meetings by reassuring employees under the guidelines established in the NLRB's *Johnnie's Poultry* decision.[30] These safeguards were articulated in the context of questioning an employee regarding the investigation of an unfair labor practice charge. Nevertheless, they are considered persuasive by the NLRB.[31]

The *Johnnie's Poultry* safeguards are as follows:
1. The purpose of the questioning must be communicated to the employee.
2. An assurance of no reprisal must be given.
3. The employee's participation must be obtained on a voluntary basis.
4. The questioning must take place in an atmosphere free from union animus.
5. The questioning itself must not be coercive in nature.
6. The questions must be relevant to the issues involved in the complaint.
7. The employee's subjective state of mind must not be probed.

---

one percent of employees threatened; enforcement denied due to union losing election by large majority); *Super Thrift Markets*, 233 NLRB 409 (1977).
[29] See *Blue Flash Express*, 109 NLRB 591 (1954).
[30] *Johnnie's Poultry Co.*, 146 NLRB 770 (1964), *enforcement denied*, 344 F.2d 617 (8th Cir. 1965) (denied on the basis that factual determinations not based on substantial evidence, did not express disagreement with the legal standards identified).
[31] The Board will quickly find an employer has violated 8(a)(1) if the safeguards are not followed in the context of questioning an employee regarding an unfair labor practice trial. See e.g. *Kyle & Stephen, Inc.* 259 NLRB 731 (1981).

---

8. The questions must not "otherwise interfere with the statutory rights of employees."[32]

Explaining these issues to an employee prior to an individual meeting should provide a significant measure of protection to any potential unfair labor practice charge.

Another legal consideration regards complaints of discrimination. Employers have an obligation under Title VII of the Civil Rights Act of 1964 to avoid discrimination on the basis of race, color, religion, sex or national origin.[33] Other statutes prohibit discrimination based on age and disability.[34]

An employer who is made aware of discrimination or harassment based on a protected characteristic has an affirmative obligation to investigate and deal with those concerns.[35] Therefore, an employer who learns of discrimination involving a protected characteristic during an employee engagement survey, must promptly conduct a thorough investigation of that claim and carefully document its investigation and any action taken.

Another potential issue regards complaints of safety problems. Employers are obligated under the "general duty clause" of the Occupational Safety and Health Act to provide a workplace "free from recognized hazards that are likely to

---

[32] Id.

[33] 42 U.S.C. § 2000e et seq.

[34] See e.g. 42 U.S.C. §621 et seq. (Age Discrimination in Employment Act); 42 U.S.C. § 12101 et seq. (Americans With Disabilities Act of 1990).

[35] See e.g. Burlington Industries v. Ellerth, 524 U.S. 742 (1998) (one factor considered in employer affirmative defense to sex harassment cases is prompt investigation of claims); Farragher v. City of Boca Raton, 524 U.S. 775 (1998) (prompt investigation of claims is one factor considered in employer affirmative defense to sex harassment cases); Montero v. AGCO Corp., 80 FEP Cases 1658 (9th Cir. 1999) (no claim for sex harassment under Title VII due to fact that employer promptly investigated and took action within 11 days of initial complaint).

cause death or serious physical harm" to employees.[36] An employer who has knowledge of a preventable hazard and fails to correct it violates this obligation and is liable under the Act.[37]

Therefore, an employer who learns of a dangerous condition through an employee engagement survey is obligated under the general duty clause to make the workplace free from that condition. While you never enjoy finding out about discrimination, in some ways, it's a good thing that these issues are brought to an employer's attention through a survey rather than a formal OSHA/EEOC complaint. It's better to find out about the racist supervisor, fire him, deal with the problem, try to repair the damage, and move forward than to let it linger and get nailed with a huge lawsuit and EEOC complaint.

Like any other employee relations tool, an employee survey is only part one component of a comprehensive employee relations strategy. Nevertheless, engagement surveys can form the backbone of a highly effective program. Surveys publicly demonstrate management's commitment to employee communication. They help pinpoint problem areas for attack, and they give companies an effective means of objectively judging the progress (or lack of progress) made on employee relations issues.

Take Action

☐ Consider the areas in your business that are already working well. What are the tactics used in these areas

---

[36] 29 U.S.C. § 654.

[37] See e.g. Pratt & Whitney Aircraft v. Secretary of Labor, 649 F.2d 96 (2nd Cir. 1981) (dangerous potential of condition must be actually known or generally recognized before employer is liable for violation of general duty obligation).

---

that make them successful? Apply those tactics to other areas that are in need of improvement.

☐ Determine the best way to involve employees and supervisors in the communication of your organization's survey results.

Chapter 10

Action Planning: Planning Your Fifty-Two Week Calendar

"No date on the calendar is as important as tomorrow"
Roy Howard, Scripps-Howard Newspapers

What You'll Learn In This Chapter
- ☐ Steps to create a concrete vision of your ideal employee relations environment;
- ☐ Three key strategies for project planning to achieve your imagined employee relations environment;
- ☐ The importance of including employees in the planning and implementation process; and
- ☐ How to utilize survey data to create your master plan.

Now that you know what to do, how will you do it? In order to transform your employee relations environment you have to do more than just learn about best practices or things that other companies have done. You must not only make concrete actions aimed at achieving specific objectives, but you must change the conversations that occur throughout your organization on a daily basis. This chapter will help you do just that.

First know this: if you fail to plan, you plan to fail. There are a tremendous number of small acts that are required in order to transform any organization. Not all of them will be planned – in fact many of them will be spontaneous. Still, you cannot change conversations or relationships without first changing yourself, and that we will plan together.

There is no one specific action or program that an employer can implement to turn around a negative culture. Just as it took thousands of actions over a long period of time to create your current employee relations environment, so will it take thousands of actions over a long period of time to improve that environment.

Think of the project like a jumbo jet sitting on a runway preparing for takeoff. At first its engines roar, even though the plane remains still. Eventually the massive fuselage begins to inch forward slowly. Later the jet begins to pick up speed, moving faster down the runway, but still moving more like a bus than a plane. However, as more and more momentum is created, forces surrounding the plane begin to add to the momentum – forces the pilot has no control over, but forces that exist nevertheless. The plane begins to lift and flies into the air. The engines do not run any faster - in fact they can even reduce their thrust, but the plane continues to fly at great speed.

Like the plane when its engines first start, your plan may at first seem like it is stalled. There will be times that you feel like you are standing still on the runway, even though the engines are going at full throttle. Sometimes you might even feel like you are going backwards. Yet eventually you will see movement. As you gain velocity you will be carried forward and the momentum will build. Soon your employee relations environment will be soaring.

While there are no shortcuts, you can set yourself up to succeed with a good plan. Understand that the plan is more about changing you than it is about changing others. It gives you a bigger picture about where you're going as an employer. By utilizing a master plan, you can avoid potential sidetracks and inconsistent actions that may derail earlier actions by creating an overall framework for change. Getting the "big picture" will help you keep things on track when you feel like the plan is slipping.

This chapter briefly explains the process I use to develop a project plan for transforming an organization's employee relations environment. It discusses the principles of project planning that are utilized and then looks at a typical Left of Boom calendar.

How to Begin

The first step to an effective improvement program is to build your Steering Committee. Depending on the size of your organization and the key issues identified in the survey you may have one Steering Committee for the whole company or a Steering Committee for each department or key work area. I will assume in this chapter that you are looking at things by department – that is most common.

Include individuals from all levels within the department. This is an important time to involve employees. Having employees involved throughout the entire process will not only show that you are truly interested in their input, but will also show your employees the high priority you place on workplace engagement. Finally, it gives you a great opportunity to get immediate feedback directly from employees about your progress and any course corrections you may want to make.

In order to use resources efficiently, top management should use the Net Promoter Vulnerability Analysis to rank each department. The departments that are considered to be the least vulnerable should be given the opportunity to go through the action planning process for their department without top management intervention. This will allow corporate resources to be used for the most vulnerable departments. It is important to remember that improvements in every department are important. The least vulnerable departments should not be ignored in favor of the most vulnerable.

Identify your Objectives

The next step is to identify your objectives. Objectives can be defined as specific goals that you wish to accomplish. These objectives are shown in your Employee Engagement Survey.

The Final Report identifies the areas that your employees are most and least satisfied with. These results are shown in the 10 High/Low Statements report. In addition you should look at the open-ended statements where employees write their likes and dislikes about the organization. Figure 10.1 shows an example of a High/Low report.

10 High / Low Rated Statements

Overall Score	Statement	Category
6.25	11. My work area is safe and accidents are infrequent.	Working Conditions
6.20	3. I am proud to be an employee here.	Company Pride
6.20	1. Considering the work I do, my work area is orderly and clean.	Working Conditions
6.18	41. The company provides a safe working environment for employees.	Working Conditions
6.11	4. The benefits offered here are fair and reasonable when compared to similar jobs at other companies.	Pay & Benefits
6.09	32. I have no problem keeping up with my workload.	Job Satisfaction
6.07	18. I have a clear understanding of my job responsibilities.	Communication
6.05	52. If I had to do it over again, I would still go to work here.	Job Satisfaction
6.03	65. This organization has a great future.	Advancement
6.01	33. Our policies and procedures allow me to provide great service to our guests.	Company Pride

Overall Score	Statement	Category
4.85	45. People here get terminated only for good reasons.	Advancement
4.85	20. The management team does what they say they are going to do.	Top Management
4.83	8. Communications from top management are adequate for me to know what is going on in the organization.	Communication
4.81	56. I believe top management at my facility knows what employees think about most major issues.	Communication
4.77	59. There is very little friction between co-workers in my department.	Work Relations
4.74	50. My management team explains the reasons for their decisions.	Top Management
4.66	28. The channels of communication between employees and management are working satisfactorily.	Communication
4.52	69. Everyone here does their fair share of the work assigned to them.	Work Relations
4.12	25. Around here, "what" you know is more important than "who" you know.	Advancement
3.95	5. The most capable employees are always the ones selected for promotions.	Advancement

Strongly Disagree 1   7 Strongly Agree

Figure 10.1 – Example of the 10 High/Low Table from Employee Satisfaction Survey

The 10 High/Low statements, along with the written statements, give you an objective measure of the best and worst aspects of your organization, according to your employees. Use these statements to start a discussion with your Steering Committee on what objectives should be identified.

This discussion should focus on <u>both</u> the high and low rated statements. The low rated statements can be used to identify improvement objectives, while the high rated statements can be used to identify maintenance objectives. The high rated statements reveal areas in your organization that are already working well, thus exposing tactics that can be applied to other areas that are deficient.

The best way to reach your objectives is to write them down. When you write down your goals, you are on your way to accomplishing them. This will also give you a list to come back to in the future to remind yourself of the goals you have set for the organization.

To begin this process, examine the 10 high rated statements and the "Like" written statements. Go through these statements within your committee and identify 5 to 15 objectives. These objectives can be the maintenance or improvement of current efforts. Write down these objectives using the format below.

Begin by listing all your objectives. Beside each objective list:

1. Why do you want to accomplish this objective?
2. What will it mean to you personally if this objective is achieved?
3. What will be the consequences if the objective is not reached?

After listing your Positive objectives, go through the process again using the 10 low rated statements and the "Dislike" written statements. Again try to come up with between 5 to 15 improvement objectives and answer the same questions.

When answering the above questions, keep in mind the reality of the issue and what it means to your organization. This information will allow you to understand the importance of each objective to both you and your organization.

Whiteacre Industries Example:
In order to illustrate this process, the rest of the chapter will use the following example:

After examining the results of their Employee Engagement Survey, Whiteacre Industries identifies communication as a low rated issue. Specifically, employees don't feel as though they have enough information on what is happening within the organization. Therefore, in order to address this issue, their objective is to "Increase the ways in which employees are informed about what's going on in the company." Here is what Whiteacre's objectives might look like:

Objective	Increase the ways in which employees are informed about what's going on in the company.
Reason for Objective	Employees are dissatisfied with the amount of information they receive about the organization.
Meaning if Achieved	Employees will be more aligned with company goals, resulting in a better understanding of initiatives. They will trust management and feel valued and respected.
Consequences of Failure	Employees will remain dissatisfied. They will view us as out of touch. They will rely on gossip and rumors. Reduced productivity.

This organization might have several other objectives identified in the survey. That is fine. You simply take each objective and map it out using the same process. When you are done, you will have each objective listed like the one above.

Prioritize your Objectives

Now that you have identified your objectives, it is time to prioritize them. The first step is to think about each objective and decide what it will take to accomplish each goal. Then, based on these factors, rate the items on (1) how much impact they will have on the organization and (2) how difficult it will be to attain. The form in Figure 10.2 can be used to aid this process.

Objective: Increase the ways in which employees are informed about happenings within the organization.

Factors to Consider:

1. Time: Need time to gather and distribute information.

2. Management Support: Need approval for all projects.

3. Budget Approvals: No budget approvals needed.

4. Needed Information: Constant Organizational and Department updates.

5. Other: N/A

Please rate the following statements by circling the appropriate number.

1. If accomplished, how much impact will this objective have on the organization?

Low Impact		Neutral Impact		High Impact
1	2	3	4	(5)

2. How easy will this objective be to accomplish?

Difficult to Attain		Neither Difficult nor Easy		Easy to Attain
1	2	3	(4)	5

Figure 10.2 – Objective Prioritization

Use the following when rating each objective on its impact or difficulty:

- The LEAST DIFFICULT goals to attain are those that can be achieved in the least amount of time and with the least amount of resources
- The MOST DIFFICULT goals to attain are those that require a large amount of time to implement, as well as the use of multiple resources.
- The goals that have LOW IMPACT on your organization are those that will have the least impact on employee engagement or impact just a small part of the organization.
- The goals that have a HIGH IMPACT will have a far-reaching effect throughout the organization and are likely to greatly increase engagement with the company.

After you have rated each objective, plot them on a prioritization grid like you see in Figure 10.3. This is a great exercise to do on a whiteboard or flipchart with your Steering Committee. Write each objective on a sticky note and have committee members put their objective where they think it fits on the matrix. Let the group debate whether they would change where the sticky notes are placed (in other words, do we have the difficulty and impact of each objective placed properly).

Based on the ratings you gave to each objective, their positions are now plotted on the grid. Categorize the goals based on (1) how easy/difficult the goal is to attain and (2) how much impact the attainment of that goal would make on your organization.

If you plot out your objectives on the matrix in Figure 10.3 you will quickly visualize that you want to focus on areas colored green for your initial projects (these are easy to attain and high impact). As you make progress you will start going after projects in the blue zone (a little harder to attain and a little lower impact than the green zone, but still very worthwhile). Eventually you may pick projects in the yellow zone (high impact but hard to attain, or easy to attain but low impact). You will probably avoid projects in the red zone that are both hard to attain and low impact.

Theory of Constraint

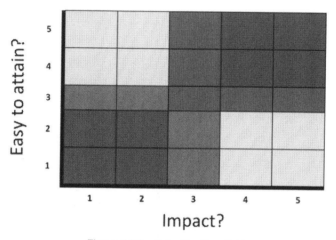

Figure 10.3 – Prioritization Grid

The Theory of Constraint (TOC) was introduced by Eliyahu M. Goldratt.[38] According to TOC, an organization, like a chain, can only be as effective as its weakest link. No matter how weak the other links in the chain, it will always break at the weakest link. In an organization, effectiveness is hindered by how weak the weakest link is. Therefore, in order to improve the organization, one must begin with the weakest link.

---

[38] Eliyahu M. Goldratt, *The Goal: A Process of Ongoing Improvement* (North River Press 1992). *The Goal* is not your normal business book. It is a novel that teaches a critical business lesson. It is a fun read in addition to being a classic text on one of the more important concepts in running a lean and efficient operation. I most highly recommend it.

We use the TOC as another way to identify which objectives to focus on first. In addition to using the matrix in Figure 3 to find projects that have a high impact on the organization and are the easiest to attain, also apply the TOC filter.

You apply the TOC filter by looking at each potential objective and thinking about the root causes of the associated challenges. Ask the Steering Committee, "What is the constraint?" Is it a lack of training? Is it a lack of resources? Is it a lack of communication? What other reasons might be the cause of this issue?

Let's say you are looking at the objective to increase the ways employees know what is going on in the organization. What is the constraint? It might be that because their equipment is never turned off, there is very little time to "hand off" or hold meetings during work time. It could be that employees are scattered across a broad area and that face-to-face meetings are more challenging. Your constraint could be that supervisors are not trained on how to communicate. Perhaps your supervisors don't even know what is going on in the organization and that is the constraint.

It is not uncommon to find one key constraint behind several issues you've identified as possible projects. Once you are satisfied that you have identified the key constraint, then identify a project that allows you to tackle that constraint. Tackle just one project at a time and begin each project by targeting the related constraint (Goldratt's book has a lot of ideas about how to deal with constraints).

Finally, try to identify a project that allows you to leverage one of the areas where you rated strong on the survey. Let's say your employees ranked safety communications as one of your most positive areas. That is a place to look for examples to leverage. How do you communicate about safety? How do these communications overcome the constraints you identified earlier? Is there a way to "bootstrap" your chosen project to some of the things you are already doing well? These are great conversation starters as you begin brainstorming how to attack your chosen objective.

Remember, although all goals are important, you should start by focusing on those goals that are the least difficult to attain and will have a high impact on the organization. As these goals are met, you can move on to the most difficult/high impact goals, followed by the least difficult/low impact goals. If you are lucky enough to get through these goals, then turn your attention to the most difficult/low impact goals. As you improve each weak link, the chain will get stronger and stronger.

Action Planning

Once you have chosen one positive area to leverage and one negative area to focus on, the next step is to dissect each one to fully understand what it will take to overcome your challenges. Under the objective you've chosen, list specific outcomes that must be accomplished in order to successfully meet your goal.

Under each outcome, list milestone achievements that will help you monitor your progress for that outcome. Think of each milestone as a step in accomplishing that outcome. Do not list every minor step that much be accomplished, but rather the major steps that will be evidence of true progress in achieving your goal.

The next step is to assign a completion date to each milestone, as well as a team member that will be in charge of accomplishing it. Figures 10.4 and 10.5 provide an example of a worksheet you can use to identify and map out the specific outcomes and milestone achievements for each objective. The example used previously is used again to illustrate how to fill out the worksheet.

Objective Plan

Objective: _Increase the ways in which employees are informed about happenings within the organization._

1) **Specific Outcome:** _Regularly communicate updates about what is going on in the business through a Company Facebook page._

   a) **Milestone Achievement:** _Survey employees to determine if stated outcome will be effective._

      i) **Date of Completion:** _August 15, 2010_

      ii) **Assigned Team Member:** _John Baker_

   b) **Milestone Achievement:** _Delegate responsibilities regarding who will keep up with the Facebook page._

      i) **Date of Completion:** _August 25, 2010_

      ii) **Assigned Team Member:** _Judy Little_

   c) **Milestone Achievement:** _Collect information about what should go on the Facebook page through researching the appropriate sources._

      i) **Date of Completion:** _September 15, 2010_

      ii) **Assigned Team Member:** _Rob Aster_

   d) **Milestone Achievement:** _Build the Facebook page._

      i) **Date of Completion:** _October 1, 2010_

      ii) **Assigned Team Member:** _Sean Timmet_

   e) **Milestone Achievement:** _Promote the Facebook page; Encourage employees to join the page_

      i) **Date of Completion:** _October 15, 2010_

      ii) **Assigned Team Member:** _Rick Lifton_

Figure 10.4 Sample Objective Plan

f) **Milestone Achievement:** _Monitor the frequency of updates on the Facebook page for the first month of operation._

   i) **Date of Completion:** _November 15, 2010_

   ii) **Assigned Team Member:** _Sarah Wester_

g) **Milestone Achievement:** _Determine how to measure the effectiveness of the outcome._

   i) **Date of Completion:** _November 30, 2010_

   ii) **Assigned Team Member:** _Pam Mistin_

h) **Milestone Achievement:** _Resurvey employees to determine if the outcome was successful._

   i) **Date of Completion:** _January 1, 2010_

   ii) **Assigned Team Member:** _Josh Street_

Figure 10.5 – Sample Objective Plan

Measuring your Outcome

Begin with the end in mind. It's not just one of the Seven Habits[39] it is a critical component of effective Action Planning. How will you know whether you are making progress toward your goal? How will you know when you've achieved it? That is why you must think about at the beginning of the project how you plan to measure progress.

After you implement a change (we consultants call this an "intervention" in the system – I guess because it sounds fancy), you must measure whether it was successful in accomplishing the overall outcome. There are a variety of

---

[39] Steven R. Covey, *The Seven Habits of Highly Effective People 25th Anniversary Edition* (Simon & Schuster 2013).

different ways you might measure the results of that intervention. Below is a list of some suggestions for evaluating your outcome and some of the advantages (and disadvantages) of each method.

- If the outcome is specifically targeted to improve a score on the Employee Engagement Survey, re-survey your employees to see if there was an increase in the scores on that item or category.
  - o Advantage: Direct, objective feedback on what you have worked on.
  - o Disadvantage: Data could be skewed if that item (or set of items) is given independently of the rest of the survey.
- If your project is going to be visible to your employees, consider conducting spot interviews or focus groups to have a conversation with your employees about whether the intervention accomplished your goal.
  - o Advantage: You hear directly from your employees how they feel about the program.
  - o Disadvantage: Employees may not feel comfortable telling you directly they do not like the program (you can counter this by being abundantly clear that you want and appreciate the feedback).
- If your project is likely to impact other observable behavior in the workplace, get a benchmark before you begin and then re-measure that area after you've intervened. You could use objective measures such as absenteeism, turnover, number of complaints, volunteers, etc.
  - o Advantage: Objective measure, independent of the intervention itself so it is less likely to be influenced by the fact we are paying attention to it (the Hawthorne Effect discussed in Chapter 5).
  - o Disadvantage: The measure may not be directly related to your specific outcome or could be being

negatively influenced by some other outside influence. You will want to think about how to "separate the signal from the noise" when using measurements like this.

Objective Outline

Now that you have dissected each objective into manageable steps, the next step is to make a timeline with all the completion dates. The timeline can be formatted as an actual timeline that can be seen by all members of management or through the use of a company calendar. As long as all members of management have access to the timeline and can view the upcoming completion dates, whatever format works best for you and your organization will work.

Figures 10.6 and 10.7 provide a couple of example formats that can be used to outline all your objectives, outcomes, and milestones. For each objective, fill out the chart accordingly.

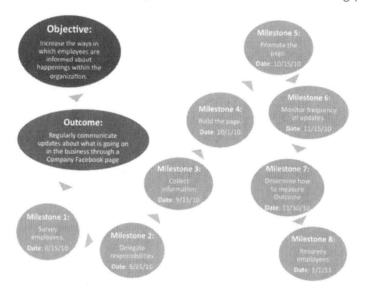

Figure 10.6 – Milestone Objective

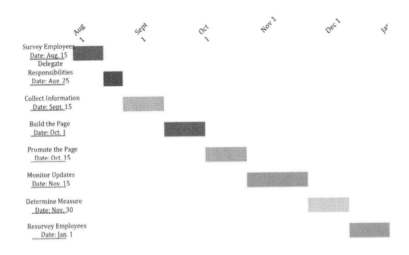

Figure 10.7 – Project Timeline

Putting It All Together

These are the key steps to develop the initial action plan. It is a fair amount of work, but it is well worth it. Once you have the plan in place, roll up your sleeves, execute on the plan, and then measure your progress. You may have to make course corrections along the way. But if you are tracking things the way I've laid out here you will know exactly where you've gone off the tracks, giving you a good idea of what interventions might get you headed back in the right direction.

I recognize that this is a lot of information and the first time through you may need a sounding board to just make sure you are on track. Anyone who has purchased this book is entitled to a complimentary 30-minute consultation with me to go over their planning documents and worksheets to discuss their specific situation. There is a certificate in the back of this book you can send in to initiate the consultation. Don't hesitate to take advantage of it – I love to hear how people are applying the lessons.

Communicate with Employees

Just as communicating the results of your engagement survey with employees is a critical step in the process, so too is communicating about your action planning process and progress. You are already aware of the issues employees are most satisfied and dissatisfied with from your Engagement Survey. Once you have put your action plans into place, you need to discuss what you're doing and how the actions you are taking are attacking issues brought up in the survey.

These meetings should discuss the objectives you have identified, the outcomes, and the milestones you are working to achieve. Allow the employees to voice their opinion on the effectiveness and perceived value of each objective. By allowing employee input, you are showing them you care about their opinions and are working to make the organization a better place.

During the Communication Meetings, you should focus on four areas:

- What the surveys told you.
- What you are going to do about the results.
- What you have done so far.
- What you are going to do next.

Figures 10.8, 10.9, and 10.10 provide a good example of what a typical action planning meeting slide deck might look like. It's only three slides, but covers all four points.

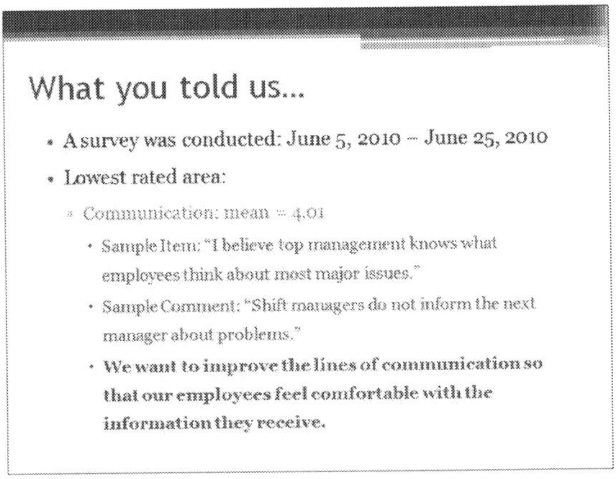

Figure 10.8 – Action Plan Communication Slide 1

The first slide should include information about the results of the survey including:

- When the survey was conducted;
- The lowest rated areas;
- Examples of the areas using sample items and comments; and
- Importance of the issue.

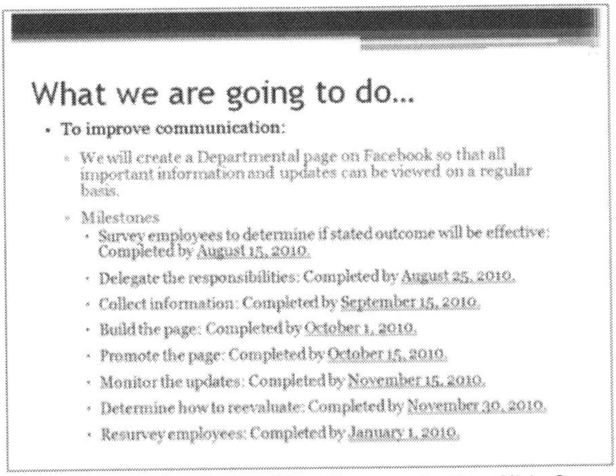

Figure 10.9 – Action Plan Communication Slide 2

The second slide should include the steps you plan to take to improve the problem area. The information on the slide should include:

- The specific outcome you wish to accomplish and
- The milestones you have set and their completion dates.

What we have done so far...

- The committee has been selected including:
  - Jeremy Bates (Dept. Manager)
  - Sarah King (Assistant Manager)
  - Leslie Plots (Floor Associate)
  - Alex Drist (Floor Associate)
- The first meeting was held on: July 10, 2010
- Next meeting will be held on: July 25, 2010
- We will report our progress via a Department-wide meeting on: September 30, 2010

Figure 10.10 – Action Plan Communication Slide 3

The final slide should outline the steps you have already taken in accomplishing this goal and what you plan to do next. Include:

- The committee members that have been chosen
- When the next progress meeting will be held
- When employees can expect an update

Another way to allow employees to keep track of the progress for each objective is to post the objectives and completion dates for everyone to see. This will let employees know what has already been accomplished; as well as, when they can expect objectives to be realized.

Figure 10.11 shows an example of a format that can be used to show employees the progress that has been made on each outcome. As each milestone has been achieved, the bubble can be filled. Once the outcome has been accomplished, the star burst at the top can be filled in to show it has been completed.

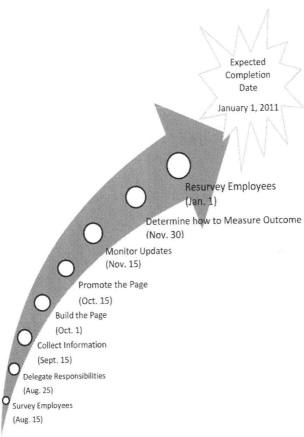

Goal: Regularly communicate updates about what is going on in the business through a Company Facebook

Expected
Completion
Date

January 1, 2011

Resurvey Employees
(Jan. 1)

Determine how to Measure Outcome
(Nov. 30)

Monitor Updates
(Nov. 15)

Promote the Page
(Oct. 15)

Build the Page
(Oct. 1)

Collect Information
(Sept. 15)

Delegate Responsibilities
(Aug. 25)

Survey Employees
(Aug. 15)

Figure 10.11 – Action Plan Progress Poster

What's Next? Rinse. Lather. Repeat.

Remember that the examples given previously only cover one objective you identified. You are also simultaneously working on leveraging and maintaining one of your strong areas. Once you feel like you've made significant progress toward reaching your first objective you may want to start on objective number 2.

When should you take on a new objective? It is not always necessary to wait until you are completely finished with one outcome to begin another. I do not recommend working on more than one objective at a time as you get started. But once you get the hang of it or have a Steering Committee that is chomping at the bit for another project it can be quite efficient to conduct more than one objective at a time. Once you have an outcome that is at a maintenance stage, it is time to consider beginning a new objective to attack.

But be careful! Dividing attention among too many objectives is the most common problem companies have with these projects. Often dividing your focus results in accomplishing none of the objectives you want to attack. Always err on the side of doing too little – you will have time (not to mention momentum) to accomplish the next objective.

Also remember that each time you intervene in a system you may create unintended (or at least unforeseen) consequences. This is another reason that picking off one project at a time, and deliberately measuring the success of that project – and dealing with any unforeseen issues – is the best way to go.

Finally, don't forget to celebrate. As completion dates from milestones are hit or objective areas have been completed, it is important to celebrate these successes. For interim milestones, this may be just celebrated among the HR department. For larger project completions, the celebrations should be firm wide. These celebrations will help keep attention focused on the organization's commitment to improve the employee relations environment and will also to help generate momentum toward the completion of still further projects and objectives.

Once you've gotten a project to completion and communicated (and celebrated) the results, you do it again. And again. And again. Keep picking off projects until your company is perfect. Considering that I've never seen such a company, this should keep you busy for a while.

Include Employees or Fail

As you plan activities to help accomplish objectives, always consider how you could include employees. Not every change effort will include employee involvement. **However, any activity that requires a change on the part of employees that does not also include those employees in the planning of that change will succeed only by luck.**

Let me repeat that because it is so important.

Asking employees to change without including them in the decision and planning for the change will fail unless you just get lucky. You might be able to change management procedures or policies without including others (although even this risks failure), but if you are asking someone to change for your reasons, you are simply wasting your time. Go bang your head against a wall instead – at least the wall won't get mad at you.

This is not to say that all problems can be solved with teams. As I will discuss later, teams are not great at solving some problems. Nevertheless, whether using a team or not, employee input (including the opportunity to object or criticize openly) is essential for a project to succeed in the long term. Forced change can be effective for a short period, but eventually employees will manage a way around the change.

Lasting change occurs through the participation and consent of those involved in the changing.

Other Tools to Consider

Your list of objectives, outcomes and milestones will guide all your actions during the action planning period. You may want to set up your calendar as a flowchart or timeline. There are a number of good project planning websites out there.

If your company or department doesn't already have one, our firm uses one called BaseCamp (http://basecamp.com) that we like. Some set up a special shared calendar for particular projects. Still others keep the project planning portions in a separate binder. Whatever system helps keep you organized is the one you should use.

I have also had success using a daily journal in a Moleskine notebook (even though I'm a geek and love technology, I've found that I go back and forth on using tech for organization and sometimes nothing beats plain-old pen and paper for this stuff). I use one page for each day and I start a new notebook for each quarter. In addition to your regular to-do items, you can keep a section on each page for your action planning guide. Look at it every morning and evening.

For example, imagine that you are working on one key objective based on your survey, like reducing feelings of favoritism by implementing a peer review or dispute resolution process. Each morning put that key objective in the box on your journal page and answer the question, "What I will do to implement a peer review process today?" It can be the most simple task, but try to do one thing each day. At the end of the day answer the question, "What did I do to implement a peer review process today?"

It is easy to get in a rut and forget about a key action area for a while – this system doesn't let you do that. Even if you do just one little thing, you are that much closer to your objective. Even if you don't do anything about your objective that day, you are forced to think about it if just for a second or two. Eventually it evolves into a habit that becomes a part of your daily routine – the first vital step to any lasting change.

You will be amazed at how much progress you make if you just do one little task each day toward your main objective. Those small tasks add up and help you accomplish big things. By the way, today my action journal has the question, "What did I do to finish Left of Boom today?" It sounds kind of simplistic, but trust me. It works.[40]

No matter which method you use, it is important to set quarterly and one year goals in your biggest challenge areas and to regularly review your progress in each of those areas. As mentioned above, you should keep employees informed about your progress toward your goals.

How Often Should You Survey?
Finally, it is an excellent idea to conduct follow-up surveys to help gauge the progress and to identify further areas for action. I recommend conducting surveys annually – this gives you a good rhythm of data to action plan from and to measure progress without creating survey fatigue. If you have significant problems you may want to survey more frequently (you can reduce the chance of survey fatigue by conducting pulse surveys and sampling just part of your employee population each month or two).

If you survey at longer intervals than this, your data tends to get stale and employees lose track of what is happening in the process. Some companies will insist on an 18 or 24-month

---

[40] If you are interested in learning more about this productivity system you can include that as an agenda item for your 30-minute consultation. Just use the certificate at the back of this book to set it up.

cycle for budget reasons (although there are some very inexpensive options to survey these days, especially if you are willing to do some of the legwork yourself). If budget is the key thing holding your organization back from regular surveys make this part of the agenda for your complimentary consultation.

I think surveying at some interval is better than not surveying at all, but the bigger the gap between surveys the less useful the data for planning or measuring progress Remember what Heraclitus said – you can't step into the same river twice. If you wait too long between surveys, too much water has flowed through the river for them to be meaningful.

Your project calendar serves as your guide through your own personal transformation into an employee relations leader. As your daily habits change, so changes the daily interactions you have with your coworkers. The change in those interactions sets off a chain reaction that can ultimately transform an organization. Be clear about your objectives and do something each day to get you a step closer to those objectives. Before long you will be amazed at what you have accomplished. Please let me know about your progress – those calls are some of the highlights of my own career.

Take Action

- ☐ Are there certain people who stand out as trustworthy and responsible in your company? Include these people in your steering committee.
- ☐ What areas within your organization are the best determiners of success?
- ☐ When was the last time you celebrated an accomplishment with your employees? Make sure that praise and celebration is a regular part of their time with your company.

SECTION III: POSITIVE EMPLOYEE RELATIONS TRAINING FOR SUPERVISORS

Employees don't leave companies – they leave managers. If they have a problem it is normally a problem with their immediate supervisor. This is not to say that employees always agree with the direction of the company or its corporate leadership (far from it). But it is a poor relationship with the immediate supervisor that tips most employees to become "detractors" vulnerable to union intrusion or other problems.

Supervisors are often employees promoted from line work, so they know the job. This is good. However, these supervisors often do not have training or experience in how to effectively supervise and manage others.

Your organization should spend a significant amount of its training resources on teaching supervisors and managers how to lead in a positive way. You should also invest in training leaders to recognize and respond to problems early, before they spin out of control.

Investing in training is one thing but getting a return on that investment is something much different. The problem with most training is that it is not focused on the right things. Companies have a hard time proving a return on the training investment or improved "soft skills" for their leaders. Because of this, it is hard for companies to justify the expense.

In the following chapters I will help you to deal with all of these issues. First, I make the argument that supervisors are a critical foundation to any positive employee relations success. If you've read this far in the book I probably do not need to spend a lot of time convincing you of this. However, I think it is useful to remind ourselves of how critical supervisors are to creating a successful employee relations environment.

Next, I'll outline how to take your current training and make it as effective as possible. Many companies already have training materials in place and this chapter will focus on how to apply the adult learning principles that we have found to be the most successful in your own training.

The next chapter talks about the underlying philosophy of our own training material. Here I will introduce some fundamental learning philosophy that underpins all of our supervisory training.

Finally, I outline the 13 key skills that are critical for any successful leader when creating a positive workplace. These are the skills that are the most predictive of whether or not a supervisor will have a successful and positive direct relationship with their employees. Conversely, most of the problem supervisors we have encountered have significant gaps in more than one of these 13 key skills.

The good news is that these are learnable skills and your organization can be successful, like many of our clients, in transferring the skills to your supervisors.

Chapter 11

Supervisors – Foundation for Your Success

"I've been married three times, so I've had lots of supervision."
Upton Sinclair, interviewed at age 85

What You'll Learn In This Chapter

☐ Why line-level supervision is the key to your successful employee relations program;

☐ The three reasons that supervisors so often form a weak foundation;

☐ What your supervisors and managers need to know about emotional intelligence;

☐ Why high supervisory scores on your engagement survey may be masking a bigger problem;

☐ How to change your promotion policies to ensure a successful supervisory team;

☐ The key "soft-skills" to teach your supervisory team; and

☐ Why training your supervisors is not enough – how to build accountability into your program.

Managers will almost instinctively agree that supervisors (who I often call line-level leaders or first-leavel leaders) are vital to the success of companies. The difficulty is that most managers never think further than the platitude. The unfortunate fact in most of the companies that we have worked with is that the most important link in the employee relation's chain, the line-level leader, is given the least amount of attention.

Companies often face many challenges with their supervisory group. In most companies, the line-level leader is the least appreciated and often most difficult job. Regularly companies will promote their best performers to line-level leaders without considering whether these individuals have the skills to be an effective supervisor. These companies lose their most productive performers and gain their worst supervisors with the same move.

This chapter briefly analyzes why the line-level leader is such a vital position in the company and further looks at the foundation on which any successful employee relations project will stand. Second, it identifies why supervisors are often the weak link in a company's employee relations program. Finally, it identifies some strategies to strengthen the foundation of your employee relations program.

Why Supervisors Are So Important

Supervisors are important because they are closest to the daily action. Line-level leaders are in the best position to identify operational problems, to make adjustments "on the fly" insuring that the operation runs smoothly, and to catch and dispel rumors in the organization.

Line-level leaders also form your first line of defense. They are your "tripwire" and your "firewall." They are the first to recognize and present employee relations problems. Line-level supervisors have the most opportunities to communicate the company's vision. They are truly the "face" of most of what an organization does.

Additionally, line-level leaders play a vital "buffer" role between top management and production employees. They are normally individuals who most recently worked as operations employees, and are often close friends with the individuals who they now supervise. While this does create challenges for a new leader, it also creates significant opportunities.

Because of these close relationships, line-level leaders are often less likely to be perceived as being on the "other side of the wall." They often have strong "relational power" (we will cover this topic at length in Chapter 12. For this reason they can be management's most effective voice for communicating reasons for change and for communicating the company's vision.

Finally, line-level leaders are vital to the company because this is typically where future leadership comes from. The future leaders of the company will use the skills and abilities developed during the supervisory period. If these skills are not cultivated in line-level leaders, one cannot expect the future top management of the company to suddenly become enlightened upon their promotion.

Setting the example for the culture early in the leadership development process ensures that the Supervisory DNA™ gets replicated throughout the management structure of the company. This concept is so important we actually created a Supervisory DNA Test™ that clients can use to determine the current leadership capabilities of front-line leaders

Why Supervisors Often Form A Weak Foundation

In companies that we work with, we regularly find supervision to be weak and ill prepared for their employee relations role in the company. There are a number of reasons that companies allow this to happen.

The first – and perhaps most common – reason is that line-level leaders have tremendously difficult jobs. They are "where the rubber meets the road" on production issues. As a result, line-level supervisors are under constant pressure to produce the numbers. Since companies often pay very little attention to positive employee relations issues, there is much less pressure on line-level leaders to deliver in this area. The leaders, logically enough, expend effort and increase skill level in areas where they are being watched more carefully.

Conversely, there is usually very little attention paid to performance management or "soft skills" of supervisors. Most companies we work with pay very little attention to the "emotional intelligence" skills of its leadership. These skills, or lack thereof, are rarely discussed by management.

Most companies feel like they have done a tremendous job in this area if they do something as little as send their leadership team to a seminar or a course on introductory management and supervisory skills. Unfortunately, given the pressures on production outlined above (and the realities of adult learning that we will cover in Chapter 13, company leaders are simply not asked to use the skills they learn. The skills become rusty and rarely, if ever, are they utilized.

Developing "Emotional Intelligence"

In the last several years a considerable amount has been written about "emotional intelligence" and its importance in predicting the success of leaders. The theory was originally articulated by professors Peter Salovey and John Mayer and famously communicated by Professor Daniel Goleman in his groundbreaking text, Emotional Intelligence.

Goleman explains what many people know intuitively; "intelligence" is a poor predictor of success. He argues that what we have come to know as "intelligence," describes "intellectual intelligence" and is less likely to predict an individual's success than a set of skills or abilities that an individual uses when interacting with others, called "emotional intelligence."[41]

Emotional intelligence refers to the ability of a person to monitor and regulate one's own feelings, as well as other's. In addition, it describes a person's ability to use feelings as a guide for thought and action.

---

[41] See Daniel Goleman, *Working with Emotional Intelligence*, (Bantam Books, 1988) pp. 317-320.

Goleman identifies five emotional competencies that are the most important indicators of emotional intelligence[42]: self–awareness, self-regulation, motivation, empathy, and social skills.

In a number of studies conducted by Goleman and others, it is estimated that while higher levels of technical competence is evident in roughly a quarter of "star" performers, the emotional competencies listed above were evident in <u>over half</u> of the "star" performers.[43] These findings have significant implications for training and developing the leadership team in an organization.

First, the technical capabilities of a supervisor are really not that important. Most critical are their abilities to be aware of and control their emotions, and use those skills to relate to and motivate those around them. Teaching technical "tools" to line-level leaders (and other workers for that matter) is less important than helping them to hone their skills at dealing with emotions at work.

This is much harder than simply sending someone to a class on performance management. It requires an individual to commit to a serious analysis of strengths and weaknesses regarding his emotional state at work (self-awareness) and developing skills to "close the gap" between his current emotional state and the desired state (self-regulation).[44] It requires individuals to pay careful attention to the emotions of

---

[42] Id. p. 318.

[43] Id. pp.319-321.

[44] LRI's Supervisory DNA™ Test is an excellent way to help supervisors become more self-aware of their natural strengths and leadership "blind spots" where they should consider development. Readers of this book can give up to 25 supervisors the Supervisory DNA Test™ free of charge (a $625 value) just by sending in the certificate at the end of this book.

others and to take them into account when interacting with them (empathy and social skills).

These changes are not easy – and while there will be breakthroughs there will be huge challenges, requiring motivation on the part of the individual supervisor. The good news is that Goleman's research, as well as the research of many others, concludes that these skills can be cultivated in individuals. As you begin to think about how you will develop your current line-level leaders or candidates for upcoming leadership positions, make certain to take time to look at ways to develop emotional intelligence competencies.

There are often few rewards for successful management of employee relations. Many companies, in fact, encourage poor leadership skills by heaping rewards onto leaders who "hit their numbers" even if their management style is threatening and abusive. In these companies, the message sent by top management is that production is valued over the human experience of working for the company.

Employees in these companies see that management rewards the supervisors who behave the worst. Young supervisors follow this example, hoping they'll be rewarded too. Even in companies where a high performing line-level leader is disciplined for his or her efforts on employee relations, this is often done with a "wink" and the understanding that management is still very happy with the results.

The final reason line-level leaders often fail is that they, like most humans, attempt to avoid pain. Honestly confronting an employee about poor performance is hard. Most managers prefer to take the path of least resistance. This means either avoiding the performance discussion altogether or deflecting responsibility for the conversation some other direction.

For example, a line-level leader might say, "my boss told me that I have to tell you this..." or "this will never work, but top management wants us to try this." In this way, the line-level leader can avoid the negative experience of taking responsibility or defending the decision and at the same time pretend to show "empathy" with the worker who is being supervised.

Unfortunately, this hurts the company in the long run. Many companies we survey have divergent leadership scores. For example, line-level leader scores may be relatively high while the top management scores will be extremely negative. Supervisors in these companies will often point to these scores as proof that they are doing a good job and that it is, "all corporate's fault."

While that will sometimes be the case, more often it is not. Many times the root cause of these scores is that line-level leaders refuse to take responsibility for their role as managers. One would expect top management to get hammered by a group of employees who are constantly being told by their immediate supervisor (also a member of management in their eyes) that the "top management" in the company is screwed up.

How To Strengthen The Foundation

There are three "legs to the stool" to ensure your company has a strong foundation of line-level leaders. If any one of the three legs is missing you'll have problems. The three legs are:
1. Want To (Values)
2. When To (Awareness)
3. How To (Skill)

Let's look at each of the three legs briefly.

Want To

This is the values component. Do your line-level leaders really care about creating a positive workplace? Do they get as upset when they see a peer doing a poor job of coaching as they do when someone violates a safety rule? Is it something they talk about as regularly? Is it something they work to improve? Those that do share the <u>values</u> of positive leadership.

You can train all you want, but line-level leaders who lack the values component will never become employee relations stars. You can teach or convince someone that they should value creating a positive work environment, but most often this doesn't work. This is why, long term, you have to hire for this trait. Awareness and skill are somewhat straightforward to train – values, not so much.

The next two chapters will explain a number of things a company can do to help improve the skills of a current group of line-level leaders. However, perhaps the most critical step to take is to promote individuals whose natural skill set is more in line with those required to be an effective leader, most especially being approachable (much more on that in Chapter 12.

There are some individuals who, no matter how much time and energy you invest in training and developing, will never be effective leaders. A company can save itself, and more importantly, save its employees a considerable amount of grief by not promoting individuals into supervisory positions when they do not have the skills for that promotion.

While it sounds like common sense, this is the step most often overlooked by companies in the promotion process. There is a tremendous amount of pressure to promote the best performer or longer-term employees to become line-level leaders. This is the path of least resistance, but often a dead end.

How To
It's not enough to want to do the right thing the right way. Just because I want to do 100 push-ups or hike the Appalachian Trail does not mean I'll do it. The second key component is

having or developing the skills needed to accomplish these goals.

If a company thinks at all about training their leadership team this is usually the part they focus on. That's the good news. The bad news is that this training is almost always designed poorly to get leaders to take action on what they're supposed to do.

In the next two chapters we will discuss some critical "How To" skills of effective first-level leadership. In Chapter 12 I describe the "one-ring" of leadership: approachability. I will teach you my research-based skill of asking three simple questions to create a culture of approachability. This simple change will move your line-level leaders far ahead of the pack.

If you equip your line-level leaders to be approachable your organization will have moved far along its journey to be an employer of choice. But there are many other skills that line-level leaders can hone to take their leadership skills to an even higher level. Those are outlined in Chapter 21.

When To
Even if you've received all the training in the world and really want to do the right thing, you will still fail if you don't see the opportunity when it is presented. The third leg of the stool is awareness, or knowing when to apply the skills you've learned. If you are missing a stool leg it is probably this one. You have to take the initiative to do the right thing and overcome inertia. That is the "when to" component.

If your current skills training doesn't seem to be delivering results, it is either because:
- It is poorly designed (we will talk about best practices for designing and delivering leadership training in Chapter 13);
- It fails to cover the topics of awareness or values; or

- If you've got those two bases covered, you probably have promoted people who don't value being a good leader.

The Power of the Want To, When To, How To Model

If you add one additional component to this model it becomes a <u>powerful coaching tool.</u> The final component is to assume that your line-level leaders actually want to be good leaders. If you make this one assumption about your leaders you will become a very successful leadership coach.

Most people make the assumption that people who are failing are broken in some way. They don't have people skills. They're too dumb to do it the right way. There is something wrong with the way they were raised or their background. They just don't have what it takes to be a good leader in their organization.

Henry Ford famously said, "Whether you think you'll succeed or you think you'll fail, you're probably right." If you think your leadership team lacks the ability or aptitude to become solid leaders it is very likely they will turn out that way. On the other hand, if your assumption about your leaders is that they really want to be great you'll be surprised at the possibilities that appear.

This reminds me of the story of an ancient guy named Pygmalion. One day he made a sculpture of a beautiful woman (for my female readers imagine the sculpture is a handsome guy). Pygmalion fell in love with the sculpture – I mean *really* fell in love with it. He was so in love with everything about the sculpture that to him the sculpture was real. Until one day his sculpture actually did come to life (the Pinnochio story is similar, but for some reason I relate more to the sculpture of the beautiful woman than the wooden puppet – go figure).

Social science research suggests that these self-fulfilling prophecies are not just the stuff of legend. One of the hundreds of different studies done in this area considers the cleanliness of classrooms. The teachers, administrators and janitors in a school were told that one class of students was messy while the other class was clean.

There was no truth to the warning – prior to the experiment neither class was especially clean or dirty. You can probably guess what happened. The supposedly "dirty" students were regularly found to have left trash in the room and had to be hounded to pick up after themselves. The supposedly "clean" students were found to be very neat (even if the teacher and janitor occasionally had to pick up the random piece of trash now and then). The bottom line: the "predicted" behavior became reality.[45]

Another study dealt with "academic spurters." In that study:

> Rosenthal and Lenore Jacobson (1968) did the same study in a classroom, telling elementary school teachers that they had certain students in their class who were "academic spurters." In fact, these students were selected at random. Absolutely nothing else was done by the researchers to single out these children. Yet by the end of the school year, 30 percent of the children arbitrarily named as spurters had gained an average of 22 IQ points, and almost all had gained at least 10 IQ points. The "spurters" were also rated much higher in their classroom performance by their teachers. Rosenthal compared his results to an expensive "total push" campaign funded by the Title I education act that led, after three years, to gains that were much smaller than even the gains for the control students in these classrooms. Something had definitely happened to the teachers of these students.

---

[45] See Daniel H. Pink, *To Sell is Human: The Surprising Truth About Moving Others* (Riverhead 2012) at p. 138.

Rosenthal was fairly certain the teachers did not spend more time with the alleged "spurters" because these students improved less on their verbal scores than their reasoning scores. Rather, he thinks the teachers were more excited about teaching these students, and maybe about teaching generally. And they must have subtly communicated respect for and enthusiasm about these students, so that the students themselves felt more capable of understanding and anticipated better performance from themselves. Rosenthal calls this the Pygmalion effect. Others call it the Rosenthal effect. And still others see it as a special case of what has come to be called "self-fulfilling prophecy."[46]

What do these littering students, academic "spurters" and a crazy old sculptor have to do with developing great leaders? You and your top managers can be just like Pygmailion, creating sculptures of your line-level leaders who come to life. You are just like the teachers and janitors in the studies. To paraphrase Henry Ford, whether you expect your leaders to fail or to succeed, you're probably right. So what kind of sculptures are you and your leadership team creating? Are they beautiful or ugly?

If you begin with the assumption that your leaders want to be successful you will have much different conversations (and deliver much different training) than if your assumption is the opposite. Now if you add the "Want To, When To, How To" model you have an extremely simple to understand way to diagnose and fix potential issues.

---

[46] Arthur Aron and Elaine Aron, *The Heart of Social Psychology: A Backstage View of a Passionate Science* (Lexington Books 1989) pp. 38-39. See also Robert Rosenthal and Lenore Jacobson, *Pygmalion in the Classroom: Teacher Expectation and Pupils' Intellectual Development* (Crown House Publishing, 2003).

Here is how the coaching model works. If you notice a person in a leadership position is having trouble dealing with a situation you start with the assumption that the he or she wants to be a great leader. That means that he or she is doing the best job possible given his or her level of awareness, skill, and values.

If this is your assumption, your conversation with the line-level leader won't focus on how or why they screwed up. Instead, you will focus on which of the three areas was missed. Does the line-level leader know how to handle situations like this (do they know How To)? Did they fail to spot the opportunity to use a skill until it was too late (do they know When To)? Or do they understand and agree with the importance of handling the situation properly (do they Want To)?

I hope you see the power of this assumption. It is critical to creating a culture of approachability, as we will see in the next chapter. It is an assumption that should permeate your entire organization – your line-level leaders need to make the same assumption about the employees they lead.

This mindset is not about blame, it is about development. In this mindset the leader takes the blame – if the line-level leader has failed it is because you haven't made sure that they have fully developed all three legs of the stool. This turns the table on the normal coaching conversation. It becomes solution-focused and win-win.

Some of the more skeptical people (they will call themselves the *realists* and they are probably right) will object that sometimes you do have a person who does not want to do their best. Some people just want to skate by and are not interested in developing their skills or becoming a great leader. And to those realists I say: "You're right – some people don't want to be great leaders." And to them I also say: "So what?"

If you have a leader who does not want to be a great leader you will eventually have to remove them (or suffer the employee relations consequences). However, in the meantime it is still much better to operate from the stance that even these folks want to be great. At some point they may prove you wrong. But you will have exhausted every possible avenue to get them where you need them to be. You will have fully documented all the work you've done to get them to the level required of them.

Every once in a while you'll see the light switch on and gain a valuable (and loyal) leader. You will be continuously improving your leadership training and development activities. And if you get to the point where you have to pull the plug it won't be a surprise to anyone, substantially reducing the likelihood that this leader's departure will be a "boom" event in your company. In the end, it's just the right thing to do.

Who Should I Promote to Line-Level Leader?
Line-level leader candidates who have experience and are high performers must also be able to prove that they have (or are willing to learn) the Supervisory DNA™ skills to be an effective leader. If they do not have these skills, then the task is to develop them <u>before</u> making a decision to promote. If this is your mindset, the quality of your leadership team will improve automatically without as much need for considerable work on the back end for development and training.

With this in mind, the key question then becomes who should you promote? What foundational abilities should you look for when identifying potentially strong line-level leaders? What skills should they have? While this is somewhat of an art over a science, there are a number of very good predictors of effective line-level leaders.

The table below lists the 7 critical categories of emotional intelligence exhibited by strong leaders. I list both the description of each category along with examples of training modules we've developed to build skills under each ability. These will be discussed at greater length in Chapters 13:

Fundamental Skill	Description	Suggested Training Modules
Approachability	This is the "one ring" of leadership that rules them all. Our research suggests that this one behavior predicts discretionary effort (or "organizational citizenship") more than any other leadership trait. It is the most important skill to select on and to teach first-level leaders.	Approachable Leadership™ Workshop
Team Orientation	While not every situation requires teamwork (and some should NOT use a team) you still want to look for individuals who are comfortable and capable of sharing information and working on a team. An individual with a high level of skill in this area can also effectively identify when a team can be effective (or not).	Situational Leadership, Managing Meetings, Coaching for High Performance
Influence skills	Effective line-level leaders are good at influencing others to take action consistent with the values and results expected of the organization. They will have high-level communication skills and be effective at communicating both positive and constructive feedback to their team members.	Persuading Others, Effective Communication, Managing Meetings
Initiative	Look for individuals who are proactive and seek opportunities to take action to avoid potentially bigger problems in the future. These individuals will also be on the lookout for potential problem performance areas and begin coaching in those areas well before an issue becomes a discipline problem.	Coaching for High Performance, The Discipline Process, Mediating Conflict, Recognizing Employee Effort, Assessing Performance

Analysis and Problem Solving	Good line-level leaders are excellent problem solvers and capable of analyzing complicated problems and coming up with effective solutions. This will often happen under high-pressure situations.	Problems & Decision Making, Managing Meetings, Mediating Conflict
Situational Leadership	Valuable line-level leaders are effective at knowing when to assume different "roles" of leadership This requires a heightened level of self-awareness. They can identify times when they need to be directive versus times when they need to be participative.	Situational Leadership, Leadership for Results
Mastery	Finally, a strong leader knows that leaders don't stand still. They work hard to develop and improve their skills and those around them. They are continuous learners.	Self-Mastery, Leadership for Results

Most companies have more people interested in being promoted to a leadership position than people who are naturally strong in all of the above ability and skill areas. Thus, most companies need a program to develop line-level employees. If you know in advance the skill sets you are looking for in a leader, it makes sense to ask your potential leadership candidates to work on those skill areas as a prelude to being considered for a promotion.

This also gives you an opportunity to compare the various skill areas among potential leadership candidates. Finally, it gives you the chance to develop "stretch" assignments and opportunities for candidates to see them in action. This is one area where a proactive company can truly "try before you buy."

As a discussed earlier, it is vitally important to remember that your highest producers may not be your best leaders. This is because a high producer who does not have good leadership skills is more likely to be a "working" supervisor and less likely to do an effective job at the actual day-to-day management of your human resources.

High producers will believe that they are doing an outstanding job of "supervising" due to the fact that they are able to continue to be high producers. If not directed regarding their roles and responsibilities as a manager, these individuals are very often the toughest to deal with since in their mind they continue to be valuable performers.

These problems are exclusively the responsibility of top management, who has done a poor job of promoting and a poor job of explaining the responsibilities and expectations to its new line-level leaders. Unfortunately, this is how most companies we work with promote their supervisors. Does this sound familiar to you?

What if your company is like most and has already promoted a number of line-level leaders who, while passable, truly do not have highly developed "soft skills"? Obviously, you will have to take steps to help train and develop these skills in your current leaders. There are really two issues you must figure out. First, what type of training are you going to conduct? Second, how will you make sure your leaders are actually using the skills that you've trained? The next chapter will help you answer both questions.

Take Action

- ☐ Examine the 3 reasons supervisors often form a weak foundation. Do you recognize any of those qualities within your own leadership team?
- ☐ Have you promoted a high producing employee that proved to be less than effective in a leadership position? List 5 qualities that should have tipped you off.

☐ Brainstorm 3 changes you can make to build leadership accountability within your organization.

Chapter 12

Approachability: The "One Ring" of Leadership

"To lead people, walk beside them... As for the best leaders, the people do not notice their existence. The next best, the people honor and praise. The next, the people fear; and the next, the people hate ... When the best leader's work is done the people say, We did it ourselves!"
Lao Tzu

What You'll Learn In This Chapter
☐ The one fundamental behavior that separates strong leaders from those who fail;
☐ How "Organizational Citizenship Behaviors" drive performance and increase job satisfaction;
☐ The ways in which Frederick Herzberg's two-factor motivation theory is still applicable today;
☐ Why "hygiene factors" like pay, rewards, and even supervision oftentimes demotivate employees; and
☐ The three simple questions that all leaders should ask.

This chapter is brand new to this edition and it started innocently enough. I was doing some research for the re-write and it had been a while since I'd looked into the academic research around leadership. I wanted to test a hypothesis I'd had for a while.

My hypothesis was this: there is some fundamental behavior that separates the strong first level leaders from those who fail. I knew from working with supervisors over many years in virtually every kind of company that you couldn't tell who'd succeed just by looking at their resume or the training they'd received.

Some of the worst supervisors I've ever seen have the education, have been to all the training courses, and look great on paper. Yet they still failed spectacularly when it came to leading people. And some of the best supervisors I've ever seen were actually pretty ham-handed at the basic blocking and tackling of supervision. Yet their people would still run through a brick wall for them.

This got me wondering. Is there a fundamental trait that separates the winners from the losers? Is it a skill or an attitude? Is it something that can be trained, or are you just born with it? Most important, what is it?

If my bow tie and glasses didn't give it away, I'm a nerd and I started referring to this quest as my search for the "one ring to rule them all"[47] for first-level leaders. I read thousands of pages of recent research. I talked to many, many people about the hypothesis and what they thought the "one ring" might be. And eventually I found it.

Look For Organizational Citizenship, Not Satisfaction

First let me tell you what the one ring is not (and this was a surprise to me). I started with the assumption that the best first-level leaders would have happier employees who would outperform the employees of poor leaders. The basic model I imagined was:

Happy Employees = Happy Customers = Better Business

I read lots of studies about job satisfaction and performance. I quickly learned that the best research shows that satisfaction

---

[47] My apologies to JRR Tolkien and Hobbit-lovers everywhere. I also note the irony here that the "one ring" in Tolkien's epic tales consumed the minds of those who wore it and lured them to their near-certain death in Mordor. This ring is not like that (although I will admit it has consumed my mind for some time).

and performance are only weakly related, and in some cases even **negatively** correlated (in case you're at a cocktail party with an organizational psychology Ph.D. you'll want to say that satisfaction is a mediator of performance). In other words, focusing on job satisfaction as a way to identify the best supervisors is a path to frustration. So I looked elsewhere.

Next I started looking at what factors did seem to drive performance. This turned me on to what are called "Organizational Citizenship Behaviors" or OCBs (a lot of people also call this "discretionary effort"). It turns out that OCBs are highly predictive of job performance (one recent study found that nearly 70% of job performance is predicted by OCB activities). If you think of this in terms of the Pareto Principle, OCB activities are the 20% of behaviors that account for the 80% of high performance. It's the tiny hinge that swings the big door.

The other thing that OCB relates to is job satisfaction. Employees who engage in these discretionary efforts feel they are making progress and getting opportunities to learn and grow. They are happier with their work. This is consistent with the two-factor motivation theory of Frederick Herzberg. His research repeatedly found that things like achievement, growth, advancement and the work itself were highly motivating. On the other hand "hygiene factors" like pay, rewards, or even supervision (more on that in a below) can demotivate but are rarely sources of motivation.[48]

Many organization psychologists have challenged Herzberg's theories about motivation. It was in an article that questioned whether Herzberg was even relevant today where I got my

---

[48] See Frederick Herzberg, *"One More Time… How Do You Motivate Employees?"* Harvard Business Review (January 2003); See also Frederick Herzberg, Bernard Mausner, Barbara Bloch Snyderman, *The Motivation to Work* (Transaction Publishers 1993).

first clue about the "one ring." This article looked at one specific OCB " activity, participation in a suggestion program.[49]

Suggestions are a quintessential OCB – you can walk by the suggestion box your whole career and nobody would care. But those suggestions can have a powerful impact on a company. And this study looked at people who had actually made a suggestion (nearly 2,000 of them). In other words, this was a population who proved by behavior that they would engage in OCB activity.

This study looked at the population of people who had made suggestions and asked what was the difference between those who made a suggestion and those who did not. The results were very consistent with Herzberg with one glaring exception: supervisors.

Herzberg suggested in his research that supervisors, like pay and company policies, were hygiene factors at work. In other words, supervisors can be major dissatisfiers (hence the truism that people don't leave their company, they leave their boss – which is certainly true). But Herzberg also found that when employees reported high satisfaction they rarely listed their supervisor as one of the reasons. This study suggested something very different.

In the suggestion study there were two factors that stood out far beyond anything else. Pay or rewards only motivated suggestions about a quarter of the time. Hope that the suggestion would improve things at work or make the job easier motivated a suggestion about half the time. However, if you thought your supervisor was doing a good job you made a

---

[49] See Nigel Bassett-Jones, Geoffrey C. Lloyd, *"Does Herzberg's Motivation Theory Have Staying Power?"* Journal of Management Development (Vol. 24 No. 10 2005) pp. 929-943.

suggestion 80% of the time. I thought that was astounding until I read the next finding. There was something else that predicted a suggestion 88% of the time.

The factor that predicted whether someone would engage in OCB " nearly 9 out of 10 times? The **approachability** of the first level supervisor. The first time I read the study I actually glossed over this point. But I re-read it sometime later and it hit me like a lightning bolt: **approachability**. Perhaps that was the one ring?

I continued to push this idea and the more and more I looked, the more I saw the power of approachability. And the more I've looked the more I find example after example of how this one behavior, more than anything else a company can do, can get employees to engage in OCB and discretionary effort. It is also highly predictive of employee satisfaction, which brings us back to Herzberg.

If supervisors are really just a hygiene factor, then how does the study about suggestions square with Herzberg? Remember, Herzberg was talking about satisfaction and motivation, not OCB " activity. And this is where approachability comes into play.

Herzberg believed (as do I) that employees are motivated internally for their own reasons and don't need a supervisor or manager to motivate them. Some employees may need a lot of help, others won't need much at all. When a supervisor is approachable he or she is creating space for an employee to do their best work. The approachable supervisor (as opposed to the micro-manager or the absent manager) provides just the right amount of supervision.

What the suggestion study showed is that approachable leaders create space for the OCB to happen. If you were to ask the people who made suggestions at work what made them happiest they would probably not list their relationship (or the approachability) of their supervisor. Instead they would focus more on the OCB activities they do every day (the kinds of things that lead to growth, achievement and development).

These employees would certainly be demotivated by a supervisor who ignored their suggestions. However, once the space is created for them to make a suggestion that they are already motivated to make, they probably won't recognize that their supervisor helped create that space.

Can approachability be taught? There is no doubt that it can. In my extensive research I've identified three simple questions that – if asked on a regular basis by first-level leaders – can significantly improve their approachability.

The three simple questions are:
1. Do you have what you need?
2. What would make your work easier?
3. Where are you going?

Each of these questions has an assumption that underlies it. The assumptions are:
1. Nobody wakes up in the morning hoping to do crappy work.
2. A leader's role is to reduce friction.
3. People want to make progress.

Let's look at the three questions and their underlying assumptions in turn so we can fully understand the power of approachability.

The First Question: Do You Have What You Need?
The first question is all about resources. When you ask someone if they have what they need you are making one very important assumption: if they had everything they need they

---

would perform great work. The corollary to that assumption is that if someone is failing to perform great work it is because they lack a resource, not because they want to do bad work. This makes the first-level leader's role simple: actively look for people lacking resources and help get them the resources they need.

There are a few important things to note about this powerful question and its assumption. First, thinking back to the Pygmalion effect, this question gets the universe working for you, not against you. It assumes our people are beautiful sculptures not ugly ones. Any flaws are the fault of the sculptor (the first-level leader) not the sculpture. As we've already seen, this point of view creates a self-fulfilling prophesy. If we assume our people want to do great work we are very likely to see just that.

Second, coaching from this mind-frame is powerful. It creates powerful win-win conversations with people. Again, if you assume people want to do great work then your conversations around performance will be related to whether the first-level leader has helped the individual understand and adopt the values, awareness and skills necessary for them to reach their full capability. It removes blame and defensiveness from the conversation. It instead focuses on possibility and potential.

Further, this question is a proactive, "Left of Boom" question. As we will see in the next question, people will actually put up with a lot of hassles without ever really thinking, "Is there a better way to do this?" Asking people about missing resources gets everyone thinking about possibilities.

Michael Gerber wrote a great book about building businesses called *The E-Myth*. The big idea of this book is that business leaders must make time to stop working "in the business" (doing the daily tasks of the work) and instead take a step back to work "on the business." This question is all about working *on the business*. Giving each employee a chance to think about what other resources could we bring to the tasks we do each day sometimes lead to game-changing opportunities that deliver BIG results.

But let's stay realistic. Most of the time times these conversations don't lead to big changes. Often these conversations lead to no changes at all. Does that mean they aren't worthwhile? No way.

One of my favorite movie scenes of all time is when Jim Carrey's Grinch runs through his schedule to see if he can make it to the holiday Jubilation in Whoville. As he goes through his agenda ("Jazzercise, wallow in self-pity, dinner with me – I can't cancel that again") he gets to my favorite item: "Solve world hunger... tell no one."

Unapproachable leaders risk creating whole departments of folks like the Grinch. They have the answer to big problems but decide not to tell anyone. Unlike the Grinch, these folks don't keep their big ideas to themselves out of spite. They tragically keep these ideas to themselves simply because no one takes the time to ask.

If your line-level leaders regularly create the space for these conversations when those rare game-changing moments do arrive they'll speak up. That is the true power of being an approachable leader.

The Second Question: What Would Make Your Work Better?

The second question is what I call the "lean" or "enrichment" question. It is all about making the work better, less painful, and more enjoyable. It is about efficiency, quality, and flow.

This question comes up a lot these days in Kaizen events, Six Sigma training and other lean activities. These events are all about how to create standard work, looking for bottlenecks and elevating constraints. The biggest difference between the questions asked during those events and the question we are asking here is two words: "your" and "better."

This question is not necessarily about how to make an operation or an assembly line more efficient (although many times the answer to this question will do just that). Instead this question is more personal. What would make **your** work better? The underlying assumption to this question is that a first-level leader's key job is to reduce friction and increase meaningful work.

Friction is the day-to-day annoyances that we all put up with at our work. Those annoyances might be very minor (a handle that doesn't work just right) or huge (a boss or a co-worker that doesn't work just right). The annoyances could be physical or mechanical or they could be relational. But everyone has them. The vast majority of them we don't even think about – we just deal with them, call them "part of the job" and go on about our business.

That approach isn't all bad. After all, if we spent our entire day thinking up and focusing on all the little things that annoy us about our work we would probably just snap. But there is an emotional and physical cost to putting up with these annoyances. They drain our energy, they slow us down and they use up valuable willpower that could be put to better use.

The power of the second question is it gives us the space to take a few minutes and think about these annoyances. Not to dwell on them, but to take a step back and evaluate whether we are ignoring something that could be fixed and would make the work easier or more fulfilling. Many times we will decide that these frictions are not a big deal. At this point they tend to stop feeling like friction (at least for now – at a later point we may think otherwise). Other times we will decide that the friction needs to be removed or that the work could be better. That begins the very productive search for how we can re-imagine the work to remove the friction and make it of higher quality.

Once again, this is a conversation about possibility and potential. It creates a space to think about what can be done to make the work itself as satisfying as possible. This is something Herzberg called "job enrichment" and it is a valuable concept. The idea is to remove as many of the "hygiene" issues from the work and to add as many of the "motivators" as you can. When you reduce friction you are removing the hygiene issues, hopefully replacing those frictions with motivators. As we will learn next, redesigning the work in this way creates more "flow" moments and satisfaction each day.

The Third Question: Where Are You Going?
Last but not least, the development question. The assumption here is that everyone wants to make progress. Herzberg showed decades ago that development, growth and advancement were the three things that created the most satisfaction at work. But it has only been recently that psychologists have really started to dig into how and why that's true.

You know that negative person you try to avoid because they always look for the worst in any situation? For most of its history that was the goal of psychologists. They focused almost entirely on the mental issues that can screw up a human. Depression, addiction, abuse, deviant behavior, you name it they studied it. Let's just say if you were invited to the local psychologist's holiday open house you might want to come up with something else to do (good advice if you're invited to the local labor lawyer's party too).

A new branch of psychology has worked hard to buck this history. Called "Positive Psychology," these folks study what makes humans happy. They have made some powerful discoveries that apply not just to general happiness, but especially to happiness at work.

One of the key findings in positive psychology is that humans achieve some of their happiest moments when experiencing "flow." Flow is that state where time sort of drifts away and you are just consumed entirely with the task in front of you. This can happen at work or away from work. I like to think of flow experiences as the "highlight reel" moments in life. A key question for positive psychologists is whether we can create these flow moments more consistently.

The guy most known for studying flow has a name that is nearly impossible to spell but not that hard to pronounce. I remember how to say it by thinking about one of my flow experiences, falling in love with my wife: Chick-Sent-Me-High (the actual spelling is Mihaly Csikszentmihalyi – see, isn't my version easier?) I'll call him Dr. C for short. Dr. C came up with an ingenious way to study these "highlight reel" moments in our lives. All it took was a journal and a pager.

The studies basically worked like this: you would carry around your journal and wear a pager everywhere you went. Around eight times a day the pager would beep and you were to stop what you were doing and write in your journal how you felt and what you were thinking about. He called this Experience Sampling Method.[50] Over time Dr. C and colleagues around the world collected countless daily experiences and began to piece together what creates "flow" in life.

There is a lot to the story, but the basics look like this. Flow experiences are times when we are challenged to do

---

[50] See Csikszentmihalyi, Mihaly, *Flow: The Psychology of Optimal Experience* (HarperPerennial Publishing 1991); see also Pink, Dan, *Drive: The Surprising Truth About What Motivates Us*, (Riverhead Books 2011) (especially Chapter 5).

something that pushes our current skill level to its upper limit but no further. If the challenge is too great it causes anxiety and if the challenge is too little it causes boredom. But when the challenge is just right we enter what Dr. C calls the "flow channel" and things get interesting.

In the flow channel we are growing and discovering. We are moving forward, getting better. If the challenge gets too easy we start getting bored and drop out of flow. Or if the challenge gets too tough we get frustrated and anxious, also getting out of flow. But when things are just right, we experience growth and progress.

We are happiest when we seek out and find these flow experiences. Positive psychology describes this search for flow moments as "The Progress Principle." The progress principle states that we are most motivated in our lives when we are making progress toward a goal. And that is what the third question is all about: how can you help your people make progress?

Discussing the goals and aspirations of your folks is important. First, it is a conversation that's tuned into WIIFM (what's in it for me). Getting a chance to talk about your goals and aspirations (or even challenges you are facing in reaching those goals) is motivating in itself. Unfortunately thinking about our life goals is something very few of us do on a regular basis. But think about the times you have – did it feel good? You can give people that feeling almost any time you want by just asking, "Where are you going?"

Second, knowing the goals that your people are working on opens up a world of possibility that you probably don't see today. Let's say you ask Jeff, one of your shipping/receiving folks, where he's going and he mentions that he wants to become a welder. Your company desperately needs welders – if Jeff could accomplish his goal it would help the company and transform his life too. You can see in Jeff's eyes that he really wants this and will work hard to accomplish it.

Once you've had this conversation with Jeff you see the world just a little different. You talk to the HR department about any tuition reimbursement that might be available for Jeff to go to welding school. You remember that one of the more experienced welders is a huge hockey fan and that Jeff used to play minor league hockey. You happen to see there is a Kaizen event coming up in the welding shop and they are looking for cross-functional help on the team. You overhear the manager of the welding department complaining that there is a bottleneck in his group because his best welders are getting diverted from the most important work to welding that, "any half-motivated guy could do with 15 minutes of training."

These conversations don't even have to be about work-related goals. Jeff might have mentioned a hockey tournament that he's trying to bring to town. It doesn't matter where Jeff's headed, the progress principle means progress toward any goal. The key is that you ask and let Jeff tell you about the next stop in his life journey.

After your talk with Jeff you are sensitized to these ways you can help Jeff make progress toward his goal. If you did these things do you think Jeff would be more or less motivated at work? Would he be more or less likely to go above and beyond in his regular daily tasks? If you said that Jeff would probably turn into an organizational citizenship machine I'd bet you're right.

And that's the fourth benefit. As we learned from Herzberg and Dr. C, making progress and growing are among the most motivating things we can do. Once people start making progress on their goals (and see that their first-level leaders are actively trying to help them reach those goals) their internal motivation soars. As discretionary effort and organization citizenship behavior increase so does overall performance.

Finally, these conversations don't just motivate the Jeff's of the world. The first-level leaders who ask, "Where are you going" get their own psychological benefit. Helping others grow and develop is a critical way for your first-level leaders to experience the progress principle in their own work. Not only will they see their people grow under their leadership, but inevitably their people will start asking them about their own goals. Plus their supervisors should be asking the same question of them.

I hope you appreciate the power of these three simple questions. There are certainly other ways for first-level leaders to behave approachably. But these easy-to-remember questions embody much of what the best recent research in organization development, positive psychology and intrinsic motivation prove are the keys to a highly engaged and high performing workplace. And now that you know them I have just one question: Where are YOU going?

Take Action

- ☐ Make a point to start performing more organizational citizenship behaviors and watch as others follow your lead.
- ☐ Pull aside two employees per week and ask them the three questions: Do you have what you need? What would make your work better? Where are you going?
- ☐ Make notes of any concerns or issues they are having and resolve any and all that you can.

Chapter 13

Designing Your Supervisory Training Program

"All mankind is divided into three classes: those that are immovable, those that are movable, and those that move."
Benjamin Franklin

What You'll Learn In This Chapter
☐ How the "knowing/doing" gap is affecting your business,;
☐ How to apply active intervals to your training programs;
☐ Tools for developing key concepts in your training modules;
☐ Strategies for enhancing communication skills in line-level supervisors; and
☐ The importance of not letting skills go stale.

You know you need to train your supervisors on key leadership skills. But many company leaders have a hard time justifying the expense. They've sent people to seminars and training and not seen a return on the investment. How do you make sure the training you offer (and spend valuable money on) is effective and gets results?

The reason most training fails is due to poor design. Adults (and children for that matter) learn best when they are active and using the content, versus passively receiving information. Therefore effective training is designed to keep the learners active and give them opportunities to use what they've learned. Most supervisors will tell you that they know what to do, but their challenge is doing it under fire. This is what is called the "knowing/doing" gap. Simulations, exercises, and skill practice are great methods to shrink that gap.

If you wanted to train your body to bench press your body weight how would you train? Would you go to the gym regularly, lift increasingly large loads, and rest in between? Or would you just go to the gym one day, watch people lift for a few hours, load up a bar and then press it?

Does that second strategy sound ridiculous (and dangerous) to you? That is how the vast majority of leadership training is designed. Instead of spacing content across a period of time and doing shorter bursts of effort, companies force people to sit in a room one time, for hours (and sometimes days) and drink content out of a fire hose.

If that sounds like your company's training you are about to learn a secret that will massively improve your training results. We call the secret active intervals.

Using Active Intervals To Get Huge Training Results
Active intervals limit what you're trying to teach to the bare essentials, and space learning content with breaks. Even though you limit what you are teaching during each learning event, the events don't last as long. You can space content over a longer period of time.

This does three important things. It reduces the burden of each training event (you are less likely to make an excuse to miss a one hour meeting than a 2-day seminar). It reduces the amount the learners have to remember and work on after each learning event. Finally, it provides space between multiple learning events, just like you rest between workouts at the gym. Similar to physical training, you are more likely to see results with supervisory training if the learner gets to practice multiple times over an extended period.

For example, our training modules typically follow a content pattern like this:
- **"Grabber" content prior to the initial learning event**: This might be an email asking the learner to

look at a YouTube video or read a short article. This content will be referred to during the live learning event.

- **Pre-learning quiz:** This is a quick check-in for learners to get a speedy assessment of what they know (and a little motivation if they see a gap that needs filling).
- **The live learning event**: We try to keep these sessions limited to an hour or so and focused on just one big idea. Each event has at least one, but often more, "leverage points" and activities that get learners out of their seats (or if delivered by webinar, interacting with a poll, quiz or other action) and working with the content.
- **Co-mentoring**: Each module ends with the creation of a co-mentoring relationship between two learners in the class. Each pair commits to engage with the learning content sometime in the next few weeks and then get together to discuss how they did.
- **Follow-up "grabber" content**: About once a week each learner gets another email reminding them of a key point from the training or pointing them to some other resource that emphasizes something learned during the live event.
- **"Capstone" event**: At some point after all the follow-up content has finished (six weeks or so after the live learning event), meet again with the class and revisit the key points and answer any questions trainees might have now that they've had a chance to put the learning to work. We normally do this at the beginning of the next training session.

If your current leadership training doesn't seem to be working look at the list above and see how many of these items are met by your training content. Do you see any gaps? That could very well be your problem.

If you don't already have training content developed you have a couple of options. You can send supervisors to training events outside the company (most communities have local colleges or community colleges who offer classes on the subject). There are also a number of national organizations that host seminars regularly at convenient locations around the country.

Another option is to have an outside consulting firm offer the training either on-site or via webinar or computer-based learning. Many consulting firms (including ours) also offer on site skill development in these areas. Whichever option you consider, make sure that the training offered hits the points covered in the list above. I'll warn you – most of them don't.

Especially look for follow up content, which is the key to actually using what is taught. If a course you are evaluating doesn't have this content, my advice is to either move on to a different offering that does or plan out these follow up activities yourself.

Next, make sure the training isn't trying to do too much. It is much better to focus on one or two big ideas and really hit these concepts hard, using multiple examples and activities. Use your follow up to create additional experiences with those one or two concepts. Keep focused until your leaders are comfortable with (and are actually using) the skills taught.

Ideas to Jump Start Your Training Program
For example, the table below illustrates the key concepts we cover in our training modules. You'll notice that we pick a core, fundamental skill. Even if supervisors just improve this one skill, it will substantially improve their capabilities. Since our last module teaches them that to truly be a leader they need to be constantly developing themselves, we obviously encourage them not to stop by incorporating this one key skill in each development area.

Module	Big Idea	Leverage Points
Approachable Leadership™	Approachability is the "One Ring" of leadership that rules all others	• How approachability drives OCB activity and satisfaction • The three questions approachable leaders ask
Leadership for Results™	Leadership is Intentional	• Theory X vs. Theory Y • Sources and use of power • Leadership "sweet spot"
Recognizing Employee Effort	Timely and Targeted Feedback	• Components of positive feedback • Reinforcing proper behavior • Accounting for differences
Coaching for High Performance	Managing Performance Gaps	• The power of developing people • Identifying performance gaps • The Access-Coach-Follow-up model
The Discipline Process	Employee Self-Accountability	• Discipline as development • Seven steps of just cause • Contracting for results
Mediating Conflict	The Supervisor's Role in Evolution	• The facilitation model • The victim-perpetrator-savior trap • Facilitation skills
Situational Leadership	Flexibility in Leadership Styles	• Key leadership styles • Personality, skill and task issues • Observing behavior
Persuading Others	Creating Alignment	• Six means of influence • Power and persuasion • Observing behavior
Effective Communication	Connecting with Humans	• The communication model • Listening skills • Timing, clarity and simplicity

Problems & Decision-Making	A Solution Orientation	• Tapping into your team • Defining and analyzing • Decisions and buy-in
Managing Meetings	Working Through Others	• Different types of meetings • Proper preparation • Using meeting tools effectively
Assessing Performance	Developing Your Team	• Methods of assessment • The appraisal discussion process • Pitfalls to avoid
Self Mastery	Power of Self-Development	• Taking responsibility • Creating solid habits • Time and work management

Review what your company currently provides for training and compare it to the table above. This will give you an idea of if there are any gaps in your current offerings and how to close those gaps. Again, simply having supervisors take a class once is not enough. You also need to make sure that key learning points are "refreshed" multiple times after the training.

Communication Training Example

Skills that aren't used are quickly forgotten. For that reason you also need to think about what your company does to keep skills fresh. For example, while you may have trained supervisors on improving their communication skills, if they are rarely asked to use them they won't stay sharp.

You can overcome this by simply asking supervisors to take a bigger role in company communications. Many companies will cut line-level supervision out of the communication process. They believe the line-level supervisors will do a poor job of communicating the information or communicate the information inconsistently.

Many companies believe that it is easier to have a single person, often the plant manager, tell everybody in one big meeting what it is they want the plant to know.

While this method does have the advantage of consistency, it is perhaps the least effective method of ensuring that a message is properly received by employees. There are often too many distractions during large group meetings. Employees can be intimidated or afraid to ask questions in such sessions. They become unwieldy and are too often an ineffective means of communicating.

Instead of avoiding the use of immediate supervisors in the communication process, these should be viewed as opportunities to train them in their communication skills. There are a number of strategies a company can use to do this:

- Arm line-level supervisors with consistent information like a check list, outline, or PowerPoint presentation;
- Assign higher level managers to attend meetings;
- Hold follow-up focus group sessions to ensure that the message is being received as intended.

If a company uses strategies like these to develop its supervisors, it need not worry about communication problems.

By strengthening the line-level supervisor's role in the communication process, the company helps ensure that supervisors are capable of answering questions from their employees. They also help supervisors feel more like a part of the management team. Most important, supervisors will know exactly what the rules are. It becomes very difficult for a supervisor to deny knowledge of a particular rule when they were responsible for the communication of that rule to their own employees.

Communication skills are just one example of skills you should ask supervisors to learn by doing. Coaching skills and performance management can also be taught in the same fashion. Line-level supervisors and managers should be held accountable for performance coaching of their direct reports. This can be done by requiring supervisors to hold performance discussion meetings with employees on a regular basis. Supervisors should be asked to review those coaching discussions with their manager before they deliver them.

Part of a supervisor's yearly review should include a review of performance discussion forms filled out during the year. A quick evaluation of the personnel files of the supervisor's direct reports would give a reviewing manager a good idea of whether or not the company's performance management requirements are being met. These reviews, in order to be effective, should ideally occur several times a year, perhaps quarterly.

Supervisors and managers can be reviewed on team building and initiative skills in a number of ways. Informally, this can be done during the quarterly review process where a supervisor is asked to describe anecdotally what issues have been solved by employee teams during that quarter.

Ultimately if a company intends for employee relations skills to be a strength in the company, it must reward those skills. If a supervisor achieves great results using less than satisfactory people skills, that supervisor should not receive higher rewards than less productive supervisors who do a good job in the "soft skills" area. Think of it like this: you literally get what you pay for with respect to performance management and coaching skills. If you do not reward these areas in your compensation system, you cannot expect them to be utilized by supervisors. It is just that simple.

The energy invested in developing supervisors and managers pays huge dividends. The first-level leader's position can be incredibly stressful – an unskilled supervisor often feels stuck, getting pushed by both company management and the employees who report to them. Many of these leaders crack under the pressure, lashing out at their employees, their manager, or even their family after work. If you can do something to make their lives easier, you will not only improve their lives and the results you get from them, but you will improve the lives of everyone around them (including yours).

Approachable and skilled first-level leaders improve the employee relations environment by increasing communication with employees about things that are important to them. It improves the management team, making it more likely that your company will actually accomplish its business goals. It also builds bench strength as you promote these leaders into higher levels of the organization. Furthermore, it improves productivity and profitability because engaged employees will provide discretionary effort and will produce better than disengaged ones.

Simply put, no action your company will take is more important to your employee relations environment than improving supervisory skills.

Proactive training, like discussed above, is not the only supervisory training you need. While your goal should always be to focus most efforts Left of Boom, you still need to be prepared for (and hopefully able to prevent) "boom" events. Therefore, in addition to proactive training we also recommend training on early warning signs of problems (this is the Tripwire™ training discussed in Chapter 3).

The core idea, whether Left of Boom or Right of Boom, is for supervisors to always be approachable and on the lookout for changes in behavior that may be a signal of employee dissatisfaction or, in an extreme case, union organizing activity. Noticing (and confronting) these changes in behavior is an essential "Left of Boom" skill.

A supervisor who is approachable and looking for changes in behavior will almost certainly have a highly engaged workforce under them. Because if you discuss these changes in behavior with your team when you notice them, you are showing your team the utmost respect. You prove through your own behavior that you pay attention to them, even when they don't know it. You prove to your employees that you care about them.

Whether you use our training materials or your own, your Left of Boom leadership development strategy should meet several key objectives. First, it should be designed to take advantage of adult learning principles. Space it out over time, include lots of simulation and "out of your chair" chances to practice the skills, and have multiple "touches" of the content.

Second, your training needs to cover multiple core "soft skills" for effective front-line leaders, especially Approachable Leadership™. Audit your own training offerings against the ones I've suggested and create your own gap analysis. This is also something our firm can do for you (this would be a great use of your free consulting certificate).

Finally, make sure the organization is aligned to ask supervisors to actually use these skills on a regular basis. Unused skills go stale. If you want highly skilled first level leaders (and remember, this is your pipeline of talent for upper level managers) you need to ask them to use these skills regularly. Look for opportunities to ask line-level leaders to use these skills. It will enrich their jobs and greatly improve your company.

Take Action

☐ Determine what kind of leadership training program would best fit your company.

☐ List 5 soft skills that you would like all line-level supervisors to possess. Then come up with real-life examples of when they could be applied.

SECTION IV: EMPLOYEE COMMUNICATION

Do you watch only one television station? Of course not. But most companies communicate with employees as if their TVs only have one channel. Worse yet, they communicate with employees as if the only way they get information is TV (ignoring all the other media out there like websites, online video, newspapers, magazines, and even – dare I say – conversations with other people).

Left of Boom companies make sure the direct relationship message is repeated regularly and across multiple channels. They think about how to market their value proposition to employees the same way they think about marketing to their external customers. This includes thinking hard about the message, how it gets delivered, and whether it's been accurately received.

Today there are an almost limitless number of tools available to companies to accomplish this task. We will cover several of them in the following chapters. However, the most important thing to remember is the basic point of communication: making sure the message you are trying to get across is understood.

This is not a one-way street – to do it well you have to put yourself in the shoes of your audience and really think hard about what will help them understand and feel the way you want them to about your message. And that is the magic of being a good communicator. If you take the time and effort (and it isn't easy to do well) in the end what you say is not nearly as important as that you have worked hard to make a connection.

This section has three chapters. The first covers the fundamentals of communication (this is derived from our Leadership for Results™ module called Effective

Communication). The second chapter talks about proactive (Left of Boom) communication and ideas about how to conduct your own "internal PR" campaign on your employment value proposition and the importance of a direct relationship. Finally, we cover some examples of how to communicate Right of Boom for those inevitable times when things don't go exactly the way you want.

Chapter 14

Fundamentals of Effective Communication[51]

"Please do not understand me too quickly."
André Gide

What You'll Learn In This Chapter

❑   The communication formula;
❑   The three keys to effective communication: mechanics, medium, and timing;
❑   10 suggestions for improving your active listening skills;
❑   The importance of asking reflective questions; and
❑   4 quick tips for effective communication.

For leaders communication is a lot like breathing. You do it every day, mostly without thinking about it. It is critical for your survival as a leader. If you have problems with communication it will slow down your performance. If you have extreme problems it can even "kill" you (or at least kill your career).

Poor communicators cause big problems, and not just at work. Miscommunication causes misunderstanding. Misunderstanding can cause everything from minor irritation to a war. Clear communicators create understanding. And understanding is important whether you are talking with your spouse, your child, your boss, or a co-worker. Understanding

---

[51] This chapter is based on our Approachable Leadership™ module *Effective Communication*. If you like this chapter contact us about options for bringing this same content to your own company as either a live-training or remote-training experience for your leaders.

is almost literally the oxygen that allows any organization to survive and thrive.

When you and your employees communicate effectively productivity improves. Errors decline. Goals are achieved. You and your team have more fun. The good news is that, unlike many breathing problems, communication is a skill that can be learned and improved. This chapter is all about the fundamentals to do just that.

As much as we think we know about getting our message across, it doesn't always happen. Often what we say is not what the other person hears. This can be baffling. But nearly all communication problems can be whittled down to one key failure: the failure to create understanding.

Communication happens when mutual understanding happens. But how do you create understanding? When two people communicate they each have responsibility for creating understanding. Most people think about communication like the "formula" below:

$$\frac{50\%}{\text{Person 1}} + \frac{50\%}{\text{Person 2}} = \frac{100\%}{\text{Understanding}}$$

Does this equation make sense to you? It definitely covers one key concept: effective communication is a two-way street. One person cannot be solely responsible for creating understanding. But does this formula get the responsibilities right?

Is it true that each person shares half the load to ensure they've created understanding? Is each person equally responsible? Can you think of a different way to re-write the formula to better reflect the realities of communication? How about something like:

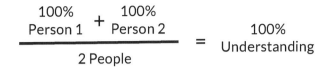

$$\frac{\frac{100\%}{\text{Person 1}} + \frac{100\%}{\text{Person 2}}}{\text{2 People}} = \frac{100\%}{\text{Understanding}}$$

The second version of the formula is a better description of how communication works in the real world. Each of us comes to any conversation with our own understanding and view of the world. You could even say that each of us always has a conversation going on in our own head. That is our individual understanding of the world. Each of us is responsible for 100% of our own "conversation" or understanding of the world around us.

When two people interact you have to account for this reality. To succeed at creating a mutual understanding the conversation in your head needs to match the conversation in the head of the other person. That's what the revised formula tries to make clear.

How does this revised formula better account for the "human element" of passing information from one person to another? If both parties to a conversation are taking 100% of the responsibility for clearly communicating, how much more likely is it they will reach an understand, than if each person is only taking 50% of the responsibility?

In order for there to be common understanding, both people must take 100% of the responsibility for communication. You are not only responsible for *telling* other people information, but for making sure they share the same *understanding* you have of the situation. Only then have you effectively communicated.

Does this formula make more sense? What does this tell you about the nature of how you interact with your employees, or for that matter, your wife and kids or anyone else?

Our objective then is to discover what it really means to take 100% of the responsibility for communicating in a way that will achieve 100% understanding. Effective communication is not sending a text message or email about something and never following up. It isn't even a face-to-face conversation with the supervisor doing all the talking, and no feedback coming from the employee being addressed.

Have you ever watched *Dancing with the Stars*? Effective communication is like a good ballroom dance. Each party has to know their moves or the whole thing falls apart. But that's not enough. Each person also needs to know the moves of their partner. When both people understand their moves and their partner's moves the dance can be beautiful and exciting. If not, somebody gets dropped on the floor.

There are three keys to effective communication:
- The mechanics;
- The medium; and
- The timing

These are like the 3 legs on a stool. Get them all right, and you've got a pretty stable platform. Leave one of them out and – like the failed dancer – you may fall flat on your face! Let's look more carefully at each of these elements.

Communication Mechanics
"Mechanics" may seem like a robotic way to look at the very human process of communication. However, it is helpful to think about the right steps in the process. Sometimes this will help you identify the source of problems that are causing a misunderstanding.

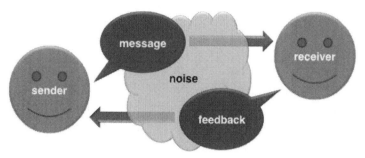

Figure 14.1 –Communication Model

What we are looking at here is a widely recognized model of the communication process, which contains five basic parts:
- A sender;
- The message;
- A receiver;
- Noise; and
- Feedback.

The sender originates a message. The receiver gets the message. The message is what the sender wants the receiver to get. Noise is anything that interferes with the message being received. Finally, feedback is the response to the sender's message that communicates the degree of understanding, or perhaps misunderstanding, of the message.

Sender > Message > Noise > Feedback > Receiver

The diagram shows how the five parts work together. The sender will send a message through some medium (more on that below) to the receiver. The receiver will act or respond to the message in such a way that the sender is able to understand that the receiver received and understood the message (feedback). In the middle of this whole process there are things that can interrupt or distort both the message and the feedback.

Here are some things the <u>sender</u> can focus on to make sure the message is received as intended:

- First, simplify the message and eliminate anything that distracts from or confuses the main point.
- Second, select an appropriate medium for the message.
- Third, attempt to reduce noise from interrupting the message.
- Fourth, evaluate the feedback from the receiver, to make sure that the message was clearly understood. Respond to the feedback, make adjustments and try again if necessary.

Remember, the <u>receiver</u> also has full responsibility for the communication process. Their part in the process is to:

- Focus on the sender and try to limit noise from interrupting the communication process.
- Provide feedback in a reflective manner, putting the message in their own words, so the sender can evaluate whether or not the intended message got across.
- Confirm that the meaning was indeed transferred – ask the sender if their restatement of the message was correct.

If the communication process works properly, the message and feedback should be mirror images of each other. Often this is not the case. Noise will interfere with the message and feedback at some point.

Think of noise like fog. In some cases it can be very light and cause almost no interference. Other times it can be dense, making it almost impossible to see. In communication this "fog" can be many different things.

We've all been on conference calls (unfortunately I spend a big chunk of my life on them). Sometimes those calls are fine, but many times they are torture. Think about some of the things that frustrate you about conference calls you've been on. A lot of that is noise. For example:

- Extraneous information that clutters up and distracts from the primary message ("Thanks for that fascinating five-minute story about the weather – now what was the question?")
- It can be physical barriers ("Oh can you hear my blender running in the background, I thought I was on mute.")
- It can be psychological barriers or emotional reactions to the message or the sender ("I'm sorry, I missed the question because I was thinking about the different painful accidents that could happen to you.")
- It can be outside distractions causing either the sender or the receiver to devote less than their full attention to the communication process ("Could you repeat the question? I've been multitasking for the last 40 minutes.")

Hopefully you are beginning to get the idea of how noise can clutter up and cloud a message. So one of the key goals for both senders and receivers should be to reduce noise.

Up to this point, you have probably been thinking of yourself as a sender – the one communicating a message to one or more receivers. The reality is, most of us are receivers far more often than we are senders!

As a leader you probably have employees regularly report to you about their work, their progress, or incidents like a safety violation or shipping error. They may report these things in a variety of ways –informally (like a quick conversation in the hall) or formally (like a safety incident report).

You also are a receiver of messages from upper levels of management. Sometimes this is just general information you aren't expected to act on (these communications can also be noise – "Let's see, I'm sure your very important email is somewhere in the 57 TPS reports you sent me this week.") Other times you are called on to interpret directives, sales goals or objectives, or process changes and make sure your team is aligned with them.

Don't ever forget that it is your responsibility to be effective at both sending and receiving communication. And this begs another question: "What if I am improving my communication skills, but my employees (or my bosses) aren't? What about their responsibility?"

Take a look at our chapter on coaching skills (we offer a training module on this as well). It has a lot of tips that will help you build up the skills of your employees. You can also use many of these tips to "coach up" and give helpful feedback to your manager. This is also a core skill of a good leader.

Either way, if you go back to our equation you know that if you handle your part of the communication equation well you will significantly improve overall understanding. Going back to our dancing analogy, if your "partner" doesn't quite know all the steps to the dance you might have a few missteps, but it's unlikely anyone will end up on the floor (or on YouTube!)

Modeling good behavior and skills is the place to start. That's how you "lead the dance" with your employees. Even without engaging in a formal coaching or training program, your team will pick up on your use of better communication techniques and skills.

The Communication Medium
Now that you understand some of the key mechanics of communication you need to think about the practical stuff: HOW are you going to try create a shared understanding?

The communications medium is how you are communicating, or the method you are using to send your message. This can be things like:
- Verbal communication
- written memo
- email
- phone or voice mail
- text message
- a physical expression
- a poster or infographic; or
- anything else where you can convey a message from one person to another.

Often when communications problems occur it is because the medium used isn't well suited for either the type of message being sent, or the person receiving the message. Some methods of communication make providing feedback difficult, especially when a response is time sensitive. Choosing the right medium for the message often makes all the difference in the world.

Think about a text message for a second. This could be a great medium or a terrible medium depending on the situation and what you are trying to communicate. Text messages are sometimes very effective because they are short (not a lot of room for extraneous chatter or noise that could distract from the message). They are also very fast (in most cases instant). If you want someone to know that you are going to be a few minutes late for a meeting text messages are the perfect medium.

But sending a text message to someone leaves out a lot of the communication mechanics. You can have a lot of noise (Did my text message actually send? Are they near their phone so they saw the message? Are they in the middle of a call or other text conversation and not see the message arrive? Did my phone auto-"correct"[52] my message so that it now has nothing to do with what I originally wanted to say?) And feedback like "K" in response to the message does very little to let us know that we've got mutual understanding.

Strengths and Weaknesses of Media

There are strengths and weaknesses involved with every type of communication medium. Whether sending email messages back and forth or speaking face-to-face, noise is always a challenge. When selecting the medium for a message the sender should consider the challenges involved with each method and choose the best method for the message and receiver involved.

As you think about communication media, consider how you currently communicate with your employees:

- What are the most common ways that you send messages to your employees (the media used)?
- What would you say are some of the strengths and weaknesses of each?
- Do you change the medium based on the type of message or do you rely on one method most of the time?
- Do you ask directly for feedback? How do you get that feedback?

Think about some of the media you could use for delivery of the following messages:

- A company tardiness policy change.
- Congratulating a small team for getting a project done early.

---

[52] If you want to kill a few minutes (or more) and are in a place where laughing so hard that you cry is OK, check out: http://www.damnyouautocorrect.com/

- Thanking an individual for staying 15 minutes late to help you close out yesterday.
- A reprimand to an employee for a safety violation.
- Instructions for making a change to an equipment maintenance procedure.

You have a lot of options when it comes to communication medium. It is important to be thoughtful about which medium is most appropriate for a particular message. An informal and private meeting might be most appropriate for congratulating the small team. You might choose to give positive performance feedback in front of co-workers. Policy changes are better communicated in a more formal and consistent manner. The medium you choose will help determine whether you will succeed in effectively communicating and creating a shared understanding.

Timing

Timing may not be everything, but it is the critical third leg of our communications stool. Even if you have the right mechanics and medium for your message, understanding can be lost if you send it at the wrong time.

Depending on the circumstances choosing the right time to send a message can be more important than any other consideration. Consider factors like:

- Are you interrupting the receiver from something important that might prevent them from concentrating on your message?
- Is the receiver in a place where communicating to them right now might be embarrassing or stressful?
- Is the message urgent and if the information required to prevent the receiver from doing unnecessary or improper work?
- Do you need an answer fast in order to prevent a bottleneck somewhere else in the operation?

If you think about the mechanics of communication, poor timing usually means more noise between you and the receiver. More noise usually means that your receiver either won't get or won't understand your message. That's why you should only send messages when you know that:

- Your receiver can concentrate and give you feedback to ensure mutual understanding; or
- You've chosen a medium that allows the receiver to choose a time when they can concentrate on your message.

The content of your message also plays a part. A very simple message that requires almost no concentration and isn't very important can be sent almost anytime (like a text saying, "I put that report you wanted in your inbox.") A high-stakes conversation that requires a lot of concentration must be planned and delivered only when both the sender and receiver can both devote the attention the conversation deserves.

Consequences

What difference does it make if you are just an "OK" communicator? What's the big deal if you use just one medium or don't think about the timing of your messages? What kinds of problems can happen? Think about these examples:

- An employee thought they were being praised for doing something that they actually did incorrectly.
- An employee misinterpreted a change to the benefit plan, and thought they were losing several paid sick days or vacation days.
- An employee didn't understand what a new employee's job responsibilities were who was assigned to their team.
- You got the dates mixed up with 3 new company objectives announced in a memo to supervisors.

How might each of these impact you personally? How might they affect performance in your department, morale among your team, and even your own career? Hopefully you see that the simple principles outlined above can prevent many common misunderstandings at work.

Each of the misunderstandings listed above are a problem in their own right. But can you see how they might build on each other? The employee who thinks they've been praised now teaches the new employee the wrong way to perform the work. The employee upset about their benefits realizes you've got the dates wrong but decides not to tell you because they are mad.

Front line leaders are the "tip of the spear" when it comes to making sure front-line employees know what's going on, what is expected of them, and when they are straying from the mark. Effective communication (or the lack of it) can make or break a department, or a company. It is a key source of friction in a company that can make the organization seem unapproachable and, as we've seen earlier, discourage employees from going above and beyond at work.

But first-level leaders are also the bridge between upper management and employees. So it is just as important that leaders take responsibility for making the communication process effective when dealing with those above them in the organization. Ensuring understanding both above and below is a key to prevent wasted effort, disappointment and frustration.

Listening Skills

Now that we've covered the process and how the various elements of the process interact, there are a few more skills that will help you communicate effectively. Whether you are the sender or receiver in a conversation, listening skills are a vital to getting communication right. Learn these skills and practice them regularly, and you will become a powerfully effective communicator.

Active Listening

Most of us think of listening as a passive process – someone talks, we use our ears to hear what they're saying, and that's it – we understand them. But we've already seen the problem with this way of thinking about listening. The presence of noise – whether external or internal – means that listening requires more than just "hearing." It requires what is called Active Listening.

Active listening is focusing your full attention on what the other person is saying. It requires practice and patience. Often during a conversation, one or both parties will be distracted by noise. You know that embarrassing feeling of drifting off while someone is talking to you, when suddenly you are surprised by a question? You panic and struggle to try to remember what they just said to you 5 seconds earlier, so you can avoid sounding stupid when you ask, "could you repeat that?" Active listening is a way to avoid that feeling.

Many times we get distracted in a conversation because we are focusing on what we want to say next instead of listening carefully to the sender. When you are actively listening you focus your attention on what the sender is saying, and not what you want to say. This requires a little more attention than usual.

Here are 10 tips on how to be a more effective active listener:

1. Pay attention to the words and body language of the sender. As you listen to what they are saying also think about what they are feeling. You might even ask them, "How did that make you feel?" or say, "Wow, that must have been frustrating."

2. Limit interruptions to the sender, but occasionally let them know you are listening carefully through your body language and even verbally. Nodding your head or uttering a simpler "Uh huh" or "I understand" helps the sender know you are present and engaged.
3. Try to really understand. Even if you disagree, listen with an open mind and try to understand the sender's point of view. If you disagree don't be defensive, but ask questions to try to understand the alternative point of view.
4. If something surprises you or gives you pause ask the sender to give you more detail or explanation.
5. Don't try to solve a problem right away or fast track the conversation – give the sender space to tell the whole story.
6. Don't be rude. Don't talk over someone's head or talk down to them, interrupt, or not let them finish what they're saying.
7. Ask reflective questions (more on that below).
8. Avoid changing topics to shift the focus on you.
9. Try not to interrupt the other person and keep your mind engaged on what the other person is saying.
10. Avoid distractions or allowing your mind to wander during the conversation (put the cell phone down!)

Active listening is about understanding the other person's message. When the other person is done, provide feedback to check that you actually understood what they were hoping to get across - restate in your own words what you think the other person was trying to say. Ask the sender if it sounds like you understood their message. Staying focused and avoiding distractions can be difficult, but practicing active listening skills will make you a better listener.

Reflective Questions
Asking reflective questions is another powerful tool. Clarifying questions can sometimes be answered with a "Yes"

or "No" response ("I'm sorry, did you just say that my hair was on fire?") just testing that you understood a particular point.

Reflective questions go deeper, testing whether you understood the entire message. They also help create rapport with the sender, because these questions show that you really were listening actively. Further, these questions prove that you really care about fully understanding the sender's message.

Here are some tips for asking good reflective questions:
- They are usually open-ended – encouraging the other party to elaborate in more detail. Avoid a question that can be answered yes or no. For example, "Did that frustrate you?" is not as good as, "That sounds pretty frustrating, how did you feel after that happened?"
- They keep the focus on the other person – on his or her intended message. Once you've established mutual understanding you may want to relate a similar experience you've gone through, but until you've proven you understand the sender is the star of the show.
- If you disagree with the sender's position a reflective question is a gentle and respectful way to get them to challenge their own view of the facts. For example, "Well, we both know Bob can be kind of aloof sometimes – what made you think that he saw the safety hazard as he walked by?"

A few good reflective questions can help clear up clutter or noise – even occasionally dealing with such noise directly – to get to the heart of the matter in a discussion or conversation.

A Few Other Tips
Here are four additional tips that will help you connect better with your employees using any medium:

1. Keep the message simple. This can be tricky for some.
Sometimes our messages get more complicated than
necessary because:
- When we stop long enough to communicate with
  someone, we take the opportunity to empty our plate
  of everything we have on our list to communicate.
- We are thinking about needing to talk to someone,
  and all of a sudden they are standing there in our
  office. We start into the conversation before we've
  really had a chance to plan what we need to say, or
  identify the crucial point of the communication.
- In our rush, we type out an email and hit the send
  button, so we can rush on to the next thing on our
  checklist.

There is an old story that is often attributed to Mark Twain
(although it is attributed to many others) where Twain once
wrote to a friend, "I was going to write you a short letter but
didn't have time, so I wrote you a long one instead." Twain's
point is that simple communication is harder than just
blathering out everything you can think of. Our
communication is often cluttered with extra details and issues,
making it harder for the receiver to understand what we are
trying to say, or at least to unravel the main point.

To keep you message simple, follow these steps:
1. Plan your communication in advance. You can have a
   simple agenda of topics you want to cover, but more
   important think about the main point you need to cover
   for each topic.
2. When possible stick to one point at a time. If you have
   more to communicate, you probably need some type of
   written communication (email, memo) versus a
   conversation or phone call.
3. Get to the point as fast as you can.
4. If you are sending an email or text message, proof read it.
   Keep it brief. Test whether the message makes sense.

5. The more clear and direct you are the less confusion there will be and the less time it will take you to explain what you are trying to say.
6. Be respectful. Follow the Golden Rule – speak to others the same way you would want to be spoken to.
7. Be positive. Communicate with enthusiasm, whether you are a sender or a receiver. Be engaged and interested in the understanding the message.
8. Be concise. Get to the point. Don't ramble.

Together, these tips will help ensure that you fully understand messages that are being communicated to you. They will also help make sure the messages you communicate are fully understood by others. Finally, these tips will help you create rapport with everyone you interact with. Others will be more receptive to anything you have to say because you have proven over time that you respect and understand them.

Communication is a more complex process than it first appears. To do it well, remember the following keys:

- The responsibility for communication (the communication formula)
- The mechanics of the communication process, along with the medium and timing.
- Listening skills – including active listening and reflective questions.
- Tips to becoming a better communicator – including simplicity, respectfulness, and being positive and concise in your delivery.

This chapter focused primarily on the theory of communication. In the following chapters we will look at some practical examples of communications you will encounter in your day-to-day work. This will help you see how to apply these keys in your daily work.

Action Steps

☐ Think back on the last experience you labeled a miscommunication.
☐ Did the problem lie in the mechanics, the medium, or the timing? Review that section for steps you can take for improvement.

Chapter 15

Communicating Left of Boom: Proactive Communication

"The following are the universally fundamental laws of literary communication:

1. one must have something to communicate;
2. one must have someone to whom to communicate it;
3. one must really communicate it, not merely express it for oneself alone.

Otherwise it would be more to the point to remain silent."
Friedrich Von Schlegel, German philosopher.

What You'll Learn In This Chapter
❑   How to apply the basic principles of communication to policies, procedures, benefits, and compensation issues;
❑   The 3 different kinds of learners and how to make sure your message is received by all of them;
❑   The importance of communicating through multiple channels;
❑   The grapevine can be your best friend; and
❑   Why you should become a proactive communicator.

When one of our consultants arrives on the scene after a "boom" event in a company, a conversation like this usually happens within an hour:

Client: "I know our employees are really frustrated but I just don't understand it – they're ignoring all these great things we've done for them over the last year!"

Consultant: "Tell me about some of the things you've done."

Client: "Oh there's tons. We added daily huddles so we can fix stuff when it happens. We've included employees in a number of Kaizen events that made a lot of frustrating processes easier. We fixed a problem with our insurance company that was causing about 10 complaints a month. We altered the shifts slightly so there could be a good handoff between shifts – that's been a complaint for a long time. We've been making a lot of positive changes recently."

Consultant: "Wow. That is a lot. Sounds like you are moving in the right direction. Tell me about how you communicated all these great things?"

Client: "What do you mean? The employees were there the whole time. They were part of the decisions being made. Why would we have to communicate about them?"

And that is the point where our consultant diagnoses one of the most common problems that leads to boom events in companies: poor proactive communication.

Proactive communication is a fancy way of saying, "tooting your own horn." For some reason people often confuse this with bragging. It's not. As Walt Whitman (among others) once said, "If you done it, it ain't bragging."

More important, assuming your employees know "you done it" is a BIG mistake. How many times have you been surprised to learn about something that happened at your company? Things that others knew about, but just never got communicated to you. Has it ever happened? More than once? More like once a week?

If that was a revelation, think about this. If you asked your CEO this same question (and you should) you will get the same answer. If the leaders of an organization – who are in a much better position to learn about these things – feel out of the loop, is it any surprise that the people below them feel this way?

Even companies that spend a lot of effort communicating good news and updates still struggle with this problem. We learned the source of it in our communication fundamentals – noise.[53] In the best of situations noise regularly prevents understanding and awareness. And let's face it, most of the time we aren't in the best of situations.

There is another problem when it comes to communicating positive information, and this one's genetic. We are programmed at our very core to be on the lookout for threats. This is what kept us from waking up in the mouth of a cheetah when we lived on the Savannah.

Our brains are hardwired to pay very close attention to news related to threats. We don't pay much attention to news about non-threats. Take a look at your favorite local newscast, newspaper or news website. Are the headlines about all the good deeds that happened today?

The same thing is happening in your company – and with you – this minute. There are threats out there on the Savannah. Did we get the big account? Is our stock tanking? Is my boss happy with that report I just finished? Am I going to get a bonus? Is there going to be a layoff? These are the threats that constantly beg for our attention. And this is the noise that must be overcome to get people to pay attention to good news in your company.

This is why proactive communication is so important. If you don't make a strong effort to "toot your horn" when good things are happening, you'll never be heard above the noise. And while I'm a big Miles Davis fan, when I say "toot" think less

---

[53] See Chapter 14 on communication fundamentals.

the mellow jazz solo and more the trumpet that starts the
Kentucky Derby.

Basic Principles

Start by looking at how you communicate inside your
organization today. Do you consistently inform employees
about what is going on in the company? Do they know about
new developments that might impact their work conditions,
their position, or their current work assignments? Is there a
system for communicating this information? How is it
working?

If important information is not being communicated now, you
need to immediately implement a system to remedy this
situation. If you already have a system, I'll give you some tips
on how to tell whether your system is covering all the bases.
Either way, the first step is establishing a system for proactive
communication.

Once you have your system in place you have to test whether
you are effectively overcoming the noise. This is the battle of
perception. Even if you feel like your company regularly
communicates proactively with employees, if employees don't
agree you are no better off than the company who doesn't
communicate at all. That's a perception problem that must be
repaired.

If you have problems with proactive communication you have
a system issue, a perception issue or maybe both. Here are
some tips on how to make sure your proactive communication
program covers all the bases. Pay close attention – these same
principles are keys to doing a good job of reactive
communication (which we'll cover in the next chapter).

Consistent Message

One common problem with communication in organizations is
message inconsistency. This manifests itself in many different
ways. For example, top management may deliver one message

while a line supervisor gives another. Written communication may transmit a third message while a fourth message is being generated through the grapevine, outside vendors or other sources. When bombarded by inconsistent messages, there is very little an employee can do besides become confused. This confusion is automatically blamed on management because employees expect their leaders to act with consistency (as they should).

This is why it is so important to regularly evaluate your communication processes to ensure that the same message is being delivered across all mediums. If you find an inconsistency, correct it.

You will have to repeat your message several times to overcome the noise in the system or to counteract inconsistent messages from others. There are some tips below for doing this without sounding like a politician, but you could learn a thing or two from politicians as communicators. While answering with the same talking point over and over (even when, in context, the answer doesn't make sense) can be annoying, it works. If your two options are bad politician or not getting your message across go with politician every time. Consistent "trumps" annoying (pun intended).

Consistency also builds trust with employees. Over time employees will grow to trust messages from management over other sources (like the grapevine we discuss below). This can take a while, especially after a union organizing campaign or other upheaval. But with time and consistency your employees will regain trust.

Keep It Simple
Another important aspect of employee communication is to keep messages simple. This is especially true when communicating complex information. Here are some tips on how to do it:

1. Before you communicate a message to everyone, test those messages and communication pieces with small groups of supervisors (good) or employees (better).
2. When possible use informal leaders in your focus groups. And don't just pick people who are always positive – try to get a few skeptics and see how they react.
3. Quiz the focus groups. Is the message clearly understood? If not let them help focus the message.
4. Can you break down the communication into smaller component parts? Sometimes it is better to communicate part of the message and build it up versus trying to "eat the whole whale" in one bite. This can also create opportunities to repeat the message multiple times.

Communication today is much different than in the past. Long-form text, for example, is rarely used at all unless it's a legal document (as a lawyer, I'd like to take this time to apologize for that on behalf of the profession). This was true when I first wrote this chapter in 2003; but 10 years later, with the advent and massive adoption of services like Twitter, instant messaging and now video messaging apps, it is even more applicable. As a society, we regularly consume content that only takes a few seconds to read or watch. Like never before, we communicate every day in the briefest way possible.

You can express disappointment in these changes, but you cannot deny them. If you are going to be a competent communicator you must keep things easy to consume, and that usually means brief. This isn't impossible and it can be very effective.

Some of the most famous advertising campaigns are one and two-word campaigns (Got Milk? and Just Do It, are two examples). Dan Pink, who we met in Chapter 11 talks about the "one word pitch" or a word that you own so completely it describes you or your business.[54] For example when you hear the word "search" what comes to mind? Google. When you hear the word "priceless?" Mastercard.

Think USA Today instead of the New York Times. Think of comic books versus War and Peace. If your message was a tweet, how would you get it into 140 characters? Your communication succeeds if the receiver gets and understands your message. The simpler the message, the more likely that happens.

Use as Many Senses as Possible
There are three primary types of learners: visual (about 75% of the population – this large group is sometimes further broken down into people who prefer reading-writing), auditory (about 20%), and kinesthetic (about 5%). Many (but not all) visual learners like to read information. Auditory learners prefer to hear the message. Kinesthetic learners learn by doing.

Research also suggests that no matter what your preferred learning style, the best approach when teaching is to utilize all three. You want your message to be received by every kind of learner. Think about what other ways you can get a message across. Can you do something visual (an infographic[55] or a video)? Could you hold a demonstration where people can actually touch and feel (and even smell) what you're doing? Each sense you involve will make it more likely your message is received.

---

[54] See Daniel H. Pink, *To Sell is Human: The Surprising Truth About Moving Others* (Riverhead 2012) at pp. 160-161.
[55] There is a sample infographic later in this chapter. Also download our infographic on Approachable Leadership™ at http://ApproachableLeadership.com

Think about a communication about 401(k) participation. You could send out a memo explaining why investing in the 401(k) program is important. It might even have a bar chart showing the difference between investing and sitting on the sidelines. How might you get other senses involved to really get the message across?

What visual options do you have besides the expected bar chart? What if you included something like:

- A brief presentation by two people: one who invested and retired early and another who did not invest and was forced to work into his/her late sixties.
- A picture of Donald Trump or Warren Buffet with a synopsis of why they invest;
- A stack of money, complete with an armed guard, on a table that people can actually flip through;
- A short YouTube video with upbeat music and some of your key points.

The options are limited only by your imagination. But don't fall into the trap of using the same method or vehicle over and over to communicate your message. There should be consistency of message, but not consistency of medium. Mix things up.

Multiple Channels

In addition to communicating in ways that appeal to each learning style, also communicate through different channels. Building on what we said about communication media, companies that post messages on bulletin boards and assume the message is communicated are typically the types of companies whose problems end up on our desks. Assuming that employees receive a message simply because someone has been told to communicate the message is a mistake and, frankly, inept management. Instead, distribute messages through as many channels as you can.

Communicating through multiple channels creates multiple "impressions" of the same message. Go back to our discussion of learning styles in school. Could you study for an exam by just reading the text once? You probably had to re-read the same text several times. You may have taken notes or created flash cards to help study. You probably attended lectures (at least the ones in the afternoon...) and maybe even recorded them to listen to again later. It's likely that you used used all the different learning styles to give yourself multiple impressions of the same material.

Advertising agencies use the same theory. Companies do not buy one ad and then stop. They will buy several months or even years of ad space. They will coordinate messages on TV with messages on websites and in magazines, newspapers and radio. In this way, through multiple impressions, advertising agencies make sure that a consistent message is communicated and received by the public.

What's an Infographic?

APPROACHABLE LEADERSHIP
THE "ONE RING" OF LEADERSHIP
HAPPINESS IS A VERB, NOT A NOUN

Organizational Citizenship Behavior: The Tiny Hinge That Swings the Big Door on Performance

Are happy employees the most productive? Workplace happiness doesn't predict performance. Discretionary activity at work (organizational citizenship behavior) again and again is the best predictor of individual and unit level performance.

■ OCB Activity ■ All Other Factors

Source: Cornell Hospitality Journal, 2010

WHAT PREDICTS ORGANIZATIONAL CITIZENSHIP?

Suggestions are great examples of organizational citizenship. They are discretionary but can have a big impact on a business. Who makes suggestions?

Desire for Money or Gift 29%
Desire to Improve Organization 45%
Supervisor Doing Good Job 80%
Approachable Supervisor 88%

Source: Journal of Management Development, 2005

80% > 88%

Approachable leaders get OCB even if not doing a 'good job'

Figure 15.1

Successful company communications utilize the same procedure. They rely on multiple, consistent impressions of the same message distributed across as many channels as possible. A few examples of effective distribution (and this is certainly not an exhaustive list) include:

- Print – bulletin board postings, paycheck stuffers, memos, infographics, signs in the break room, etc.
- Auditory – team meetings, one-on-one meetings, broadcast over loudspeaker, audiotape, podcast, quarterly meetings, etc.
- Electronic – e-mail, sms, twitter, company intranet, YouTube, PowerPoint slides, etc.

What About The Grapevine?

When deciding how to communicate a message, consider all the ways employees receive messages in your company. One method mentioned before, but worth repeating, is the grapevine. Many companies allow the grapevine to become their downfall by ignoring it, failing to correct the rumors, or pretending that it doesn't exist at all.

Every business has informal networks. In fact, when you map an organization these informal networks dwarf the "formal" networks of communication. This is where the literal and figurative "water cooler" conversations happen. In fact, surveys often indicate that the grapevine is the number one source of information for many employees.

Do not ignore the grapevine. Instead, learn to use it as another method to communicate messages. If management is not managing the grapevine, it is allowing the grapevine to manage the communication of its messages.

How do you take advantage of the grapevine? Informal network leaders should be used as sounding boards for the communication of important messages. You should test whether these informal leaders understand your message.

You may be concerned about whether you can trust informal leaders with key messages. Like any trusting relationship, you have to build it over time. Don't try to figure out if you can trust someone to be confidential with the first conversation. Confide in them with low-risk messages first and see if they maintain confidence. Then build from there. Eventually you will have a few key individuals you can trust to give you solid feedback about how messages will be received (and who will often help communicate the messages themselves once they become public).

When the grapevine is communicating false information, it is critical for management (and other key informal leaders) to immediately attack that misinformation. The company must then reinforce the correct information. This ensures consistency of the company message. There are a number of tools you can use to do this. Consider some of the following:

- Create talking points documents that supervisors and first-level leaders (the level of management most likely to overhear incorrect rumors) can use to make sure employees have the "full story."
- When rolling out a message make sure to include all leaders first, and role-play answering some of the most common rumors you anticipate after the announcement.
- Consider creating a "FAQ" document that answers some of the rumors you anticipate (this will parrot much of what you have in your talking points).
- For important messages we will sometimes create a "message wheel" that has the key message in the middle and has follow-up points as the spokes. The idea of a message wheel is to get communicators to always end up back on the key message.

While there is no way to stop all misinformation flowing through the grapevine, you must always consider this channel when dealing with your communication strategy. The more attention you pay to the grapevine, the more likely you can use it as an ally.

Test Your Success

One often-ignored aspect of communication strategy is determining whether or not the message has actually been understood. After communicating an important message to employees, it is a good practice to conduct some sampling to see if the message was clearly understood by your target audience. This sampling can be as simple as asking a few people to repeat what they understood, to something as formal as focus group meetings or a communication survey.

The best time to sample is after a little time has elapsed from the initial communication of the message. This lets you evaluate not just the initial communication, but also whether the message is lasting and has stood up to the grapevine. Most important, this counts as another impression for purposes of communication strategy.

What Should I Be Proactively Communicating?

The flip answer to this question is, "anything you wish people understood better about your company." However, I think the flip answer is also the truth. Whenever an employee asks you or another manager a question, that's a possible topic. If someone doesn't understand a key policy or benefit, that is another opportunity for some proactive communication. If one of your employees is worried about something happening in the business, it is likely that other employees are worried about the same thing. Use these concerns as a topics for proactive communication.

In addition to the regular questions and concerns that come up at work, here are some other topics you might want to consider for proactive communication:

- **The value of a direct relationship.** Some companies utilize proactive communication to make direct comparisons to unionized companies, but that's not the only way to get this important point across. Communicating stories about how your company responded to a customer need with flexibility (maybe out-maneuvering a slower competitor) is a great way to promote direct relationships. You can also highlight policies and benefits that create flexibility. These all must explain why this flexibility makes the business more successful and improves work-life balance. We have had several clients communicate this type of information on a monthly basis, changing the specific example but always illustrating the key message of "we accomplish more working directly together."

- **Benefits.** Communicating about key benefits like your 401(K), health care, tuition reimbursement, disability insurance, vacation and personal leave, incentive pay, and all the other benefits you offer is a big opportunity for most companies. You can let your imagination run wild here. Focusing on one benefit for a month or two and then switching to another is a good way to keep things fresh and to illustrate over a course of time the large number of benefits your employees enjoy. Think about ways to get employees involved in learning more about each benefit and remember to communicate across multiple channels.

- **Company mission and goals.** After the posters go up on the walls most companies don't do much to communicate anything about their mission, core values or goals. These topics provide great opportunities for the company to "level set" everyone on the organization's True North. Think of ways that you can illustrate how day-to-day activities help the company reach its mission. Highlight individual employee contributions that illustrate your core values in action. Tell stories about customer experiences that reinforce the value your business creates in the world.

- **Help solve problems.** Another great way to use proactive communication is to ask people to report on their challenges, or to ask for suggestions on how to help solve these problems. You can also use these communications as a way to go over all the different ways someone can get help overcoming an obstacle at work.

Isn't This Over-Communicating?

When we work with companies, particularly ones that have done a poor job of communicating in the past, a question we often get asked is, "Isn't this over-communicating?" The answer is yes. But over-communication isn't the problem. In fact, over-communicating is a critical strategy for companies with communication problems. There are a couple of reasons companies with communication problems should respond by over-communicating.

First, these businesses must learn how to communicate. Simply, practice makes perfect. A lot of time and effort should be devoted, particularly in the early stages of revamping communication capabilities, to repeatedly communicating your messages. Assess whether these messages have been communicated through as many channels as possible; additionally, ask if they have actually been received and understood by employees.

Second, over-communication is an intentional strategy to overcome the perception that a company is not communicating well. Overcoming the ingrained belief that your company does a poor job of communicating will not happen overnight. A large increase in the number of impressions of company messages is required to change the perception and will be seen by others as a change for the better in the company.

This is especially important on the heels of a union organizing campaign. Most companies communicate more regularly and more effectively during a union campaign than they ever have before. If the company goes back to its normal pattern of communication after the campaign, employees will sense a huge vacuum of information flow. This jeopardizes relationships built during the campaign and feeds claims by union supporters that the company's interest in employees during the campaign was simply a tactic and that no long-term improvements will be made. Without public evidence to the contrary, these claims can be very persuasive.

While employees may at first feel bombarded by the number of messages directed to them, they will form the distinct feeling that management is trying, (maybe even trying too hard), to ensure they are receiving the information needed to effectively do their jobs. While eventually management can back off from this approach, in the early stages the overload of information is critical. In addition, this strategy gives management the opportunity to test as many different communication methods as possible in the only environment that matters – their own.

Methods of communication work differently in each company. Every business is unique and requires its own system for communicating messages. By experimenting with as many different methods as possible, management can evaluate which are most effective and then rely more heavily on those methods in the future.

Don't Forget Humor
People remember and will repeat something that is funny, so humor is a good tool to add to your employee communication toolkit. In companies that have recently gone through serious upheavals (like an organizing campaign) it can be helpful to lighten things up a bit.

The inclusion of topical cartoons and humorous messages as part of a communication program helps retention, creates additional impressions, generates buzz, and reduces tension provoked by tough issues. Using these strategies effectively can defuse what might be considered a negative employee relations problem in an at-risk business.

Be careful not to overdo humor. It has its place and can be very effective, but you don't want to come across as dismissive or flip about serious issues. You are not a comedy act - use humor as a supplement to your regular communications.

Your employees are no different than you. You want to know what is going on. You want to know where the company is headed. If you have a problem you want to be able to get it resolved quickly and without a lot of hassle. You want your leaders to think about how to make your work experience the best it can be. You want them to talk to you about your achievements and your progress.

When you think about proactive communication, think about these same topics. Talk about the kind of information you'd like to know. Focus your communication in those areas and you will be miles ahead. You'll truly be communicating Left of Boom.

Action Steps

- ☐ Does your organization have a system for communicating important information company-wide? If not, start there.
- ☐ Once you do, make a habit of reviewing it on a regular basis. There is always room for improvement.

Chapter 16

Communicating Right of Boom: How to Communicate When Things Go Wrong

"What we've got here is a failure to communicate."
Captain, Road Prison 36 (Strother Martin), in Cool Hand Luke

What You'll Learn In This Chapter
- The three "rungs of response to workplace disruptions;
- "First aid" for workplace disruptions;
- The two core components of "unfair administration" complaints;
- How to communicate around pay and benefits; and
- Becoming the best bearer of bad news.

Boom events happen in every company. You will face one soon (if you aren't facing one now). Companies that struggle with communication take bad situations like these and make them worse. Companies that shine, however, take the bad situation and use it to reconnect and even grow their relationship with employees. This chapter will give you some ideas about how to do that in your company.

One boom event that our consultants see on a regular basis is what we call a "workplace disruption." This would be something like a group of employees marching into their manager's office to protest a new change in the schedule. It could be an anonymous letter slid under the door that complains about harassment by an employee or a supervisor. It might even be a group of employees who call off work on the same day to complain about a benefit change. Any of these activities represents a threat and an opportunity for the leaders of an organization to improve their relationship with employees.

I have seen many union campaigns that begin with boom events like the ones described above. In most of those situations, if the company had handled the initial boom event better, the union campaign never would have happened. Communicating well during boom events can literally be the difference between facing (or, even better, avoiding) a union campaign or other expensive workplace disruption.

We teach an entire course highlighting the nuances of dealing with workplace disruptions.[56] In this chapter though, I want to focus specifically on the communication challenges that occur when your company faces one of these boom events.

In any situation like this, there are three "rungs" of response you need to consider. At the very lowest level you have the law. You don't want to say something illegal. When it comes to employee protest activity, your main concern is making sure you aren't threatening or disciplining someone for protected concerted activity. That is a whole book in itself (and lucky for you this isn't that book). For our purposes here, understand that there are legal land mines your leaders need to know how to avoid.

Not breaking the law is just the first rung in these situations. The next rung up is responding in a way that reflects the company's values. We call this level "don't be a YouTube sensation." Consider the situation of employees marching in on the manager. In today's world, it is increasingly likely that this march will be recorded – sometimes even without the manager's knowledge. You want to make sure that the

---

[56] To learn more about our Workplace Disruption Workshop check out http://LRIonline.com/workplace-disruption

manager behaves in a way that won't embarrass the manager or the company.

Leaders need to know what employees (and yes, sometimes unions) are trying to accomplish when they engage in workplace disruptions. This is why it is important to provide leaders with a framework for dealing with these events. Think about these incidents as situations where your leaders need to provide "first aid." They should:
1. Assess the situation.
2. Do no harm.
3. Secure the scene.
4. Restore operations.
5. Accurately report what happened.
6. Limit the impacts.

The third rung is perhaps most important, and yet is oftentimes paid the least amount of attention. We describe the third rung as leveraging disruptions to build engagement. Workplace disruptions create a lot of risk for an organization, but they also create opportunities. Anytime a leader is faced with disruptive activity they have the opportunity to not only show what kind of leader they can be under pressure, but also use the event to build stronger relationships with co-workers.

Protests, marches or other disruptions can be highly emotional events for everyone at work. Employees involved in the protest are upset enough about an issue to take part, but are also probably worried about making their boss mad and the impending discipline that might happen because of it. Employees not involved in the protest may be scared, confused or even upset with the co-workers involved. They may be concerned about how these disruptions will effect their jobs. And of course the leaders involved often feel attacked, betrayed, and may also be angry.

These emotions are raw right after the event. But they are great opportunities to build connections and understanding that can pay long-term dividends. A disruption event creates a chance to get to know someone's issues and concerns in a way you never did before. You have a chance to show that even after an emotional event, you remain approachable and interested in their well-being. Sometimes you will learn about issues you never considered before. If a union is behind the disruptive activity you can actually reverse field on the union.

Every time you communicate around a "boom" event you need to keep these same three goals in mind:
1. Don't say something illegal;
2. Don't say something stupid; and
3. Do honor and build the relationship

If you focus on these three steps your chances of communicating effectively will increase exponentially. As you plan your communication, it is often best to start with goal number three and work your way backward. Let's look at some real-world examples to get a feel for how this works.

Client Story: Intentional Non-Communication?

During union organizing campaigns, companies are regularly hit with unfair labor practice charges. These charges are often used strategically by unions to create the impression that companies are "bad actors" who deserve a union. The vast majority of these charges are subsequently dropped by the union or not pursued by the National Labor Relations Board. Most of those that remain are settled by the NLRB.

Companies that settle unfair labor practices are often asked to post a notice stating they will refrain from committing unfair labor practices in the future; business owners who already feel railroaded by the process generally protest this last step. "I'm not posting a notice - they are making me look like a criminal in my own work place." This is the point where we explain to them that their poor communication methods of the past can actually work to their advantage.

First, I would calmly walk them by the company bulletin board (where such notices would be posted) and point out to them the now age-stained and faded memos from years gone by posted on the same bulletin board. "When was the last time you looked at this bulletin board?" I would ask rhetorically. "If we wanted to make sure no one read something, this is exactly where I would post it."

In fact, during one hotly contested campaign, we were asked by the National Labor Relations Board to issue a memo to all the employees of a company. When asked how to distribute the information, we were told to do so through normal channels. In that particular case our "normal" channels had worked dismally in communicating just about every other important message over the preceding year. That woefully ineffective method was an "all hands" memo stacked in the employee break room. While historically these memos proved a terrific source of scrap paper for employees, they were almost never read and essentially created a litter problem.

Therefore, we dutifully distributed the memos by stacking them in the employee break room. Weeks later, stacks of memos (the ones that had not already been thrown in the trash) remained right where they were originally placed. "Communication" accomplished.

Today the NLRB will sometimes make an employer read a notice in front of employees, but this is the exception.

Most employers violently resist this (and I don't disagree with that). But I will also say that the few cases I've seen where the Board insisted on the notice being read were quite anti-climactic. Think about it. Would you pay attention to someone reading a notice from the NLRB out loud? It's hard enough to get the lawyers involved in drafting them to read the notices to themselves!

Application of Strategies – Two Particular Problems

Policies and Procedures

Your company has decided to change its attendance policy. Instead of having supervisors decide when an absence is excused or unexcused, you are going to a "no-fault" point system. You have been asked to communicate this change. Many of your employees are going to hate it.

This is a common potential "boom" event. You know you have your work cut out for you. Some of your best employees, the ones who rarely ever miss work, are now going to start getting "points" for routine doctor appointments or school events for their children. Many of them may feel like they are being punished for the fact that others abuse the current policy.

The employees who regularly miss work will also complain about the new rule. They will argue with the number of points, or the fact that excuses that used to get them out of trouble now get them points. Pretty much nobody will be excited about this change. That's a boom event.

What do you do? Think about our three goals and start with goal the third goal first: communicate this change in a way that honors and builds the direct relationship with employees. Explain the aspirational reasons for making the change. Describe ways this change improve things.

Make sure you explain the need for the change in business terms. What are the business reasons for switching to a point system? Explain how much time supervisors waste verifying excuses. Discuss how difficult it is to administer the policy consistently. Show how other companies you benchmark against use a similar policy. Describe how making this change improves productivity, quality and customer care.

Also think about how the current rule negatively impacts employees. The "excused" absence is very reminiscent of grade school. Having to justify every time you're late or leaving early can feel demeaning. How does the new policy treat people like adults? What kind of conflicts does the new rule avoid?

You also want to describe the resources and flexibility the company provides to help avoid absences in the first place. Present the ways an employee can work directly with their supervisor to deal with the most common situations. Explain how the new rule accommodates employees in a way the old rule could not. Identify all the other ways time off can be dealt with other than a recorded absence. Ask for feedback from employees for any potential problems they see.

It is also important to express understanding for the panoply of legitimate reasons people need to leave work. Discuss the importance of work-life balance and how the new policy better accommodates those goals. Explain how the new policy will be monitored and, if necessary, tweaked to make sure it is actually working the way the company hoped.

Next think about your other two goals. Don't say anything illegal. Depending on your timing this probably isn't too big of a concern. But if you are in the middle of a union campaign, it can be a problem. Since changing policies during a union campaign can be objectionable conduct, you'd want to make sure you explain that this was a change being considered for a while (that obviously must be true).

You also want to take care in explaining the reasons for the change in policy. For example, blaming the change (or making the change for that matter) on abuse of protected family or disability leave could be used against you in a future FMLA or ADA case. Focusing on excuses made by particular work groups could generate complaints of discrimination.

Your final goal is to avoid saying something stupid. Again, focusing on the aspirational business reasons for the rule change is a great place to start. The more time you spend talking about past abuses, the quicker you are going to say something you'll regret. At best, you'll embarrass someone (or many) who have used an excuse before. At worst, you'll bring up something that creates potential PR or legal issues ("*Can you believe he just said that if fewer people had babies maybe we wouldn't need to change the policy?*") Murphy's law dictates it will happen at the worst possible time, probably while being recorded. That's dumb.

Thinking about this communication using our three goals and remember to work your way backwards. Focus the bulk of your message around the positive business reasons for the change. Make sure that you express your understanding of how the change impacts employees. Ask employees for their feedback and help to make sure the change is a success. Emphasize the company's commitment to creating a great work experience and illustrate how this change fits into that goal. Finally, make sure that you understand any potential legal issues and steer clear from comments or actions that could embarrass the company.

Other Ideas Around Policy Communication

A common complaint among employees is that policies and procedures are unfairly administered. This claim of "unfair administration" usually has two core components. First, supervisors may be applying rules inconsistently due to their own misunderstanding of policies and procedures in the company. Second, employees never fully understood the company's policies and procedures to begin with. Both of these problems are communication issues.

Whether communicating policies and procedures to employees or supervisors, make sure to use multiple channels of communication. The first channel is, of course, the language of the handbook or policy and procedure itself. They are often written by lawyers, who aren't always easy to understand (hopefully I'm an exception). These policies should be regularly reviewed not just for legal reasons, but also to make sure they are clear and easy to understand.

Handbooks should be kept as simple as possible, since they have the broadest distribution and will be relied on most regularly by employees. Policies and procedures, while more detailed, should also be reviewed for ease of administration and understanding by supervisors.

Consider asking focus groups of employees and supervisors to review policies. Ask them whether they understand the documents. Ask how they would apply the policy to hypothetical situations. Once satisfied with the language, handbooks and policy manuals should be printed and distributed to all employees. The employer should also consider making policies, procedures and employee handbooks available online if the company has an intranet.

Other channels of communication should also be explored. Review your orientation process to see how effectively policies, procedures and handbooks are explained. Video presentations or multimedia computer sessions on the handbook are excellent tools for creating another "impression" on the policy and procedure issue. These tools can also be used later for retraining purposes.

To create another impression, training sessions on policies and procedures should also be considered. Even consider a Kaizen-type event where HR goes over handbook provisions with supervisors. Discuss how they can be better administered and communicated, talk about common misapplications, and rewrite things that can be made clearer or easier to administer.

Sessions like these can also be held with hourly employees to make sure that they understand a particular policy or procedure. Most important, employees need to understand why various policies and procedures exist in the first place. What are the business reasons for the rules? These sessions don't need to cover all policies and procedures at once. Rather, choose one and handle each in its own session.

Also consider rotating long-term employees through the employee orientation process every so often. This practice serves several purposes. It gives current employees a chance to review the orientation process for possible changes and improvements in how to get new employees up to speed. It also creates an additional impression on policies and procedures, along with the other issues covered in orientation. Finally, this process will involve employees in the development of training in an area in which they have significant expertise – their own jobs.

Another communication strategy surrounding policies, procedures or handbook provisions is using bulletin board posters, paycheck stuffers, memos, and articles in company newsletters that cover a particular rule that has generated confusion or problems.

Finally, supervisors should be trained to manage the grapevine regarding operational issues. This requires that they be thoroughly familiar with various policies, procedures and handbook provisions. In addition, they should be trained to correct improper statements they overhear regarding company procedures.

Supervisors and managers will usually be the first to hear employees complain about a policy or procedure and it's important that they pay close attention to these complaints as they are great opportunities for the supervisor or manager to communicate the reasons for company policies; the company's commitment to fairly and consistently apply those policies; and, if a complaint appears to be valid, ensure that the company investigates the issue in question. It is critical that employees receive feedback from the supervisor about any promised investigation.

Compensation and Benefits

It is time for annual reviews, and your unit has been performing exceptionally well – they've set both production and profit records this year. Other divisions of the company, however, have been getting killed, which is why the corporation is limiting raises for top performing employees to 2%. And guess who is told to communicate this news to your workforce?

Again, think about our three goals. First, how can you communicate this information in a way that honors and builds the relationship with employees? It is important to empathize with employees about their feelings and frustrations (this shouldn't be hard – you are probably feeling the same way). It is frustrating when your unit performs well but you still suffer because other parts of the business aren't doing well (and doesn't it seem like that is *always* the case?) Are top managers getting increases? Are they more than 2%?

You obviously need to be well versed in the compensation package in your own business and, if possible, in other parts of the business. It is easy for news such as this to sound defensive, so make sure employees understand the relevance of these facts. Make sure employees can see the big picture.

Try to think of examples when your business unit benefitted because other units were performing well. Be able to explain the ways that working in a diversified business provides long-term security and protection, even if it can create challenges in the short term.

Also remember to keep the wage issue in context. As we learned from Herzberg's research, wages are not real motivators, but they can be demotivators.[57] Your challenge here is to make sure that this single wage issue is seen in relation to the entire employment experience. Make sure employees remember the other aspects to their compensation (see the suggestion about "total compensation" communications below). A big part of the frustration here is feeling unappreciated and not being able to do anything about it (lacking control). Show employees that their hard work is appreciated, that this one event is just a small part of a bigger picture, and that they do have control over their future.

Times like these are a great opportunity to talk about development opportunities. Let's face it: if your financial plan is to stay in a job for 30 years getting a 2-3% wage increase each year, you haven't got much of a plan. Instead, encourage employees to think about how to get a big raise by developing more valuable skills. Helping employees see the connection between development, growth and an improved financial future may be the nudge they need to get to work on their development. And as Herzberg taught us, that is the path to true motivation and engagement.

Now that you've honored and tried to build the relationship you still need to think about any legal issues or "Doh!" moments you want to avoid. The biggest mistake companies make around pay communications is trying to discourage people from talking about pay. You don't have to encourage people to wear a sign with their pay rate on their chest, but pay discussions are protected concerted activity. Anything

---

[57] See Chapter 12 on Approachable Leadership.

you say or do to try to limit those discussions is a problem (and let's face it, not going to prevent anyone from talking about their pay anyway).

Not only are pay discussions protected activity, but attempts to limit them just make you look defensive and weak. Thinking back to our strategies on honoring and building the relationship around pay, remember that you have many positive things to talk about. By focusing on these messages, you avoid the need to be defensive about pay.

Also note that things you say about pay can be used as evidence of discrimination (*"if we didn't have so many old-timers here at the top of their scale maybe we could afford bigger raises"*). If you focus on positive messages about total compensation, how the pay strategy fits into the bigger business strategy, and encouraging development opportunities, you will avoid these legal and PR land mines.

Other Ideas Around Pay and Benefits Communication

Employers create a lot of problems for themselves when they poorly communicate about pay and benefits. These are issues that rate low in employee surveys time and time again. It's especially true in companies that have recently suffered a union organizing attempt. A union organizer can take virtually any pay or benefit (even industry-leading packages) and transform it into a big fat stink-bomb. Unrealistic promises made by union organizers during campaigns can cause employees to be frustrated with what may very well be a perfectly generous and competitive benefit package.

Union organizers know something about pay and benefits that most company leaders do not. They know that pay and benefits are "hygiene factors" – not great motivators but good ways to <u>demotivate</u> people.[58] And that's just what organizers do. This tactic is especially effective when a company does a poor job of communicating its pay and benefit practices and procedures.

Employees often do not understand how pay is administered. Without accurate information they automatically assume the worst – that pay it is done in an unfair or haphazard fashion. Therefore, it is important for companies to regularly communicate to employees why their pay and benefit package is what it is. Explain how they are developed and administered. This assumes that your wages and benefits are properly developed and fairly administered, a subject that is dealt with in Chapter 19.

Communicating around pay and benefits should be considered a continuing process. Obviously, the place to start is to look at what you currently say about pay and benefits. Is it up to date? Is it simple to understand? Does it adequately summarize the pay system or benefit plans? Is it easy to digest (infographics and other visual communications are becoming popular ways to get across sometimes dry and complex information).

Your communication material should explain the principles behind the pay and benefit plan. It might explain, for example, that the company wishes to pay in the top third of the market for the various jobs it offers. It should go on to explain how the company implements that goal. This could include explanations regarding the types of wage and salary reviews conducted, the geographic areas and industries reviewed, etc. The piece might then describe a yearly review process to make sure that wage ranges are within market rates and comply with the company's philosophy on pay. Finally, it could

---

[58] See Chapter 19 on pay and benefits where we go into this concept in detail.

include examples of how the pay policy is actually administered to employees.

Consider all the ways you can re-purpose this content. This type of communication can be used in the recruiting, hiring and orientation processes; it can be used during the yearly appraisal analysis; and it should definitely be used as a follow-up or retraining piece during supervisory meetings regarding pay and benefits.

In addition to the printed communication, a company should also consider providing training sessions on pay and benefits. Again, this could be included as part of the orientation process and then subsequently used in retraining sessions for supervisors and managers (some companies hold "in-service" or lunch and learn sessions – this would be great content for those kind of meetings). If groups of employees have questions about the pay system, this training session could be available as a way to address those concerns.

In addition, managers and supervisors should be prepared to talk about pay and benefits during individual employee development discussions. They should be trained to discuss the company's pay principles and procedures with employees during the appraisal process and at any other time a question arises. One-on-one meetings on these issues often defuse potentially negative situations (see "Being the Bearer of Bad News" below). Individual meetings, of course, can also take a turn for the worse and it is important to train supervisors to effectively deal with these situations.

Another popular communications strategy is "total compensation communication," a method used by many businesses today. In this method, you create a statement that can be used either as a paycheck stuffer or handed out in individual meetings. This statement analyzes each employee's total compensation, including taxes paid by the employer on behalf of the employee, cost of benefits, cost of vacation and holiday pay, etc.

A total compensation statement can graphically illustrate to each employee the significant amounts of compensation that are often hidden from view. It shows employees that their compensation is significantly more than what they normally believe to be the case. An important point to remember about this and any other communication strategy is that, standing alone, it is insignificant. Each piece must be utilized as part of an overall communication strategy on the compensation and benefits issue.

Being the Bearer of Bad News

An important part of every management team's communication strategy includes dealing effectively with bad news. The natural reaction for most people, whether at work or at home, is to avoid uncomfortable situations or conflicts. These are unfortunately common occurrences in a workplace setting and, if avoided, can lead to misunderstandings and hurt feelings. In some cases, these situations can lead to union campaigns.

We've already talked about the basics of communicating bad news (don't break the law; don't be a YouTube sensation; and honor and build the relationship), but there are a few other principles to consider when bad news is imminent. First, don't "beat around the bush." Most people see hesitation as a lack of strength or leadership. Even worse, it can be viewed as guilt or avoiding responsibility.

Second, consistency is even more crucial during a period of bad news. Whether the issue is a layoff, an increase in benefit costs, a termination, or other serious incident, managers and supervisors must have a consistent message to employees. Dealing effectively with negative situations demonstrates leadership and increases respect for managers and supervisors.

As discussed earlier, we often see a paradox in employee surveys conducted in companies that have recently fought an organizing campaign. In many of these companies, immediate supervisors rate much higher than top management. Supervisors often point to this as a sort of redemption for them (*"top management was the problem all along"*). But looking more closely, we often learn this is not the case. What it really reveals is an important communication problem.

Many times supervisors, siding with their employees and against management, refuse to take responsibility for negative news. This reveals a lack of leadership and over time leads employees to believe that their complaints are legitimate. Employees will take the fact that their supervisor agrees with them as validation of their complaint against top management. While occasionally the supervisors are right – top management is the problem – the majority of the time supervisors will just agree with employee complaints because they prefer the path of least resistance. This is unacceptable.

Supervisors must not take part in disparaging the company. Instead, they should take responsibility for explaining the company's actions. Employees do not have to agree with everything the company does, but if they understand the process behind the company's decisions and feel that their well-being is a top priority for the company, they will be more likely to listen and accept the policies for what they are. Employees must also understand that what is best for the health of the business won't always mean immediate good news for them. But if you can get them to look down the road a bit they will inevitably see that what is good for the health of the company is good for the welfare of all employees. In this way, effectively delivering bad (or just uncomfortable) news can actually create desirable results.

Client Story: Bearing Bad Benefit News

One company we helped was nearing the end of their "certification year," about 12 months after narrowly defeating a union election. The last election occurred right after a poorly communicated benefit change and rollout – indisputably the primary cause of the election.

Over the course of the ensuing year, the company made great strides in many areas, and conducted a second employee survey just prior to announcing benefits changes again. That survey showed that employee engagement had increased dramatically.

However, just weeks before the next benefit enrollment period (and, unfortunately, also just weeks before the union could file another petition) the company received horrible news. The cost of the benefits plan that created so much anguish the year before was now going up again. Premiums would cost, on average, 25% more for employees. The company was not in a financial position at the time to absorb much, if any, of the increased benefit cost. This was indeed a gray day.

After absorbing the news, the management team went to work. They had made significant strides with employees over the course of the year and built up an increased level of trust. Management had gained experience communicating on a variety of workplace issues, and employees noticed the positive changes. Given this new backdrop, we trained managers and supervisors to meet individually with employees to go over the news and the benefit options.

Those meetings included several themes. The managers and supervisors began by stating they had some tough news about the benefit program. They explained the upcoming cost increases and the steps the company had taken to limit the costs. Those steps included providing new and different coverage options.

Each supervisor was then prepared to discuss benefit options with each employee. The discussion included the increased premium cost under the current plan and an explanation of other available plan options. Many of these options would reduce coverage while also reducing the benefit expenses for families. The supervisors then helped their coworkers figure out the package that best balanced needed coverage with the costs.

The supervisors and managers empathized with employees about their situation (which was not difficult since many of them were absorbing the same benefit cost increases). The meeting closed with an explanation to employees of the enrollment process and an opportunity to resolve any questions or issues they had regarding benefits.

Much to the company's surprise, the benefit rollout during this period was extremely smooth. Obviously, many employees were frustrated and there were negative comments regarding the increase in rates; but nevertheless, employees understood that this was an industry-wide situation and their employer was truly between a rock and a hard place. Supervisors had been educated about all the options the company considered and effectively shared this information while explaining that the company was looking at the matter as a total compensation issue. In fact, employees witnessed several changes in compensation during the course of the year that were consistent with the employer's efforts to stay within market rates.

Honesty, empathy and individualized treatment on the issue defused what only a year before had been a core organizing issue.

Always Respond

The final lesson in communicating around "boom" events is to always respond to employee requests. One of the most common communication complaints from employees is that they ask questions and receive no response. There is no doubt that this is sometimes a perception problem. It is very easy for employees to ignore an answer they don't want to hear. That's why companies should make every effort to ensure that employee requests are responded to <u>every time</u> and handled in a prompt and transparent manner.

Whenever possible document your answers to these questions. After all, if one employee has a question the chances are pretty good that many others have the same question and just haven't asked. While this can increase workload, it ensures that both supervisors and employees know what's going on.

Not every request requires a formal response (and by formal we are not talking about long and carefully crafted letters – short notes, handouts, or emails are fine). But verbal responses should be used for only the most routine issues. As mentioned before, for companies that have recently undergone organizing campaigns or have had employees complain about communication, it is best to over-communicate in your response to requests.

One strategy I have seen work is the use of 3x5 cards, small notebooks, or even PDA's. When an employee makes a request, it is routed through the company to the individual who can answer the question (like a support ticket at a software company). The card is to be returned, with the answer from the appropriate person, no less than 24 hours from the time it is submitted. This practice is a simple and effective method for combating perceptions of supervisory aloofness or lack of empathy with employee problems.

Communication is a fundamental issue in every "at-risk" company. It becomes an even bigger issue when you are communicating bad news. Whatever strategies you decide to use, the key is to focus on whether the message has been received, not just on whether it has been delivered. The good news is that this is a "keystone habit"[59] and effort spent fixing this issue helps resolve many others. It is a foundation of good management and a cornerstone to highly productive and engaged work forces.

Action Steps

- ☐ Think about the last time you encountered a workplace disruption. Were your employees engaging in protected concerted activity? Did your response reflect the company's values? Did you leverage the disruption to build engagement? Make a list of how you could have improved in any of these areas.
- ☐ Hold a training session for your leaders on the six "first aid" components to workplace disruptions.

---

[59] Keystone habits are behaviors that, when changed, cause a cascade of other behavior changes. These can be positive or negative. See Charles Duhigg, *The Power of Habit: Why We Do What We Do in Life and in Business,* (Random House, 2012) pp. 97-126.

SECTION V: HIRING AND ONBOARDING

As famously discussed in Good to Great, it is vitally important that you get the right people "on the bus" to begin with. Many times poor engagement is not so much caused by the way employees are treated, but because you have a square peg in a round hole. If you have the right people on the bus to begin with, you don't spend near as much time swimming against the current and your engagement training is much more useful and effective.

Once an employee is hired, the orientation and onboarding process provides the first (and prime) opportunity for the company to present its philosophy with respect to work environments, and particularly, unions. The messaging should reinforce the desire for, and benefits of, a direct relationship between all levels of management and the employee. Companies that have high external vulnerability should also include a message about the company's position on unions.

Chapter 17

Recruiting, Hiring and Pre-Employment Screening

"You can't be all things to all people. But I can be all things to
the people I select."
Donald Neuenschwande

What You'll Learn In This Chapter
❑ How selection techniques can transform your employee relations environment;
❑ Why an effective hiring program is the first step to employee retention;
❑ The disadvantages of relying on "historical" data when hiring instead of present evidence of competency;
❑ Strategies for creating narrow, objectively observable interviewing criteria;
❑ The five keys to conducting a good interview; and
❑ Whether job simulations can improve your selection process and hints on recruiting.

Some employers today settle for less and less when it comes to hiring. They'll end up hiring anyone who walks through the door – an absolute a recipe for trouble.

You've heard this (or maybe even said it) before: "I knew that guy was trouble the minute I hired him. I bent over backwards to give him a chance to work out, and the thanks I get is an NLRB petition! How could I be so stupid?"

Of course there are also those "high standards" folks with big impact interviewing techniques like:

"What's your name?"

"Joe."

"Ever been in a union, Joe?"

"Yeah, I was in one back in the 70s when I was bagging groceries for my local supermarket. High school job."

"Well, Joe, let me tell you how things run around here. We don't have a union and we don't need your kind coming in here with your bright ideas trying to change that. You know Joe, I haven't liked your look from the start. I think maybe you better just find work somewhere else."

While these people make good clients for labor lawyers, they make even worse hiring decisions than companies that don't interview at all.

Employers should not be concerned with prior union membership;[60] instead they should focus on hiring people who are self-directed, team-oriented, committed to their work quality and open to coaching from co-workers and supervisors. Research indicates that self-directed and independent-minded people with a strong sense of commitment to the quality of their work performance are typically less likely to vote for a union[61] (I must stress that this

---

[60] This should go without saying, but in addition to being a poor hiring practice, it is a violation of Section 8(a)(3) of the National Labor Relations Act to select people based on their prior union membership, their suspected union sympathy, or even the fact that they are known to be professional organizers seeking employment solely to organize the employer. *See e.g. Phelps Dodge Corp. v. NLRB*, 313 U.S. 177 (1941) (union members); *NLRB v. Electrical Workers Local 322 (Bechtel Power Corp.)*, 597 F.2d 1326 (10th Cir. 1979) (non-members); *NLRB v. Town & Country Electric*, 516 U.S. 85 (1995) (paid union organizers). For more information on this or other labor law questions, talk to your labor counsel and see Hardin, et al. eds, *The Developing Labor Law*, (BNA Books, 1996 and supplements).
[61] For many examples, see Brofenbrenner et al., eds., *Organizing to Win: New Research on Union Strategies* (Cornell University Press, 1998); the best

is not a reason for adopting such a program; it is, however, a potential side-effect of focusing your hiring on these qualities). These individuals are also more likely to be involved in community activities, prefer pay-for-performance arrangements and are normally high performers in their jobs.

Community and Work Involvement: Union Prevention Tools?

Studies by scholars friendly with organized labor suggest that workers involved in their communities are significantly less likely to be involved with a union. One such study concludes:

> "To summarize, the effect of community involvement, net of the effects of standard model predictors, is to lower the likelihood of voting pro-union in a certification election. The findings suggest that community involvement effectively competes with unionization for individual allegiances. In addition to the influence of employment and workplace issues on respondents' desires to unionize, involvement in community organizations tends to reduce the desire of respondents to unionize their workplaces"[62] (emphasis added).

These studies also suggest that worker involvement in Employee Involvement Programs (EIP's) significantly reduces the likelihood employees will turn to unions. Another study concludes:

> "The difference in the union win rates between campaigns in which employee-involvement programs existed and those in which they did not is striking: the union won in 48 percent of all the elections when there were no EIP's but in only 30

---

explicit discussion of the issue from a hiring policy standpoint I have ever read is in Saltzman, "Job Applicant Screening By A Japanese Transplant: A Union-Avoidance Tactic," 49 *Industrial and Labor Relations Review* 88-104 (1995).

[62] Cornfield, McCammon, McDaniel and Eatman, "In the Community or In the Union?" *Organizing to Win: New Research on Union Strategies* (Cornell University Press, 1998), p. 255.

percent of all the elections when there were EIP's"[63]
(emphasis added).

The following table summarizes some more of this research.[64] This study suggests that employee involvement in community organizations or churches can reduce the likelihood of support for unionization by over 15%. This table describes the percentage increase or decrease in the odds of voting pro-union in a certification election for respondents with specific characteristics compared with those without such characteristics.

Characteristic	Increase/Decrease In Union Support
Has high job autonomy (versus moderately high autonomy)	-9.7%
Perceives that employer gives raises for performance (versus respondent who does not have such perception)	-22.0%
Agrees that unions have too little power (versus indifferent respondent)	54.7%
Disagrees that unions hinder economic progress (versus indifferent respondent)	132.3%
Black (versus white)	37.7%
5-9 years' work experience (versus <5 years)	-1.9%
Has two organizational memberships (versus one membership)	-18.2%
Attends religious services monthly (versus several times a year)	-15.0%

---

[63] James Rundle, "Winning Hearts and Minds in the Era of Employee Involvement Programs," *Organizing to Win: New Research on Union Strategies* (Cornell University Press, 1998), p. 218.
[64] See Cornfield, McCammon, McDaniel and Eatman, supra note 62.

Unsophisticated, uneducated or simply unscrupulous employers often try to discern union sympathy during the interview process. These employers will ask people about whether they are prone to vote for a union or not. Of course, this question is illegal. The other option is to try to hire independent, self-directed individuals committed to their work, without reference to (and without caring about) union sympathy. Not only is this legal, it is just smart business.

Take this opportunity to improve your employment selection process. First, start asking the right questions – look for people who value on-the-job autonomy, want to be paid for high quality performance, are interested in employee involvement and appear to be committed to their employers. Look for people who have proven their leadership and team orientation through their involvement in community organizations. Look for people who have participated in employee involvement programs at prior companies.

Stop worrying so much about whether someone has been a union member and start worrying about what kind of a performer they'll be. The good news is that this practice will not only keep you out of court, it will be better for business. It is also the best predictor of whether someone will be a good performer and a valuable contributor to your organization.

Hiring for Results
The best place to start an employee retention program is during your hiring process. This may seem counter-intuitive, but the evidence is overwhelming. Companies that do a good job of hiring have fewer problems with turnover and enjoy the benefit of a generally happier workforce.

Companies that hire anybody who walks in the door usually have turnover problems. They also tend to experience lower employee morale among the employees who do stay. By hiring individuals without a thorough selection process, you are more likely to employ someone who is either unskilled or otherwise unable to perform the job well.

If the prospective employee does not have an accurate picture of what his job duties will be or is not screened sufficiently to ensure a proper fit into your work environment, he will not remain an employee for very long. He may self-eject, i.e. quitting because the job wasn't what he thought it to be, or because the work was too difficult. His tenure may also end by termination due to his inability to perform the job properly.

Additionally, employees who have been with the company for some time are unlikely to accept a procession of new hires with open arms. They are often frustrated by this "revolving door" of new hires who (due to the poor screening process) are unable to do the work.

This frustration will show up in many ways. New employees will not be welcomed. (Why attach yourself to someone who won't be there in 90 days anyway?) Management will constantly be blamed for production problems because of all the new hires unable to do the job. The workforce will be negative – new hires and long-term employees will be equally frustrated and unhappy.

Ineffective hiring practices perpetuate the problems of constant turnover and poor morale, creating a vicious cycle. How do you create a hiring process that puts the brakes on this treadmill? It's not complicated but it does require some work up front and consistent attention to the hiring process. Perhaps the most important step is to develop a process and stick with it in every hiring decision. What follows is a description of how we assist companies in developing such a hiring process.

Focus on competencies, not on history. The fact that someone has done a job in the past is certainly worth knowing. What is much more valuable is to know how they performed that job and, even more important, how they will perform in the future. This information is rarely discovered when reviewing historical data on a job application or a resume. It must be demonstrated either during the interview or, better yet, by conducting a simulation. A simulation or "in-box" activity can help you evaluate both the "hard" skills and "soft" skills necessary to effectively perform the job.

The place to start when developing a list of competencies is to look at your high performers. Begin with a list of jobs you hire for most often. Underneath that list, make a list of high performing employees currently working in each of those positions. Underneath that list of names list specific competencies or job performance behaviors that make those individuals high performers.

For example, look at attendance, willingness to help others, professionalism, work quantity and quality, or other characteristics that make those employees high performers. These factors may be different for each job, but there will be many crossovers within the organization. It is very important that this list include objective, readily observable behaviors.

The table below lists some factors often used in hiring. The first column describes the factors in language that is too broad. The second column outlines narrower, more objective factors. Again, it is important to understand that the specific competencies required by a particular job will differ across job categories and companies. The key is to specifically identify the performance behaviors of high performing employees.

Good Attitude	• Willingness to make changes based on work demands • Willingness to pitch in on projects not technically part of employee's everyday job • Ability to influence co-workers to jointly solve problems

Good Attendance	• Almost always at work/meetings promptly and on schedule
Communication Skills	• Clear communicator in written and spoken form. • Able to understand verbal and written instructions
Organized	• Identifies most efficient or convenient order when accomplishing assigned tasks

Another important part of this exercise is to list objectively identifiable characteristics that are evident in poor performers. Therefore, a second list should be generated identifying poor performing employees and the objective considerations and behaviors of their performance.

This project can be very valuable when conducted in group sessions with supervisors or managers in charge of supervising the particular jobs in question. You could also involve high performing employees in these sessions. If these same supervisors or managers make hiring decisions on those jobs, the information gathering process gains even greater importance. It can greatly improve the interviewing and selection skills of the hiring supervisors.

Once competencies are identified, the next step is to identify the interview questions that will get the right information from a prospective employee. Questions must be carefully crafted to determine whether candidates have the high performance characteristics or not.

Once again, these questions should ask for objective examples from the prospective employee regarding the competencies that you have identified with high performers. Of course have any interview questions reviewed by labor counsel to ensure that they are lawful under the myriad laws in place regarding discrimination and employment.

The following table includes some sample questions in various competencies.

Competency Area	Interview Questions
Initiative	• What ideas have you sold to management in the past? Why? What happened? • How much information do you need to get started on an assignment?
Participative Culture	• Tell me about a team you were on. • What was the biggest success of your team? • What was the biggest challenge your team faced? • What characteristics make it hard for someone to work on a team? • What do you find challenging about working on a team?
Interpersonal Skills	• Give me an example of a co-worker, manager, or customer whom you find most difficult to communicate with. Why? • What would you do if a co-worker made a derogatory comment about another co-worker?
Creativity and Innovation	• Describe a great idea that you have seen in your job recently. • Why was it unique? • Give an example of a situation at your previous employer when others knew more than you. How did you close the gap?

It is good practice to brainstorm a long list of possible questions and then have a group identify and evaluate the best ones. Next, create a form that provides consistency to the interview process.[65] Once the form is developed, it should be used in all interviews. Each potential candidate for a job should be asked the same questions in the same environment. The idea is to create, as closely as possible, identical circumstances for the interviewing process. In this way, candidates can be evaluated against each other more accurately.

There are a few golden rules of interviewing that should always be observed:

- Conduct interviews in a location that is private and free from interruptions.
- Make sure you have fully prepared a consistent and objective interviewing process before seeing the first candidate.
- Enlist at least two individuals to separately interview all finalists for the job. This helps to reduce subjectivity.
- Rely on open-ended questions versus closed-ended or "yes" or "no" questions. Give the candidates an opportunity to respond fully using specific examples from their lives. Insist that candidates answer all questions. Even if this causes uncomfortable silence sometimes, wait for them to answer the question. If a candidate gives an answer that is not specific enough or skirts around a question, repeat the question. Part of the interviewing process is to get comparable and objective answers to the questions.

---

[65] If this is an area of focus for your company I recommend you start with a book called *Topgrading*. See Bradford D. Smart, *Topgrading: The Proven Hiring and Promoting Method That Turbocharges Company Performance*, (Penguin Group 2005)

- Take notes during the interview period and accurately write down the candidate's responses to the questions you have asked so that you can accurately compare responses at a later time.

These are some of the basics for conducting a good interview. There are, of course, a number of excellent texts and training courses available to help hone interviewing skills.[66]

Pre-Employment Screening and Job Simulations

Many organizations today use pre-employment tests and job simulations as an important part of their hiring process. Again, the use of these tools is important to create a consistent and objective hiring environment where candidates can be compared rather than the "gut feeling" approach often utilized by companies with a poor hiring record.

The decision on what screening tools to use depends primarily on the job for which you are hiring. A number of pre-employment screening tools are available on the market today. These range from competency-based computer software tests to high-end psychological profiles. The types of tests used in hiring for a particular position will depend on the competencies required to perform the job. Entry-level manufacturing positions probably do not require high level psychological testing. Requiring a candidate for the CEO position to take a typing test is likewise an ineffective use of screening time.

An increasing body of literature suggests the importance of emotional intelligence skills in our knowledge-based economy. Soft skills are tremendously important in today's work environment. The ability to work together to solve complex business problems is increasingly what separates winning companies from losers. Today, perhaps more than ever, it is critically important to hire people with high "soft skills" and

---

[66] There are a lot of other great tips in *Topgrading*. See supra at note 65

put into place systems that allow them to learn the technical or "hard skills" necessary for job performance once they are hired.

Many companies have turned to soft skills profiles as a way to make better hiring decisions. A word of caution, however, about using any pre-employment test. In today's highly litigious environment it is very important that any pre-employment test pass the scrutiny of discrimination laws. Before using a test, it is always a good idea to talk to both the vendor and your labor counsel about the validity and appropriate use of pre-employment screening tools.

At risk of oversimplifying the legal issues involved, the bottom line is that the employer must be able to prove that any test administered is job-related and predictive, in that the test accurately predicts existence of the job-related skills for which it tests.

Once the test is proven job-related and predictive, it is also a good idea to periodically review the impact of that test on various protected classes of workers, i.e., minorities, gender and age. If a test appears to have an adverse impact on any protected class, you should alert labor counsel immediately and review whether or not use of the test should continue.

Job simulation is another very productive screening tool. Whether we like to admit it or not, people often lie about their qualifications and skills on job applications and resumes. Job simulation is a way to observe skill levels of candidates by watching them perform a sample version the actual tasks they will be required to perform every day. Another advantage of job simulation is that it provides a good preview of the job to prospective employees. This allows employees to decide, prior to accepting a job, whether the tasks required by that job are ones they want to perform on a daily basis. Many companies find that this preview further reduces turnover in the workforce.

Clearly, some positions are better suited for performance simulation than others. For instance, simulating a receptionist or assembly line job is significantly easier than simulating the duties of a CEO. Often companies will pick parts of a job to simulate in order to make administration simpler and repeatable. Again, the concerns related to job simulation are similar to those for other types of employment tests. The simulations should be objective and as similar as possible for each of the candidates tested. There should be an objective way to identify a "passing" or "failing" score or performance on the simulation. This test should be used as part of an overall hiring scheme, not as the only factor.

Client Story: You Want Me To Build a Swingset During My Job Interview?

Have you ever been asked to help build a swingset on a job interview?

One of my clients asked people to do just that during their final interview. After completing an interview with a cross-functional interview team and the teammates they would actually work with, the final candidates would be walked outside, shown a big box, and asked to put together the swingset inside. The candidates would be timed and observed.

This seemed like a curious final interview step to me. Would they ever be asked to do this task at work? No. Were the tools or instructions they'd be following job-related? Not really. Then what was the point?

The point was to watch people behave under pressure as a team. They were asked to do it in an environment that would be pretty unfamiliar. They would have to work together with a group of strangers who, at some level, had an incentive to make them look bad. It was a very interesting simulation.

The interviewers would observe the team as they unpacked the box and started laying out all the parts and going through the instructions. They would watch as the team figured out who would do what work and who naturally assumed leadership. They would look at who got flustered under pressure and who seemed to get along even in an uncomfortable situation. They would watch the attitude of people who were being asked to do something a little (OK, a lot) out of the ordinary.

This exercise reveals a lot about people. It is impossible to hide behind stories of how you work with others when you get to see it firsthand. While you might try to be on your best behavior there is no getting around the fact that you are also competing with some or all of these people. You want to shine. You want to produce.

A simulation like this isn't for every company but it really worked for this client. Their production people were salaried and had to work well in small teams without a lot of supervision. The swingset exercise, combined with the other pieces of their selection process, gave the team members great information to make a good decision (voluntary turnover at this plant was virtually zero).

And what about all those swingsets? They were donated to local pre-schools.

Recruiting

When I start talking about tightening standards in the hiring process employers often complain about just getting bodies in the door. These organizations do not understand the relationship between poor selection procedures and high turnover. High turnover creates great pressure on the recruiting process – more bodies must get in the door to fill the spots left by former employees. On the other hand, great companies that do an excellent job of hiring have significantly fewer problems with recruiting. This is due in part to the fact that there are fewer positions to fill. Nevertheless, candidates must be sourced, and recruiting is an important part of the hiring process.

The recruiting process is tough. This is a good place to get creative. The days of sourcing candidates by just putting up a help-wanted sign or running a newspaper ad are over for everything but the most menial jobs. High performing employers have learned that recruiting is an ongoing process, and if you wait until you have an opening before recruiting for that opening, you are likely to have continuing difficulty with filling positions.

The recruiting process should be approached in the same manner as identifying competencies in the hiring process. For example, look at high performing employees and identify how those individuals were sourced to your company. In this way you identify a broad list of recruiting sources – often much broader than people applying off the street or responding to newspaper ads. Ask high performing employees to refer people who they know – this can be an excellent source for new hires.

In addition to this list, think of other innovative recruiting methods. Companies today use many resources, including their web sites, networking sites, open house receptions, job fairs, radio and cable television ads, along with many others. An almost limitless number of opportunities exist for finding potential candidates. Reaching out to minority and non-traditional communities (disabled, retirees, veterans, etc.) is another great source for rounding up talent.

Implementing a consistent, ongoing recruiting process is vitally important. When you network and search for talent on an ongoing basis, you ensure you always have a qualified pool of applicants and potential employees. As good candidates identify themselves, stay in touch with them, even if there are no jobs available at the time.

The recruiting, selection and hiring process is complicated and difficult. It is, nevertheless, one of the most important things a company must do in order to sustain its success and to grow. Decisions made about hiring are some of the most important decisions made by organizations. As we proceed further into a knowledge-based economy, this importance will only solidify.

Companies that concentrate and invest time and energy on the hiring process will see great returns, not only in employee morale, but also on the bottom line. In addition, companies that do a good job in hiring are substantially less likely to face a union organizing campaign.

Take Action

- ☐ Develop an easily repeatable hiring process that focuses on competencies rather than histories.
- ☐ Construct interview questions that reveal whether prospective employees contain these compentencies.
- ☐ Determine whether or not you will use pre-employment tests or job simulations as a part of the hiring process.
- ☐ Review your recruiting methods. Make a list of innovative ways those might be improved.

Chapter 18

They're Hired, Now What? Orientation Programs

"A vision is not a vision unless it says yes to some ideas and no to others, inspires people and is a reason to get out of bed in the morning and come to work."
Gifford Pinchot

What You'll Learn In This Chapter
❑ You never get a second chance to make a first impression – why the orientation process is critical;
❑ Common mistakes made in the orientation process
❑ Strategies for planning new hire orientation;
❑ Why you should consider lengthening the time of your new hire orientation; and
❑ How to involve co-workers in the new hire orientation process.

Think back to your first day of work at your current job. What do you remember about that day?

One often overlooked employee relations opportunity is new hire orientation. It is overlooked because of the pressure involved in getting a new employee into the job. Most don't start looking to fill a role until there is an opening. Therefore, after several weeks spent sourcing, recruiting, interviewing and then making a job offer to a candidate, there is immense pressure to get the new person started. This is especially true in high turnover companies.

Like companies that do a poor job of hiring, companies that make little effort to orient new employees reinforce the turnover cycle. Employees often begin work feeling unsure of their responsibilities or not knowing how their job fits into the overall services of the company. They become frustrated and anxious, which can lead to poor performance.

During this critical early period, these feelings can cause people to self eject. (*"That job just wasn't what I thought it would be."*) Even worse, some in this dilemma are terminated before their "90-day probation period" is even up. This sort of discharge often occurs when supervisors give up on a new employee – one who is lost but could have gotten there with the right help. (*"They just don't get it... why do they keep hiring these idiots?"*) Companies with these problems often fail to teach even basic skills during the orientation process.

A second reason it is so important to utilize the orientation period is because at that time the company has the full attention of the new hire. Newly hired employees are typically happy to land a job and are willing to default to the employer's opinion on most employment issues. It is critical during this "honeymoon" period to deliver as much positive information as possible about the organization and the work the new hire will be performing. This is also a good time to communicate negative information or challenges that the employee may face during his or her employment. You have an attentive audience and should take the opportunity to explain these issues before the naysayers of the company get hold of them.

This platform is really important if your company is vulnerable to union organizing. It is a prime opportunity to communicate the high value the company places on working directly with employees to resolve issues and overcome challenges. Tell the key stories that illustrate how working directly together has saved a customer, solved an especially tough employee problem, or helped the business accomplish an important goal.

It also gives you a chance to explain the reasons behind policies and procedures that are complained about by a vocal minority of the work force. While the purpose of the orientation process should be positive and not concentrate on lots of rules and regulations, it is an excellent opportunity to "choose your battles" and place the company's position on key issues in the forefront.

Orientation is also one of the few opportunities a company has to communicate, with the full attention of the employee, the important stories that establish the company culture and build loyalty. These might include company history, discussion of the business environment and market in which the company competes and the company's philosophy.

Many organizations communicate some of this information through an orientation video. Video is an excellent way to communicate the direct relationship message and, if appropriate, a message about unions.[67] A video message doesn't change; you know that the exact same message gets repeated every time. A video can be sent home with employees so they, along with their families, can learn more about the company at their convenience. It is a very effective tool to communicate background information that doesn't change often (company history, key principles, "folklore" that reinforces company culture). Orientation videos should not be utilized to communicate information that might change on a frequent basis, like benefits or policies.

Finally, new hire orientation should be fun and enjoyable for the employee. Many companies fall into one of two extremes in their orientation process. They might adopt a "trial by fire" approach, where the employee is dropped into his or her new position with very little information, if any. Other companies go to the opposite extreme, trying to make their employees experts on every possible issue they might face. These

---

[67] LRI produces custom orientation videos and PowerPoint presentations for use in new-hire orientation. You can view examples of orientation video at http://LRIonline.com/orientation-video-demos (this is a password protected page – call 800-888-9115 to get a password to view the videos).

companies use a very rigid process, which may include testing on policies and procedures, signing tons of documentation, and a general overload of information. Neither of these two approaches is much fun for the employee being oriented.

Instead of these extremes, think about the orientation program from the perspective of the new employee. What can you do to make sure the employee leaves the first day feeling great about their decision to join the company? What can you do to make sure there are 2 or 3 great stories the employee can tell when they are inevitably asked, "How was your first day?" You need to acclimate employees to their new position and communicate the valuable information they need to get started on the right foot. But the process should first and foremost be designed to give the new employee a sense of belonging and make them confident in the decision they made to work for the company.

It is very important, even if there are a number of candidates for a position, to make sure that the one chosen feels good about his or her decision for the long term. If this effort is made consistently with every new hire, the company is setting itself up to succeed.

Mistakes will surely be made in the hiring process, and some employees will be "bad eggs" and feel unhappy immediately after the work starts. But by treating the orientation process as an opportunity to motivate and instill good feelings toward the company, there is much less likelihood of a new employee bad-mouthing the company when given an opportunity. More often, these employees will forcefully defend the company even in the face of negative incumbent employees. Over time you can transform the company culture by doing a good job of orienting new employees.

An effective orientation process will improve employee morale and increase good will toward the company. Every organization should rapidly respond to employee discontent and deal effectively with concerns. Issues will not snowball out of control in a work force that is positively inclined toward the employer from the start.

Common Mistakes

Think for a moment about your current orientation process and compare it to some of the common mistakes companies make. We've already discussed some of these, but they are listed again here for easy reference:

Employees are given a voluminous handbook or policy manual with little or no explanation (or worse yet, sat in a room and asked to read the whole thing and then sign it).

Employees are given a lengthy policy manual or handbook and extensive instructions over minor policies with which they will have little daily experience.

Employees are immediately placed on the job with little or no "low pressure/low risk" opportunities to learn the job.

Failure to give employees enough opportunity to meet co-workers and supervisors.

Spending an inordinate amount of time filling out forms and paperwork.

Including too much information in a short amount of time.

Failure to include social activities as part of the orientation process.

Failure to devote personalized attention during the orientation process.

Not being prepared for the employee once they start.

Strategies to Improve the Employee Orientation

There are a number of strategies to improve and invigorate the orientation process. A few are outlined above. Here are some additional suggestions for creative ways to improve orientation.

Plan the Orientation Day

Plan the orientation day with the goal of making it as interesting and enjoyable for the participant as possible. First impressions are most important, so it is critical to have the first morning well planned. Activities could include a reception for the new employee hosted by the employee's supervisor and work group.

Avoid beginning the first day of orientation by forcing the new employee to fill out a lot of forms. If this must be part of the orientation process, save it for later, toward the middle of the day. Better yet, let employees fill out forms on their own time before (or after) they go through the orientation day. Structure the day (or days) of orientation around a core group of ideas or a particular area of training. Establish an agenda and a set of goals for each day and communicate that to the employee. Most important, include as many pleasant and enjoyable activities as possible during the orientation period.

To paraphrase the famous saying, the fastest route to a person's heart is through their stomach – TAKE THEM OUT TO LUNCH ON ORIENTATION DAY! It's simple, easy, and inexpensive but it can mean a lot. CAREFULLY pick the employees they will interact with. Pick the "welcome wagon" types (this could even be a perk for employees) to be ambassadors during orientation. Avoid sending them to lunch with Dan or Debbie Downer. You don't want a new employee to feel that they made a mistake from the get go. Only use your best employees for this ambassador role.

Lessons From Orienting Executives

Several cutting-edge businesses incorporate innovative orientation strategies in their new-hire process for executives. These techniques offer some insight into potential orientation techniques for all positions in an organization.

Jack in the Box, the fast-food chain, requires its new regional vice presidents to spend a month working in the restaurants they will ultimately manage. This includes everything from mopping floors to flipping burgers. These managers will have a better understanding of the day-to-day pressures faced by the people reporting to them and have a clearer understanding of the business environment than those who have never worked in a fast-food store.

For another month, they shadow other executives and develop a personal strategic plan for their first year in their new position. The results? Retention among executives who have gone through the program is much higher than in comparable businesses.

The Limited, a clothing retailer, has a program called on-boarding for new executives. These employees spend the first month with none of the responsibilities that will be required of them for the rest of their career. Instead they spend that time selling clothes, investigating competitors and learning about the company's history and future plans. For the ensuing several months, these executives only gain responsibility for their new positions part time. The idea, once again, is to ensure that executives thoroughly understand the company, its philosophy and its people.

While giving new hires a month or two to learn about the business may seem a little extreme, these examples show the importance that some companies place on the orientation process. Knowing your day-to-day job tasks is important. Understanding how your job fits into the business and knowing the responsibilities of others can help individuals at all levels. It sets up workers for long-term employment. They feel like they are part of a team or family. This should be the goal for any orientation program.

Include Co-Workers and Supervisors in Orientation

This makes it more interesting for new employees and also makes the orientation process more inclusive in the company. It creates buy-in from the rest of the employees. The more people involved, the more exciting it will be. Including employees in the process also creates an opportunity to empower co-workers. If employees are involved in orienting new hires, their feeling about the value of the orientation program will increase dramatically. Employee involvement also creates additional opportunities for interactions between co-workers and supervisors.

Even though involving employees in the orientation process can create strains, particularly during periods where the workload is high, the effort is worthwhile. Time to get acquainted must be allocated for co-workers and the new employee. This time should be in addition to actual on-the-job training. If possible, job training should occur first in a classroom setting or some other environment where there is little risk (i.e. a simulated operating station designed for training purposes) so that the new employee can practice without worrying about messing up job production.

Increase the Length of Time
Don't try to hurry the orientation schedule by compressing the allotted time. This does not mean that orientation must last days on end, although some jobs do require extensive training. Consider spreading out the orientation program across weeks (the examples above spread out orientation over several months). The time should be sufficient to thoroughly acquaint the new employee with the business, the coworkers and the culture. Throwing an employee handbook to new employees, then sending them out on the line for their first day is unacceptable.

The key aim for orientation is to acquaint new employees to their jobs and the company. Most orientation programs will include sessions on:
- Company history
- Company culture, mission, and core values
- Business issues and market considerations

- Overview of the various departments of the organization and how they fit together
- Tour of the facility
- Review of important company policies and benefits
- Filling out the necessary paperwork and forms
- Skills training
- Safety training
- At least one social event (welcome reception, lunch with supervisor, welcoming party, etc.)

Depending upon the complexity of the job, the orientation process may last a week or longer. The bulk of the additional time may be spent in skills training with some on-the-job training as a follow-up.

All orientation programs should be designed to include some sort of regular follow-up during the orientation or probationary period. Again, this practice creates a habit of communicating performance expectations and development with employees. This will hopefully carry on beyond the orientation period. A human resources representative and the immediate supervisor should be involved in these development "check ins."

You know the old cliché: you never get a second chance to make a first impression. This is exactly the way companies should approach the orientation process. Getting employees started on the right foot creates a stream of positively motivated employees that are ready to work and knowledgeable about the culture and goals of the company. These employees will be better prepared to defend the company if they understand the reasoning behind rules, procedures and business practices. Well-oriented employees are also more productive. Finally, including co-workers in the orientation process improves teamwork and maximizes opportunities for empowering highly effective hourly employees. As the saying goes, don't miss this opportunity, you never get it back.

Take Action

- ☐ Does your organization have an orientation program in place for new hires? If so, take a moment to review its components. If not, begin the process of developing one.
- ☐ Make a list of individual ways in which your organization can make orientation day interesting and enjoyable.
- ☐ Come up with a few employees who are especially friendly and outgoing. Ask them if they would be interested in showing new hires the ropes.
- ☐ Develop a strategy that spaces out the orientation process, keeping new hires from being overloaded with information.

Chapter 19

Show Me the Money – How to Deal Effectively With the Challenges of Pay and Benefits

"Money is better than poverty, if only for financial reasons."
Woody Allen

What You'll Learn In This Chapter

❑ The paradox of pay and benefit frustrations;
❑ How your exit interview process can identify key pay and benefit concerns;
❑ Conducting a pay and benefit survey to attack external fairness issues;
❑ Designing a pay and benefit plan to avoid internal fairness issues;
❑ The disadvantages of keeping pay issues secret; and
❑ Legal issues regarding pay and benefit changes.

Remember professor Herzberg, who taught us about "hygiene factors" that can de-motivate but not motivate?[68] His research repeatedly found that pay and benefits are hygiene factors. They don't motivate, but can easily become de-motivators.

Pay and benefit issues are common complaints in every organization. Do you feel overpaid? Well neither does anyone else. Virtually everyone longs for more money and better and cheaper benefits. Employees often feel that people at other companies have a better deal. Given what Herzberg observed, employee frustration over pay and benefits seems inevitable; and thinking you can create employee engagement using pay and benefits is a "holy grail" you can't attain.

---

[68] See Chapter 12.

Frederick Herzberg fully explained this paradox in his classic article on employee motivation in 1968.[69] Professor Herzberg explained that wages and benefits are not motivators of employees. He used the metaphor of "hygiene" factors. In other words if you feel like your pay and benefits are bad, you feel frustrated and "dirty." But improving pay and benefits is just like a shower – you will get the momentary satisfaction of being clean, but before you know it you're dirty again. Wage and benefits improvements are simply not a long-term motivator.

Recent research on students in the US Military Academy at West Point illustrates the point even further. Professors Amy Wrzesniewski and Barry Schwartz asked over 11,000 incoming West Point cadets about their motivation to go to the Academy and then watched how they performed during their tenure.[70] Like Herzberg, they too found that cadet motivations fit into two categories. The first they called "instrumental motives" and included things like wanting to get a good job after college (this would be more like pay and benefits, one of Herzberg's hygiene factors). The second they called "internal motives" and it included things like wanting to develop new skills as a leader (more like growth and development, one of Herzberg's motivation factors).

After following cadets through their college and military career, they found that those who were mainly motivated by instrumental factors were more likely to quit the academy, or perform poorly at school and in the Army after graduation. Those motivated mainly by internal motives graduated,

---

[69] "One More Time: How Do You Motivate Employees?" *Harvard Business Review*, January-February 1968.
[70] See "The Secret of Effective Motivation," *New York Times*, July 6, 2014 (available at http://www.nytimes.com/2014/07/06/opinion/sunday/the-secret-of-effective-motivation.html)

performed better in school, and had more successful military careers.

Wages and benefits are instrumental motivators. They satisfy basic needs for most employees. And a pay and benefit system that isn't fair in comparison to others in the market is certainly a de-motivating factor for employees. It can be a key issue in a union organizing campaign. However, even the most generous wage and benefit package cannot prevent frustration among employees if the other internal motivators aren't part of the employment experience. Any good organizer will tell you that you win union campaigns on treatment issues, not pay and benefits.

Most of the rest of this book explains how to create an environment rich in these internal motivators. But to understand the strategy it is important to also understand what you can reasonably expect pay and benefits to do for your employee relations environment.

With this as context, here's the strategy. Focus your efforts on ensuring that your wage and benefit packages (and administration of those packages) meet two factors: external and internal fairness. If these two qualities are met, you will avoid the de-motivation that comes from poor or unfair wage and benefit packages and then can focus on other non-hygeine motivators.

External fairness refers to how the wage and benefit package compares to other companies. A company that pays wages or provides benefits less favorable than those of its competitors or other businesses in its region will be perceived more negatively. Chances are that companies suffering under this perception will also experience high turnover if the area job market has any fluidity. This factor can be identified by reviewing turnover statistics and exit interviews.

Internal fairness refers to whether the system and procedures by which employees are paid or receive benefits are handled fairly within the company. This relates to appraisal systems, merit increases, equal pay issues, the way raises are handled, decisions regarding who receives benefits, and similar issues. Each of these areas will be discussed separately.

Conducting Effective Exit Interviews

Many companies fail to take advantage of one of the best sources for identifying problems in their company – ex-employees. There are a number of excuses. Lack of time and the feeling that departing employees will not give honest feedback are two of the most frequently cited.

These objections are misguided. First, good companies do not have time to ignore input from departing employees. In today's fast-paced economy, companies must constantly seek to increase efficiency and productivity. Unfortunately, many corporate cultures do not go out of their way to encourage feedback on these issues. Many employees are reluctant to offer suggestions, fearing that their managers may feel like they complain too often. Exiting employees are an excellent source of information about processes and procedures that are frustrating or need improvement.

Questions regarding the honesty of feedback are not without merit, but still do not make exit interviews worthless. It is certainly good to take exit interview complaints with a grain of salt – you have to investigate any complaints that come up. Disgruntled employees (particularly those who have been terminated for cause) may have an axe to grind during the exit interview process. On the other hand, some employees are afraid to "burn bridges." These employees may sugarcoat the problems they observed while working at the company. Nevertheless, it is still valuable to ask exiting employees what they thought about their employment experience and what the company can do to improve.

Terminated employees may have anger toward their supervisor or manager. They also have the least amount to lose by complaining. Both details should be considered when reviewing feedback from exit interviews. Still, they often have good insights about the problems of the company, even if they are slanted negatively. In addition, their complaints, if looked at in the context of many other exit interviews, can help management spot trends that are causing turnover.

Employees anxious to leave a good impression may try to put a positive spin on issues, but will still answer most questions truthfully. Once again, if their input is viewed as part of a trend of data it can be very valuable in identifying problem areas. Assurances of confidentiality can also help to get these individuals to open up during the exit interview process.

One method to help improve the data collected from exit interviews (and to reduce the likelihood that the circumstances surrounding an individual's exit will taint the data set) is to use an anonymous forced response exit interview questionnaire. This way, all exit interviewees answer the same set of questions and the data collected, over time, can be analyzed as a larger sample. This reduces the likelihood that a single comment or incident will result in an overreaction while ensuring that the company receives accurate information about why employees leave the company.

Another valuable use of the exit interview tool is its assistance in limiting legal liability often associated with ending the employment relationship. For example, many companies will ask questions about incidents of discrimination or workplace injury. If these issues are raised during the exit interview, it gives the employer an opportunity to respond to potential lawsuits very early in the process – perhaps initiating dispute resolution techniques before a charge or lawsuit is even filed. Should the employee fail to identify issues of discrimination or workplace injury during the exit interview, then suddenly remember an incident after they leave the company (perhaps after running into their local plaintiffs' lawyer), the exit interview form can become terrific evidence for the employer.

The exit interview is not a cure-all, but it can provide valuable information for any employer. For an example of an exit interview form, see Appendix 4.

External Fairness Issues
There are a number of issues to examine when determining the external fairness of a company's pay and benefit program. First, what's your philosophy on pay? Is your goal to compensate employees at:

- The top third of the industry?
- The mid-point of the industry?
- The mid-point of the local community?
- Or to pay a fair day's wage for a fair day's work?

Whatever the philosophy, it should be clearly stated and understood. Once a philosophy is clear, how will you make sure it is implemented? If the company wants to pay in a certain range within its industry, you have to conduct regular wage and benefit surveys of other employers in the industry. If the benchmark is to meet the level of local competitors, then survey that group. You need to regularly accumulate this information to make sure you are keeping up with the benchmark you set for yourself.

What If We Can't Keep Up With Our Benchmark?
Most employers do not pay below their benchmark because they want to. Sometimes business conditions require

companies to hold labor costs in line for extended periods of time. These circumstances are difficult for both employers and employees. When this situation arises, you have to be up front with employees.

People recognize a huge difference between someone who is being "cheap" and someone who is being financially responsible. Most employees understand when things are tight because of legitimate business factors. They know that these factors, if ignored, could hurt or possibly end the business. Employees won't like it, but when faced with the alternative of no job at all, most will help out.

Asking employees to forgo pay raises and work for less than market value to help the company isn't a long-term strategy, but it can work during tight times. If you have communicated your philosophy about wages and benefits effectively and employees have bought in, they will be willing to make sacrifices for the long-term success of the company. This is particularly true where other "non-hygiene" factors are handled well.

To maintain external fairness you have to regularly monitor your comparison group. Do this as thoroughly as possible, benchmarking wages and benefit packages against key competitors for talent. It is not uncommon for an employee looking for a raise to approach their line level leader with anecdotal evidence about wages or benefits paid by other companies in the area. To effectively respond, it is crucial for the managerial team to have data to support its case that the current package is in line with the stated compensation philosophy.

Conducting an effective wage and benefit survey is complicated – a full description is beyond the scope of this text. But here are several key principles. First, conduct surveys at regular intervals. Data more than a year or two old is no longer valid.

Second, conduct the survey in a statistically valid manner. Clearly identify the job classifications and employers who fit the benchmark group. There are a variety of sources, like salary and benefit surveys conducted by consulting businesses, Chambers of Commerce, and industry groups. You may also choose to conduct your own survey. No matter your source, here are some tips on getting useful comparisons:

- Make sure that job descriptions for the jobs being compared are explicit and reviewed carefully. Small differences in job descriptions or duties can make significant differences in the compensation required for the position;
- Include not only hourly rates but also bonuses, stock options, 401(k) programs, lump sum payments and the variety of other methods of compensation that are used in businesses today. Failing to account for these additional areas of compensation can skew estimates in survey comparisons;
- Make sure all elements of benefit programs are examined, including medical and dental networks, deductibles, co-pays, premium sharing arrangements, significant exclusions, out-of-pocket limits and the like. This is especially important with health care costs being so high these days;
- Ensure confidentiality of the information in order to obtain accurate, specific data. This can be accomplished by promising to share benefits without company names, or by asking an outside party to conduct the survey.

Once you have good external data, compare this to your current package and against your competitors. Are you missing the mark? Then you either need to make and adjustment or explain why you can't do so at this time.

Internal Fairness

It is equally important to analyze the internal fairness of your pay and benefit package. Internal fairness primarily considers how the company evaluates performance and administers increases. You want to be fair and consistent. The first step in examining internal fairness, like external fairness, is to describe the company's philosophy. Examples could include:

- Merit pay for performance
- Pay for longevity
- Across-the-board increases
- Gain sharing or profit sharing

Whatever your philosophy, clearly state and follow it.

There are ethical, legal, and employee relations reasons to be concerned about internal compensation fairness. From a legal standpoint, lack of fairness can be viewed as discriminatory. The EEOC regularly initiates pay-based discrimination and equal pay claims against employers. Class action lawsuits on wage and hour violations are skyrocketing, resulting in large verdicts or settlements against employers, often due to poor administration of a policy that on its face is valid. Lawsuits like these are incredibly expensive and create a terrible public relations problem. Discriminatory pay practices are also just wrong.

Unfair pay practices (or even the perception of unfairness) are those "hygiene" factors that create significant employee morale problems that negatively impact business performance. If employees believe the pay system is unfair, they start wondering what other policies are administered unfairly and they lose trust in top management. They inevitably become de-motivated, distracted, and simply don't work as hard.

To avoid this, many companies try to keep wage and salary discussions under wraps. Some even try to discipline employees who discusses wage and salary information. The NLRB considers discussions about pay and benefits protected concerted activity. Therefore, these discussions are protected and discipline for talking about pay and benefits is an unfair labor practice.[71] Even if it weren't illegal, policies like these are dumb. Companies who try to limit discussion about pay are deceiving themselves. Your employees talk about money. There is no way to get around this fact.

Employees are going to talk and (worse yet) speculate on all areas of wage and salary administration. The better job a company does of hiding pay and salary information, the more likely unreliable sources like the grapevine will be the only source. This often creates even bigger problems. It is far better for the company to be up front about pay and benefits. I'm not suggesting you post everyone's pay on the wall, but pay ranges and how people move through them should not be a secret.

Some pay systems tie salary increases to individual performance or skill level. Using performance appraisal scores or some other performance measure, these systems reward higher performing employees. If you use a system like this it is very important to have a transparent and well-implemented performance appraisal process. This is hard to do well.

Other systems base rewards on company performance, not individual performance. Gain-sharing and profit sharing are popular versions of this approach. These systems avoid the inherent difficulty in appraising individual performance (many companies feel that tying performance appraisals to pay decisions is too difficult and subjective). They focus attention instead on company goals. When done properly, these

---

[71] The NLRB has ruled (and Circuit courts have enforced the decisions) that blanket policies prohibiting salary discussions among employees violate Section 8(a)(1) of the NLRA. See e.g. *NLRB v. Main Street Terrace Care Center*, 164 LRRM 2833 (6th Cir. 2000).

programs are very good. The challenge is tying individual employee performance to the larger company performance in a way that lets employees understand how their work impacts the bonus payout. If employees do not understand this connection, the bonus payout is seen simply as an extra check. When company performance lags, this creates a de-motivating situation (almost like announcing a wage freeze or cut).

Still other companies just do across-the-board pay increases based entirely on wage survey information. These organizations either decide to keep things simple or wish to avoid other more difficult pay programs that tie pay in some way to performance. There is nothing inherently wrong with such systems – in fact, given what Herzberg says about pay, it might be the most realistic solution. But policies like these do not take advantage of pay as a potential motivator for short-term performance.

These are just a few examples of many that are available. The bottom line is that whatever system you use must be externally and internally fair, fit your company philosophy, and be well communicated to employees.

Legal Issues

A company involved in organizing activity must take extra caution when making changes to pay and benefits. As discussed earlier, you cannot promise or offer inducements to employees for the purpose of discouraging them from engaging in union organizing activity under Section 8(a)(1) of the NLRA.[72]

Changes in pay and benefits are sometimes used by unscrupulous employers to sway the outcome of a union

---

[72] See Hardin, et al. (eds.), *The Developing Labor Law, 3rd Edition* (BNA Books, 1996), pp. 115-119.

election in their favor.[73] The United States Supreme Court stated in 1944 that "[t]here could be no more obvious way of interfering with these rights of employees than by grants of wage increases upon the understanding that they would leave the union in return."[74] For this reason, the NLRB presumes that giving benefits during an organizing campaign is objectionable unless the company can prove the timing was due to factors other than the election.[75] The employer is cannot offer any inducement to employees when either the timing or impact leads the Board to conclude that the employer's purpose is one of "impinging upon... freedom of choice for or against unionization, and is reasonably calculated to have that effect."[76]

The NLRB examines a number of factors to determine whether a pay or benefit increase is unlawful. The Board will rule against an increase where it is:
- Given in the context of repeated references to the union;
- Made effective just before an election;
- Conforms to an earlier request by a union during the campaign;
- Announced before an election when it could reasonably be delayed until afterward;
- Otherwise announced in a way calculated to influence employee choice ;
- Given to fulfill an illegal promise of benefits made during the campaign.[77]

---

[73] See *Medo Photo Supply Corp. v. NLRB*, 321 US 678, 686 (1944).

[74] See Id. at 686.

[75] See *American Sunroof Corp.*, 248 NLRB 748 (1980), enforced in part, 667 F.2d 20 (6th Cir. 1981); *Honolulu Sporting Goods Co.*, 239 NLRB 1277 (1979), enforced, 620 F.2d 310 (9th Cir. 1980); *Micro Measurements*, 233 NLRB 76 (1977).

[76] *NLRB v. Exchange Parts Co.*, 375 US 405, 409 (1964).

[77] See *St. Francis Federation of Nurses & Health Professionals v. NLRB*, 729 F.2d 844 (DC Cir. 1984), enforcing 263 NLRB 834 (1982); *NLRB v. Exchange*

Any change to pay and benefits must be made independent of union organizing activity. Document any discussions about potential changes and understand that any decision in this area will be carefully scrutinized by the NLRB if a union shows up on the scene. Obviously, any employer involved in union activity should not make a change to pay and benefits without talking to their lawyer.

Conclusion

It's tempting to think that approving a raise is a quick way to improve employee happiness, but ultimately pay and benefits are less important than the other aspects of the employment experience discussed in this book. You can't ignore these issues, but you can't focus on them too much either as it diverts your attention from other more important areas.

This is not to say that pay and benefit changes won't be appreciated – they will; but realize that the positive effects of pay and benefit changes are short-lived. Improving in other areas like approachability, communication, and recognition provide much more leverage (and cost very little).

Your employees can be distracted by pay and benefit issues, particularly if your organization does a poor job of ensuring external and internal fairness. Their attention can be diverted from the good things your organization is doing if the "hygiene" factors of pay and benefits are not handled well. If this is your situation, you may have to "clean up" pay and benefit issues early so employees can focus on other changes.

Don't try to eliminate all pay and benefit complaints. It's a fool's errand. If your pay system is fair, legally sound, and

---

Parts Co., supra note 76; *Seneca Plastics*, 149 NLRB 320 (1964); *NLRB v. Arrow Elastic Corp.*, 573 F.2d 702 (1st Cir. 1978); *NLRB v. Rich's of Plymouth*, 578 F. 2d 880 (1st Cir. 1978); *Rupp Industries*, 217 NLRB 385 (1975).

---

competitive within your defined market for talent, you should focus on other areas. You may have to work on communicating it, but you will not make large gains trying to make additional improvements. Are pay and benefit issues distracting you or your employees from paying attention to (and appreciating) the other changes taking place in the organization? If your answer is no, move on.

Take Action

- ☐ Review your pay and benefit packages to insure that it meets both internal and external fairness and is legally sound.
- ☐ Construct and implement a process for effective exit interviews.

SECTION VI: "NET PROMOTER" CULTURE

Bain Consulting has done some fascinating research on customers as "promoters" for a company, and how the ratio of promoters to non-promoters creates a "Net Promoter Score" for the company and its products. This score is an indicator of the company's future performance.[78]

Bain's work is devoted primarily to customer engagement. However, we have reached very similar conclusions in our employee engagement research. The key takeaway in the Bain research is that there is really only one measure that matters when it comes to customer engagement: whether or not customers would tell their friends or acquaintances to do business with the company. Likewise, one of the key measures of employee engagement is whether or not your employees would recommend (or perhaps defend) the company to others.

There are a couple of important implications of this research: You can leverage your employee engagement research by focusing on this promoter statistic. Our Employee Engagement Surveys ask 3 specific statements related to net promoter score. It is also a key component of our Multi Dimension Interview (MDI) Vulnerability Assessment process. You want to create a culture where your employees are active promoters of your organization, and where you are stressing projects and engagements that increase the number of employees who are promoters.

If you have a lot of promoters in your organization, you disrupt the network of non-promoters (what we call net-detractors) of the organization. In Iraq, you are more likely to

---

[78] For a quick overview of the research watch the presentation at: http://resultsbrief.bain.com/videos/0402/main.html

find people who will engage in or support the insurgency in communities where they are surrounded by likeminded individuals (even if many of those individuals on their own would not take action in support of the insurgency). The same is true of the workplace. You do not want to create an environment where these negative people are surrounded by others who, even though they may not actively promote a union, would still not notify the employer if union activity was occurring around them. By focusing on creating a promoter environment you increase the probability of obtaining promoters who will notify the company if there is union organizing activity going on around them.

Chapter 20

Employee Involvement – A True Win-Win

"I tell you and you forget. I show you and you remember. I involve you and you understand."
Eric Butterworth

What You'll Learn In This Chapter
- When to use a team – and when <u>not</u> to use one;
- Choosing the issue for a team;
- Common causes for failed teams;
- Examples of teams in action – safety and work conditions issues; and
- How to avoid the legal pitfalls that can be associated with the use of teams.

Two common areas of frustration in the companies we survey are work conditions and workplace safety. These issues impact employees daily. They can be areas of intense frustration, and trigger great employer expense. Unions often take advantage of these frustrations during organizing campaigns.

Employees surveyed after a union campaign oftentimes express continued dissatisfaction. While we don't applaud employers with poor work conditions or safety problems, it is important to acknowledge that these problems create opportunities. They provide a chance for quick, public wins; and are also excellent opportunities to generate employee involvement.

A Word About Teams
Team-based solutions are so regularly recommended that the suggestion has become almost trite. Most company leaders have read (ad nauseam) about the advantages of team-

oriented problem solving; yet, when many try to use teams to deal with issues in their workplaces, they have little success.

One reason for this disconnect is that teams are often formed to solve problems that they are ill-suited to attack. Therefore, before determining whether or not to solve a problem using a team-based approach, you must understand the strengths and weaknesses of teams.

Using teams to solve the wrong type of problem has two important negative impacts on a business. First, it gives teams bad publicity. It discredits the team concept and reduces the likelihood that teams will be used in areas where they should be the most effective.

Second, using a team to solve a problem that is inappropriate for employee involvement de-motivates team members and discourages employees from getting involved. At its worst, a team-based experience can create tension and dissatisfaction among groups of employees. The table below describes the categories of problems best suited for team-based problem solving and those more appropriate for individual problem solving.

Consider a Team	Don't Use a Team
Complex issues, with few readily identifiable solutions	Readily identifiable solutions
Team members' areas of expertise could help identify solutions	Team members share little expertise
Limited or identifiable time line	Solution requires long-term and continued attention
Scientific analysis and measurement is possible	Analysis and measurement is difficult or impossible
Clearly identifiable end point or "finish line"	No readily identifiable end point

The projects you select to implement a team-based approach should meet a number of criteria (this is particularly true for your first team effort). Don't randomly select a project; and do not pick a project just because it is popular (decided on by means of a vote or other such process). It should be carefully selected for its suitability for a team approach. It is also important to select a project that has a direct impact on internal and/or external customers. This ensures the project will have visible effects that can be experienced by employees not directly involved in the process.

Make sure the project is meaningful to employees. Solving a minor problem or something generally perceived to be a "non-issue" among employees will not generate much excitement. Employees may feel that the company is just "tossing them a bone" or trying to mollify them if given unimportant problems to solve. Rather, pick a project that has the potential to show measurable results on a daily or weekly basis. By picking this sort of project, you not only create a scale to identify whether the team has been successful or not, you also reinforce to your employees that they are valuable.

Choose a project that cuts across departments. This increases the visibility of the project throughout the company. It also allows employees from different departments to work together toward a common goal, which is often out of the ordinary. This gives employees from different departments the opportunity to experience some of the challenges their coworkers face. This can create empathy and a new respect for the employees of other departments. It also provides fresh perspectives to problems that may have perplexed others in the past.

Finally, the project should not involve a process in transition. The process being dealt with should be well settled. This way accurate data regarding the process and progress made by the team can be assessed. If it is a process in transition, there is little way to meaningfully measure results.

Characteristics of Good Team Projects
Selected by management
Direct impact on internal or external customers
Meaningful to employees
Measurable results that cycle regularly
Cuts across departments
Not a process in transition

Once you've identified the right issue to attack, the next step is to select the employees for the team. Consider several issues when identifying team members. First, and most obvious, the individuals should be able to work well with others. They don't have to be made up of volunteers exclusively – this can be a disadvantage – and they don't have to be cheerleaders (more on that below). However, participants should be open to participating.

It is also important that team members have skills or expertise in the area being considered. For general problem solving on issues that impact the whole company, finding employees with expertise may not be hard. On the other hand, specific safety and work conditions issues may require individuals in specialized job categories or even outside consultants with relevant expertise. Some employers even go a step further and evaluate their workforce to discover hidden talents that might be brought to bear on a specific problem.

Team members should also be skilled at working together as a group. This is not the same thing as being willing to work together. Team-based solutions to problems require excellent meeting and problem-solving skills. We recommend two Leadership for Results™ Modules for every new team: *Getting Together* (Managing Meetings) and *Finding Solutions* (Problem Solving and Decision Making).[79] These modules provide solid

---

[79] For more information on Approachable Leadership™ check out http://LRIonline.com/leadership-for-results

---

baseline skills that the team will use again and again. Starting each new team out with these two modules lets more experienced team members refresh their skills and allows new members access to a set of competencies to bring to future meetings.

Finally, choose good communicators and natural leaders from the company to be team members. Volunteers are not always the best members for a team. Often, it is better to handpick team members based on the individual skills and team dynamics you think are important to solving your specific problem.

Team members won't necessarily be the most popular or most positive employees in the company. Sometimes it is good to pick a known "naysayer" or skeptic to be part of the team (see The People Team has a Breakthrough below). If you have just won a union election, you might consider someone who actively supported the union (so long as they are open-minded and willing to help solve a problem with their teammates). This can have a very positive long-term impact on the employee relations environment.

When you move to pick leaders for your team, remember that there are two kinds: formal and informal. It is very important to include leaders in the informal network of the organization. This is especially true if team-oriented solutions are either new to the company or negatively perceived due to problems in the past. Committee members should be individuals who are respected for their objectivity and commitment to the business.

Client Story: The People Team Has a Breakthrough

One of my favorite professional moments happened just a year ago during a team project. Our client, an industrial equipment manufacturer, had recently started a lean transformation. As part of that project they developed a new company mission and vision and created a People Team.

This team had members from all areas of the plant, including production, engineering, software design, and sales. It was made up of informal leaders and was a cross-section of personalities. There were several company cheerleaders, intermixed with a couple of skeptics. Some of whom were outspoken, while others were quiet.

One of the People Team's projects was an employee survey. This company had successfully used our off-the-shelf survey for years. But the People Team wasn't sure it fit the new company mission or vision. Long story short they decided to "fire" me!

I was asked to talk with the team about some of the new surveys they were considering. In the end, we decided not only was our off-the-shelf survey unsuitable, but so were all the other surveys they were considering. We were stuck.

After quite a bit of brainstorming, we decided on a different path. The team would create a new survey that aligned with the main goals of the People Team (sustaining a culture of respect and development). We worked up a survey that fit the new vision and mission (the company's "true north" was to improve lives). The team then administered the new survey to their coworkers.

Once the survey results were compiled, the People Team faced a new challenge – how to best communicate the results. Prior surveys had been handled almost entirely by the HR department and our firm. This year the People Team took ownership of the communication process. They developed communication slides and worked on a process to deliver the results and get feedback.

The team decided on a small number of actions to take as a result of the survey. These focused around their two main goals – respect and development – and the company's mission of improving lives.

There is a saying that, "a beautiful answer to he who asks a beautiful question." I'll never forget one meeting where this team was asking great questions. The lowest rated statement on the survey related to whether employees felt like the company was delivering on its "true north" goal of improving lives. Everyone around the room was disappointed.

The People Team was struggling with how to get coworkers engaged in creating a culture where they believed they were genuinely improving lives when a heated discussion started about who was responsible for creating this culture, the employees or the company. Someone suggested that employees ask at least one coworker each day what they could do to help the other.

One of the "skeptics" on the team jumped in. "I've got a problem," he said. "If I was to go up to someone and ask that question they would literally laugh in my face. This isn't some fairytale land." In a lot of meetings a comment like that would end the discussion. This wasn't one of those meetings.

Another team member replied, "OK, so they laugh in your face. What do you do then?" Now that was a great question. It started everyone thinking about how do we deal with this natural skepticism about the overall goal of improving lives.

I got up and drew a Venn diagram on the white board (after all, I'm a consultant and what consultant can walk by a whiteboard without drawing a Venn diagram?) The three circles asked three questions. Have I done something in the last week to improve:

- Me?
- My Coworker?
- My Community?

The People Team then began their action planning. They decided to incorporate these three questions into their own scorecard. They would survey coworkers and simply ask the three questions. Then they would track the responses, just like all the other lean manufacturing statistics. This would be their measure.

Next, the People Team went to work delivering the survey results, talking to people about their action plan, and getting feedback from coworkers about possible follow-up actions. The results were overwhelmingly positive. Coworkers commented about how professional and thorough the meetings were. Even the quiet and reserved team members seemed to grow right before our eyes.

The People Team is just at the start of their journey, and they will face obstacles and resistance as they go. But they did some incredible work, started a terrific process to really get their coworkers involved in living the company's values, and developed themselves in the process. All while continuing to do their "day jobs." Not bad.

Once the issue has been picked and committee members chosen and trained, the next step is putting it all to work.

What Can Go Wrong
Never ending teams
Unfocused teams
Teams focused on the wrong issues
Wrong people on teams
No follow-up
Poor leadership

Not all businesses can effectively use teams to implement responses to problems. The following are good predictors of whether or not a company will be able to use teams:

- The company regularly shows a commitment to the customer and to continuous improvement;
- Employees have a clear understanding of their jobs and how they fit into the overall production of the company;
- Employees feel their jobs are important, and they are committed to the success of the company;
- Individual contributions are valued and employees are encouraged to act in their area of expertise;
- Data and information are accurate and used regularly in the decision-making process; and
- The feedback of results and performance from customers to suppliers is regularly evaluated as part of the system.

This does not mean that companies that do not share all of these goals or fail to implement them effectively will find it impossible to use teams. After all, gaps in these areas are often a symptom of companies with labor relations problems in the first place. We have successfully assisted many companies whose business culture would not immediately meet the criteria listed above with implementing team processes. However, companies that wish to use teams will want to push their business culture in this direction as part of their plan.

Keys to Successful Teams

There are several key principles for a successful team process. First, clearly define the goals, action plans, responsibilities and deadlines for the team. It is critical for team members to know how their efforts will be measured and when their goal should be accomplished. Otherwise, it is impossible to know whether the team process has been a success or failure. It results in the team losing focus. The team should be able to regularly refer back to its action plans, goals and deadlines to keep its bearings.

The team members should communicate up and down the line regarding the progress of the team. In other words, the team should be communicating to people at its level and below regarding the information being collected and the process the team is undergoing to resolve the issues. The team should also be communicating above to managers, notifying them of progress made toward its goal.

Keep the team together until the results are in. Disbanding a team before knowing whether or not its efforts were successful is a problem. First, the team loses the opportunity to celebrate its success – it is not enough to celebrate, "We worked together as a team!" There must be a moment where the team can collectively celebrate, "We worked together and this is what we accomplished."

Second, and more important, if the project fails, the team loses the opportunity to make an honest assessment of its methods. Finally, it is critical to talk to the people affected by the team's decisions. Those people directly impacted should know and understand the recommendations of the team, measurements used to identify success or failure, and the team's assessment of its results.

What Makes a Successful Team
- Clearly defined goals, roles and ground rules
- Straightforward communication
- Beneficial behavior by members
- Well-defined decision procedures
- Balanced participation
- Use of a scientific approach

Failed teams share a number of common symptoms. The first is "floundering" or indecision over the next action to take. This happens when the team either doesn't have clearly established goals or failed to set deadlines. It is best resolved by going back to the initial team action plan and goal statement and assessing what that plan requires the team to do next.

Another common problem with teams is the dynamic between the participants. Overbearing or dominating members can derail the team process and trivialize others' opinions. Reluctant participants are the flip side of this problem. These people are either unable or unwilling to provide feedback or suggestions and do not contribute to overall team success. There are a number of other personality types that can negatively impact a team, but variations of these two kill many teams.

If these problems exist, bringing in a skilled facilitator can move the conversation forward. Facilitators are trained to reduce the impact of overbearing or dominating participants (this is one of the key skills we train in our *Getting Together* Leadership for Results™ module). For example, there are a number of exercises a facilitator may use that get each participant to add a comment or suggestion. This reduces the ability of overbearing participants to "take over the floor." Facilitators can also effectively encourage reluctant participants to increase feedback in order to gain input from all members of the team.

If you don't have a skilled team facilitator in-house or the ability to train your internal teams, it is imperative to engage an outside facilitator. This is especially true if this is one of your first team projects. If you plan to use team-based solutions, you should invest the time and money to get it right from the start. You need early wins, particularly in a work unit where trust is an issue like in a post campaign environment.

Unquestioned acceptance of opinions as facts is another symptom of teams that fail. Team members must be properly trained to identify the difference between fact and opinion. The use of the scientific method of fact gathering (i.e. defining a hypotheses and an experiment to test that idea) and other data testing tools are critical aspects of the team process. In our *Finding Solutions* module we teach teams to use tools like a fishbone diagram, decision matrix, and mind-mapping that encourage testing facts and discourage decisions based on opinion.

How do you know if your team is successful? This question is why it is important to agree up front on the goal and how it will be measured. By doing this, you help force the team to make decisions based on objective data and not simply opinion. A skilled facilitator will push the team members to examine information carefully. He or she will ask questions like: "What can we do to verify this conclusion? Do we have enough data to prove this? Would more information be helpful here?"

Some teams fail because they experience a rush to "accomplishment." They ignore the best opportunities because they want to show quick success. When this occurs, a facilitator should remind team members to explore all possibilities before deciding on one (the decision matrix is a great tool for this). The facilitator's job is to teach team members how to balance what is fast with what is best.

Finally, failing teams often face problems of attribution (who gets credit), discounting contributions (who doesn't), tangents and feuds. Sometimes team members want to take individual credit for team accomplishments. They may divert attention from the specific goals identified at the beginning of the team process because of private agendas, jealousy or ill will. These behaviors can also derail the progress of the team. A skilled facilitator will keep the team focused on the goal, counter these selfish behaviors, and encourage the group to act as a team.

Let's look at examples of how employee involvement can work effectively on those two most common issues we see in employee surveys: safety and work conditions.

Team Based Approach to Safety Programs

Safety programs are well suited for employee involvement. They meet many of the criteria listed above for good team-based problem solving:

Complex problem with few readily identifiable solutions: Safety problems often require significant investigation and analysis of how possible solutions will impact the performance of the company.

Problem where team members' areas have valuable expertise: Safety issues are particularly well-suited for employee input because employees are affected daily by workplace safety decisions. They typically have the best view of where safety problems arise and how proposed solutions will impact them.

Problem with limited or identifiable timeline: Many safety problems have readily identifiable end points, like a procedural change or the addition of a safety feature. Other safety issues are continuing projects – an ergonomics program, for example. It is important to identify a project with a limited timeline if employee involvement is the goal.

Issue where scientific analysis and measurement is possible: There are numerous opportunities to measure and scientifically evaluate both company history and the success of prior programs. These are great areas for employee involvement.

Direct impact on internal or external customers: There are clearly direct impacts on internal customers – the employees directly affected by the safety program. Impacts on external customers are less visible, if they exist at all. Evaluate projects with the impact on customers in mind.

Meaningful to employees: Projects that directly impact the safety of employees are among the most meaningful of all.

Cuts across departments: Many safety programs (depending on the one chosen) will cut across departmental lines and can be exceptional projects for employee involvement.

Not a process in transition: This is another area where potential safety projects will have mixed results, depending on the nature of the project. It is best to choose a project where the process or procedure is in place and there is a measurable safety history to review.

There are both advantages and disadvantages to choosing safety programs as employee involvement initiatives. Let's first review the many advantages. Employee safety programs show compassion on the part of the employer. They prove to employees that the company takes employee welfare very seriously. Managers exhibit concern. Companies also benefit through reduced costs associated with insurance claims, workers compensation, absenteeism and lost time due to accidents.

Employees benefit as well. Group participants get direct access managers to understand their concerns about important safety issues. They develop better relationships with managers and co-workers. They share safety tips and can warn the company of unsafe practices before an injury occurs. Finally, if successful, they have the satisfaction of making their workplace safer.

There are some disadvantages to consider, particularly if this is your first employee involvement program on the heels of the union organizing campaign. Safety issues are often used during organizing campaigns to inflame voters. Unions may have employees file OSHA complaints to harass an employer during organizing drives. These complaints may still be pending at the conclusion of the NLRB election process.

In addition, safety rhetoric is well suited for inflammatory action by extremely negative employees. These employees will simply not effectively participate in a team. They may attempt to derail discussion by continuing inflammatory rhetoric. In this environment, the best advice may be to avoid employee involvement.

This is not to say that the issues should be ignored. However, you might first handle these issues directly through management with limited employee involvement. You can decide this during the management evaluation of potential team projects. Careful issue selection avoids creating additional issues in contentious areas.

Team Based Approach to Work Conditions
Work condition issues are also well suited for employee involvement. Once again, they typically meet the criteria of good team-based projects:

Complex problem with few readily identifiable solutions: Many work condition issues meet this criteria, particularly ones that have a history of being contentious with employees based on unpopular management action. Management normally responds to the simple issues, so those that remain normally require more difficult solutions.

Problem where team members' areas of expertise could help identify solutions: Depending on the particular work condition issue, team members are perhaps in the best position to identify potential solutions to problems and how they would impact the operation.

Problem with limited or identifiable timelines: Work condition projects are perhaps the best example of problems with limited timelines, or where a "finish line" is easily identified.

Issue where scientific analysis and measurement is possible: Measurement and analysis of work condition problems are often readily available. Many have been analyzed before (as we shall see, financial constraints after analysis are often the most important obstacle to resolving these issues).

Direct impact on internal and external customers: These issues directly impact internal customers – the employees who are required to deal with the unsatisfactory work condition. These conditions may also reduce productivity or quality, having a direct impact on external customers as well.

Meaningful to employees: By their very nature, work condition issues are usually the most meaningful to employees.

Cuts across departments: Work condition issues are very likely to impact more than one department.

Not a process in transition: Sometimes work condition problems are a result of transitional issues in companies. Those issues are less resolvable in a team-oriented situation. In order to meet this criteria, managers should look for problems that are not transitory.

The advantages to choosing work condition projects for teams are similar to those of safety projects. They tend to express compassion for employees. They are typically very popular causes. They directly impact the day-to-day work life of employees.

The disadvantage to most work condition programs is that they can be expensive. Most employers do not allow poor working conditions as a rule (if you do that's a whole different book!) Therefore, where poor work conditions are not due to simple laziness or poor management, they are usually a result of limited resources or expense.

Expense is a very important aspect to the process of identifying whether an employee involvement initiative should be used on a work condition issue. If management is not prepared to respond to the work condition or to expend resources on solving it, it should never be chosen as a team topic. This may potentially be an unpopular decision, in which case you face a potential "boom" event and need to develop a communication plan around that. The good news is you just have to jump back one chapter for a number of tips on how to do that.

If you do choose to tackle a project with budget constraints one of the best approaches is to identify those right up front and allow the team to work within the constraints. This forces the team to make business decisions just like managers. They are encouraged to use creativity in solving the problem. They also usually gain increased appreciation for the resource issues managers face.

Client Story: Work Conditions Teams in Action

A manufacturing client of ours fabricates wood and metal products. We surveyed the company, and it received relatively typical scores. Work conditions rated very low, next to advancement and pay and benefits issues. However, the client was in a very competitive industry and regularly conducted wage and benefit surveys to ensure the company was competitive in this area. We decided that frustrations about pay would be better attacked through employee communications.

Therefore, we identified the work conditions issue as a potential win-win for the company. Focus group sessions were conducted in conjunction with communicating survey results to identify the work condition problems in the plant. It became evident during the course of those meetings that the biggest complaint was over the amount of dust in the air.

Some employees treated this as a safety issue, but most simply complained that it was hot and sometimes uncomfortable to breathe. A few months earlier, the employer had a safety analysis performed at the plant to ensure that there was not a breathing hazard. There was not. Nevertheless, employees still complained about the work condition, and some still viewed the workplace as unsafe.

Upon identifying this issue in focus groups, we went back to the company's top management and explained that this met our criteria of an effective subject for team-oriented problem solving. The employer noted that this issue had been examined several times before and any potential solution was just too expensive to implement.

This impasse existed before the union organizing campaign. It had to be overcome to make any improvement in the dusty work condition frustrations among the employees in the plant. After discussing the possible options for dealing with the problem, we suggested that the employer consider if there was *any* money that could be budgeted to solve the problem. After some debate, a modest budget was established to be put toward a solution.

Once the budget was established, we asked for a team of employees, including an engineer and several employees from both the wood and metal departments, to work together. The difficult task was to come up with a solution to the ventilation problem within the identified budget.

Team members initially received training on facilitation of team meetings and on team-oriented problem solving. An outside facilitator from our company conducted the training. The facilitator explained the budget and helped the committee establish its mission, goals and timeline. After this, the only assistance from our company came in reviewing minutes from the meetings and suggesting ways to overcome roadblocks and obstacles. The onsite facilitator (an hourly employee from the company) handled the rest of the meetings.

The team met a half dozen times over the course of the next several weeks. The employees identified vendors of high-powered fans that they believed, if properly placed, would relieve the ventilation issues within the budgetary limitations. The team had two vendors bring in samples. During the course of this process, the vendors began to bid against each other. Ultimately the employees were able to secure a large fan and install it in the area where the majority of the dust was created.

The same group of employees was surveyed approximately a year later. The overall score on working conditions improved over 12 percent, with almost 70 percent of the employees responding favorably to statements regarding the work environment in the company.

Legal Issues

Like the use of employee surveys, employers who use teams in a post-campaign environment must take extra care to understand the legal landscape. The NLRB rules that govern the use of workplace teams apply equally to all organizations covered by the NLRA (even those who have experienced no union organizing activity). Nevertheless, it is usually those companies who have been through organizing activity (and whose activities are therefore being closely monitored by unions) who will need to pay closest attention to the rules that follow.

Section 8(a)(2) of the NLRA prohibits employers from dominating or supporting any group of employees that fall under the broad definition of a "labor organization" in section 2(5) of the Act.[80] In several cases, the NLRB has found that teams or committees of employees constitute "labor organizations" and, due to the fact that they are supported or under the control of the company, are unlawful under section 8(a)(2).[81]

The prohibition of 8(a)(2) was originally intended to prevent "company unions," a common response by employers in the first half of the 20th century to avoid a true "arms length" bargaining relationship with an independent union.[82] In the years since section 8(a)(2) was enacted, particularly in the last two decades with the increased use of more decentralized and empowered work teams in the workplace, the NLRB and the courts have struggled with distinguishing between cooperation (which the courts allow) and domination (which is prohibited by the Act).[83]

---

[80] Section 2(5) defines a "labor organization" as an entity that "exists for the purpose, in whole or in part, of dealing with employers concerning grievances, labor disputes, wages, rates of pay, hours of employment, or conditions of work."

[81] See e.g. Electromation, Inc., 309 NLRB 990 (1992), enfd. 35 F.3d 1148 (7th Cir. 1994); E.I du Pont & Co. 311 NLRB 893 (1993); Keeler Brass Co., 317 NLRB 1110 (1995).

[82] See Hardin, et al. (eds.), The Developing Labor Law, 3rd edition (BNA Books 1996), pp. 298-299.

[83] See Id., pp. 299-300.

This struggle to distinguish between cooperation and domination turns on the NLRB's interpretation of the phrase "dealing with." The NLRB described its formulation in its decision in *Crown Cork & Seal Company*, 334 NLRB No. 92 (2001):

> One of the required elements for "labor organization" status under Section 2(5) is that the entity "exists for the purpose, in whole or in part, of dealing with employers concerning grievances, labor disputes, wages, rates of pay, hours of employment, or conditions of work." (Emphasis added.) The Board explained that "dealing with" contemplates "a bilateral mechanism involving proposals from the employee committee concerning the subjects listed in Section 2(5), coupled with real or apparent consideration of those proposals by management." *Electromation, Inc.*, 309 NLRB 990, 995 fn. 21 (1992) *enfd.* 35 F.3d 1148 (7th Cir. 1994). "That 'bilateral mechanism' ordinarily entails a pattern or practiced in which a group of employees, over time, makes proposals to management, [and] management responds to these proposals by acceptance or rejection by word or deed. ..." *E.I. du Pont & Co.*, 311 NLRB 893, 894 (1993).[84]

Not all employee committees or work teams are "labor organizations" subject to the restrictions of 8(a)(2). In *Crown Cork & Seal Company*, 334 NLRB No. 92 (2001), the NLRB outlined the factors it considers when determining whether an employee committee is "labor organization" under section 2(5) of the Act.

In *Crown Cork & Seal Company*, the company had seven committees examined by the Board. They were part of the "Socio-Tech System" the company designed to delegate to employees substantial authority to operate the plant. The seven committees in question included combinations of management, production and maintenance employees. Four of the committees were production teams – every employee in the plant participated on one of these four teams. The

---

[84] *Compare General Foods Corp.*, 231 NLRB 1232 (1977) (job enrichment program delegating responsibility to employees normally assigned to management not "dealing with" under Section 2(5)).

remaining three committees were the Organizational Review Board (ORB), the Advancement Certification Board (ACB) and the Safety Committee. Many of the decisions of these committees were reviewed by the management team *Crown Cork & Seal Company*, 334 NLRB No. 92 (2001).

The ORB monitored plant policies to ensure they are administered fairly and consistently by each of the plant production teams. The ORB regularly recommended changes to the plant manager or management team in policies, hours, layoffs, smoking rules, vacations and other terms and conditions of employment. The ORB also reviewed recommendations by the production team to terminate, suspend or discipline an employee. The plant manager testified that he rarely, if ever, rejected a recommendation of the ORB. *Crown Cork & Seal Company*, 334 NLRB No. 92 (2001).

The committees were not allowed to operate outside of established parameters. One example identified was when the ORB recommended a layoff procedure with a provision for seniority. The management team returned the recommendation to the ORB with a note that "we do not have seniority in this plant" and the final version did not include seniority as a factor. *Crown Cork & Seal Company*, 334 NLRB No. 92 (2001).

The ACB, which administered a pay for skills program in the plant, certified skill levels of employees and recommended them for raises. The Safety Committee reviewed any accidents in the plant and would make recommendations to help make the plant safer. The plant manager never overruled a recommendation of either the ACB or the Safety Committee. *Crown Cork & Seal Company*, 334 NLRB No. 92 (2001).

The NLRB found that the Socio Tech System, like the job enrichment program in General Foods, was a flat delegation of management authority to production employees. The Board found that the power exercised by the committees was "managerial." However, the Board held that the committees do not "deal with" management but instead they "perform essentially management functions." *Crown Cork & Seal Company*, 334 NLRB No. 92 (2001).[85]

The Board rejected the argument that the act of making recommendations to the plant manager that could be rejected by him is in effect "dealing with"management. The Board distinguished the act of sending recommendations between levels of authority from the exchange of proposals in a bargaining context. The Board compared the sending up of recommendations by the committee to be very much like the sending up of a recommendation by a supervisory employee in a more traditional plant. The Board felt that the Socio Tech committees simply played the same role as a supervisor in the traditional plant. "[T]he seven committees are management," in their respective areas of authority, the Board held. *Crown Cork & Seal Company*, 334 NLRB No. 92 (2001) (Emphasis in original).

Therefore, an employer wishing to avoid difficulty under Section 8(a)(2) should take great care to ensure that any employee committee or team is given broad discretion to act within its area of authority. The factors considered most important in Crown Cork & Seal were:

- The number of times a committee recommendation was rejected by higher levels of management

---

[85] *See also Georgia Power Co.*, 342 NLRB 192 (2004) (no violation where "Workplace Ethics Committee" made management-level decisions regarding ethics complaints); *Syracuse University*, 350 NLRB 755 (2007) (no violation where committee adjudicates employee claims against employer and does not recommend changes to terms and conditions of employment). *Compare Reno Hilton Resorts*, 319 NLRB 1154 (1995) (quality action teams violate Act when they occasionally made recommendations for management to accept or reject).

- The weight given to committee recommendations (when faced with contrary recommendations from other managers)
- The types of tasks delegated to the committee (typically "managerial" tasks)
- Whether there appears to be any "back and forth" between the committee and management (versus simply forcing committee to act within its area of authority)

Obviously these cases are very fact-intensive, and there is no way to be certain that any committee or team will satisfy the NLRB requirements. This fact often frustrates employers (we guess the Board wonders why this issue should be any more certain than the remainder of labor law). As frustrating as the law might be, this should not in any way diminish the incentive to use teams where they can be effective. The key is to clearly identify the parameters for the team and then give them substantial authority to act within those boundaries.

Conclusion

Teams are not for everyone. Employee involvement takes effort and commitment on the part of both management and employees. This work of team problem-solving is above and beyond the normal day-to-day activities of employees. Some employees are motivated to participate while others are not; just as some projects are well suited for this approach while others are not. However, if you identify projects suitable for teams and groups of employees who want to participate, the programs can be highly successful.

Ultimately, employees who participate in employee involvement programs feel they are more connected with the company. These employees make a real contribution and have control over their work environment.

Studies conducted by pro-union scholars also suggest that participation in Employee Involvement Programs (EIP's) significantly reduces the likelihood employees will turn to unions. One study concludes:

> "The difference in the union win rates between campaigns in which employee-involvement programs existed and those in which they did not is striking: the union won in 48 percent of all the elections when there were no EIP's but in only 30 percent of all the elections when there were EIP's"[86] (emphasis added).

Our experience is that effective implementation of team-based approaches when solving problems results not only in increased satisfaction over contentious issues, but also increased credibility of supervision and top management. The use of teams significantly reduces the chances a union will ever win an election in your company. Most important, the use of teams increases involvement and engagement at work. That's what I'd call an employee relations "triple threat."

Action Steps

- ☐ Consider some of the problems your organization has recently experienced. Do any of these meet the criteria for a good team project? List them.
- ☐ Start with the most pertinent potential project and select employees for the team.
- ☐ Choose and train committee members.
- ☐ Make sure goals, action plans, responsibilities,and deadlines are clearly defined to team members.
- ☐ Step back and let the team get to work.
- ☐ When the project is completed, review the process and results for improvement.

---

[86] James Rundle, "Winning Hearts and Minds in the Era of Employee Involvement Programs," *Organizing to Win: New Research on Union Strategies* (Cornell University Press, 1998), p. 218.

Chapter 21

Recognition, Positive Feedback and Motivation Strategies[87]

"What every genuine philosopher (every genuine man, in fact) craves most is praise—although the philosophers generally call it 'recognition'."
William James

What You'll Learn In This Chapter

❑ The top motivators of employees (hint: it's not money);

❑ Why recognition and motivation is so difficult for most companies;

❑ Low and no cost motivation programs;

❑ Informal and formal recognition strategies; and

❑ Legal issues with implementing recognition or motivation programs.

When was the last time your boss gave you a "pat on the back" or a "high five" for something you did well? Was it just last week? Within the last month? Within the last year?

Now answer this. How did that make you feel? Did you:

• Feel good?
• Want to work harder?
• Try to repeat your good work?
• Feel better about your job?
• Feel better about your boss?
• Feel better about yourself?

---

[87] If you enjoy some of the tips outlined in this chapter take a look at our Approachable Leadership™ module *On Time, On Target: Recognizing Employees* which covers the basics of recognition and positive feedback.

Survey after survey shows that money is <u>not</u> the biggest motivator of employees. Instead, as we learned in Chapter 12, the top motivators for employees are things like growth, producing quality work, and making daily progress toward goals. Always near the top of the list is receiving recognition for a job well done. While low pay or poor benefits are great ways to de-motivate workers, recognition is the route to high performance.

Once you issue a pay raise it tends to show up every paycheck without interruption. Recognition is much more difficult to consistently deliver. Perhaps this is one of the reasons it is such a motivating factor. There is no "off the shelf" program that makes this happen – only consistent effort and practice by managers, supervisors and ultimately co-workers.

Recognition can take a variety of forms. It can be a formal recognition, like a trophy, certificate, or some other physical recognition. It can be an informal "atta boy" (or "atta girl") at a department meeting. It can literally be a high five or a pat on the back. Whatever the form, it is a powerful motivator.

Let's define positive feedback. Good positive feedback is **timely**, it recognizes **specific behavior** that is both **desirable** and **repeatable**. Telling an employee "way to go, chief, you're the best" isn't very valuable feedback. Positive feedback is somewhat difficult to get right. When you see an employee doing something you want them to keep doing or repeat in the future, the idea is to reinforce that behavior. Here is a little more detail on the key components of positive recognition:

> • **Timely**: You want the recognition to happen as close to the observation of the behavior or action as possible;
> • **Specific**: Name exactly the action or behavior you want to reinforce;

- **Focused on Behavior**: Focus on an objectively describable action or activity of the employee – not the motivation behind it, or even the outcome;
- **Desirable Behavior**: Make sure the behavior is one you want to reinforce, not just the outcome;
- **Repeatable Behavior**: If the idea is to get more of it, it must be something that the employee has control over – not just a lucky happenstance.

A great way to think about the proper delivery of positive recognition is the phrase, "on time and on target." A helpful way to construct good positive recognition is to put it in an "I message" format, which consists of the following elements:

- I saw what you did (the desired, repeatable behavior)
- I appreciate it (be sincere)
- It's important (how it contributes to our work or productivity)
- It makes me feel....

Be **truthful**. Don't embellish the impact of the behavior. When someone does something well that you want to recognize, just tell it like it is. If the impact was small that is okay, you don't need to make a production out of everything. If on the other hand, your employee did something that saved many lives, maybe a parade is warranted. The things that you want to target are those behaviors that can be repeated and that will serve as models of behavior you would like to see other employees engage in. When giving recognition, keep it simple, and keep it honest.

Whenever appropriate, make it **public**. There is nothing like being recognized in front of people you know and respect. It lends validation to the positive feedback. When one, or all, of your employees do something well, recognize them in front of others. Public recognition is free and a great tool to build morale.

There are a couple of caveats to this. First you need to know your employees. Although most people thrive on being praised in front of others, a small percentage will be embarrassed. In these cases, there are some options: You can send out an email to your group or in some other way post the feedback so that everyone sees it, but the recipient is not necessarily standing in the glare of the spotlight when it happens. Some DO appreciate the public recognition – they just don't like it to happen "live" in front of others.

You could also send the person an individual email, and perhaps copy only your boss. This way, the employee receives the positive strokes, and knows that someone else significant is aware of the job well done, but they are not called out in front of their peers.

Or you can call the person aside individually, let them know that you understand that they don't like a lot of public attention, and deliver the feedback privately. They will appreciate both the feedback, and your understanding. You could couple this strategy with some strategic "positive gossip" – in other words repeat the story about what happened to others. This lets you make sure others have the opportunity to learn from the experience and word will probably get back to the employee that you bragged about them to others.

The bottom line: get to know your employees, so you know whether they thrive on public recognition or whether they are more reserved.

When it comes to formal awards and recognition, there are a number of strategies you can use. Ultimately any strategy employed must be consistent with the business, its culture, and the goals of the company. An impromptu trip to a movie theater, for example, probably will not motivate employees of a movie theater. The same reward may be highly motivating to employees of a retail store. A contrived recognition program will be seen that way and may have a negative impact on employee motivation. Instead, think of as many strategies as you can to give sincere acknowledgement, then adopt the ones that seem to fit best with your particular group of employees.

Bob Nelson, a nationally recognized expert on motivation strategies for employees, has written several books on motivating, rewarding and energizing employees.[88] He focuses on three important aspects of rewards that bear repeating. First, match the reward to the person. A program providing the exact same reward to all employees will be less motivating than one rewarding individual performance on an individual basis. The more personal the reward, the more motivating it is.

Nelson believes the second component of a successful reward program is matching the reward to the achievement. In other words, significant achievements receive greater rewards than small achievements. This is not to say that small achievements should not be rewarded or recognized, however. Instead, achievements should be rewarded in proportion to their value to the company, the effort of the individual, or the degree of innovation required.

Nelson's third strategy, like we discussed earlier, is to be timely and specific. This means that you reward successful performance when it occurs and specifically identify what is being rewarded.

Another important consideration with any reward program is to assess your recognition and change it, if need-be. No matter how great or how well conceived a reward program you develop, after a period of time it will be considered "part

---

[88] See *1001 Ways to Energize Employees*, (Workman Publishing, 1997) and *1001 Ways to Reward Employees*, (Workman Publishing, 1994).

of the package" and no longer motivating. This is the irony of rewarding only through compensation. A $1,000 bonus in one year may be highly motivating. However, a $500 bonus the following year, while certainly a bonus, is seen as a demotivator by many people in the context of prior rewards. For this reason, it is very important to mix up rewards and recognition programs using a variety of different methods consistent with business goals of the company.

The reason reward and motivation programs are so difficult to successfully implement is that they require more attention than compensation-based programs. There are no shortcuts. Employers must know what their employees are doing at work, know what they are proud of outside of work, and know what they like and don't like. Lapses in any of these areas will make the program less effective and potentially de-motivate employees.

The programs also have to be stepped. An employee who is consistently performing a function that was recognized and has now become a habit, no longer needs to be rewarded for performing that function. Instead, they should be rewarded for performing some additional function. In this sense, there will be a continuous improvement aspect to the reward program.

There are a variety of strategies, both no cost and low cost, that employers can use to inexpensively reward employees and increase employee motivation. It is beyond the scope of this book to list all the different methods available. I will highlight a few good options and resources below. Most important, pay attention to the implementation of these reward and motivation strategies and how they might fit as part of your overall employee relations program.

No Cost and Low Cost Motivation Strategies
There are numerous little to no cost strategies to motivate employees. These can be both informal and formal. Start

simple. Have lunch catered to celebrate an individual's recent accomplishment. Host an impromptu ice cream social (at our company we have recently held a Cinco De Mayo party, wine tasting, Octoberfest lunch, and other themed lunches to celebrate reaching business goals). Make a plaque commemorating a great accomplishment. Give an employee a partial day with pay to donate to his or her favorite charity. Hold short meetings for the express purpose of commemorating a success. Ring a bell to signify a new sale or client.

Look for motivational opportunities in your "normal" daily routine. Fast Company magazine used to run an article each month called "Meeting I Never Miss," which has given us several ideas for motivational meetings. One issue recently discussed a meeting called "First Friday," held at a startup company in Atlanta. This meeting includes all 120 employees of the company and begins by welcoming any new hires. New employees introduce themselves and explain why they joined the company – each is also given a standing ovation by their peers. Next, each department updates the company on their successes and projects. Each team decides on the format for its presentation – often teams will use skits to help educate the company on their projects. These sessions are highly motivational and provide plenty of opportunity for recognizing successes of individual team members.

Train your supervisors and managers on recognition strategies. As mentioned earlier, one of the best resources on the subject is a book by Bob Nelson titled *A Thousand and One Ways to Reward Employees*. He has a companion book titled *A Thousand and One Ways to Energize Employees*. These two books are great references to use when developing motivation programs and we encourage you to get both of them when thinking about your program. Below is a list of just a few of the excellent ideas Nelson suggests for informal recognition rewards.

Informal Rewards

- Congratulate employees with personal notes or cards
- Give employees personal recognition – supervisor can have the president or the supervisor's manager call employees and thank them for a job well done
- Give employees a pat on the back when you catch them doing something right
- Take out newspaper ads thanking employees by name
- Host a day of appreciation, office parties
- Purchase a trophy to pass around
- Present a personal gift related to the employee's hobby
- Make a batch of cookies for the employee
- Give tickets to an event, hand out movie passes, pay for a round of golf or give service gifts – free car wash, lawn service, etc.
- Give time off or cash

Formal Reward Programs

Formal rewards are obviously more structured than their informal counterparts. These rewards, while not always expensive, do tend to have more resources allocated to them. Since these are more formalized, more effort should be put into communicating the parameters of the program to ensure employees understand clearly any "rules" associated with earning the reward. While more trouble and expense than informal programs, a few of the ideas on this list (also suggestions from Nelson) can be highly motivating – the types of programs talked about for years. Suggestions include:

Formal Rewards

- Name an employee of the month (all stars, rookie of the year, etc.)

- Give performance "bucks" that can be redeemed for prizes or contests where winners get to participate in company advertising
- Implement employee suggestion programs where employees are rewarded a percentage of the savings their idea brings to the company or where there's a drawing for everyone who contributes a suggestion during a period of time
- Give stock options or "phantom stock options"
- Ask customers or guests to nominate or even reward employees based on good service
- Send a team on an outing (fishing, baseball game, golf, cruise or other vacation) after completion of a project
- Award perfect attendance bonus (cash, stock, drawing)
- Host quiz shows to promote knowledge of company information, a company-wide "Olympic" event
- Award tuition for college, match donations to an employee's college of choice or make a donation in the name of an employee to the charity of his or her choice
- Send employees to special seminars, workshops or meetings outside the company
- Allow high performing employees to make presentations to top managers on issues or to mentor during the orientation process
- Give time off to work for community service, political campaigns or to give blood

These lists are not intended to be exhaustive and are merely designed to suggest starting points for thinking about motivation and recognition programs.

Legal Issues
For businesses worried about third party intervention, the implementation and development of the motivation program in your company must be handled diligently and conscientiously. An employer is not allowed to promise or

offer inducements to employees for the purpose of discouraging them from engaging in union organizing activity under Section 8(a)(1) of the NLRA.[89] The United States Supreme Court acknowledged in 1944 that employee free choice "may be induced by favors bestowed by the employer" and is therefore unlawful. See *Medo Photo Supply Corp. v. NLRB*, 321 US 678, 686 (1944).[90]

As with grants of pay and benefits, an employer is prohibited from offering an inducement to employees when either the timing or impact leads the Board to conclude that the employer's purpose is one of "impinging upon... freedom of choice for or against unionization, and is reasonably calculated to have that effect."[91] This includes not only pay increases, but also favorable changes to other aspects of the employment relationship.[92]

Companies should avoid any action or communication that in any way implies that a recognition or motivation program is in any way related to organizing activity. Take particular care to look at the timing of any such program. If recent union organizing activity has occurred in your company, it is a good idea to have your labor counsel review any plans for implementing motivation or recognition programs in this environment.

Bear in mind a couple of additional strategies with respect to implementing a formal motivational program (as opposed to informal recognition of organizational citizenship behavior). First, the program should be public. All employees should be

---

[89] See Hardin, et al. (eds.), *The Developing Labor Law*, 3rd Edition (BNA Books, 1996), pp. 115-119.
[90] For an in depth discussion of the legal issues surrounding the unlawful grant of pay or benefits changes, see Chapter 12.
[91] *NLRB v. Exchange Parts Co.*, supra note 76.
[92] See Id. at 409 (employer announced changes in birthday holiday, and more favorable holiday and overtime scheduling before NLRB election).

aware of the program and the standards should be well communicated. Second, the implementation of the program needs to be consistent and fair. Managers and supervisors must be encouraged to consistently recognize good performance within their work group. Don't play favorites.

Perhaps the best way to make sure managers are motivated is for top management to evaluate managers and supervisors based on how effectively they recognize and acknowledge excellence among their employees. A good plan is to tie part of the appraisal process (and even better, part of the compensation process) directly to implementation of these motivational strategies.

One could, for example, reward managers whose employees give the most suggestions in a suggestion program. You might choose to track the number of formal and informal incidents of recognition that occurred under various programs that are implemented. You could even evaluate how their employees rate them on recognition related survey scores.[93] The key factor in sustaining the program is to hold managers accountable for the recognition and motivation of their employees.

If formalized programs are used where cash or other monetary incentives will be distributed, employees should have a say in the development of those programs. While they do not have to be involved in every motivation program, it is a good idea to have at least one program that is developed and preferably even managed by a group of employees. This group should have the authority to change the program and monitor its implementation.

---

[93] Two of our regular survey questions are: "My supervisor has talked to me about my performance in the last week," and, "In the last week my supervisor has given me positive feedback."

Managing a program in this way has the dual advantages of relieving some of the pressure on management and ensuring that there are several alternative routes to recognition and motivation. Allowing employee participation also empowers employees, which we have seen is a critical aspect of any positive workplace. Employee recognition is a high impact, low cost way to motivate and engage employees. It is a high-leverage opportunity that should be a key part of any positive employee relations program.

Take Action

- ☐ Think about the last few times one or more of your employees impressed you with a job well done. Make a list of ways in which your positive feedback could have been improved in line with the key components of positive recognition.
- ☐ Two heads are better than one. Assign your direct supervisors with the task of coming up with five suggestions to improve your reward and motivation programs.
- ☐ Get to know your employees better so you may learn how to reward and motivate them better.

Chapter 22

Performance Feedback That Works[94]

*"Failure is only postponed success as long as courage coaches
ambition. The habit of persistence is the habit of victory"*
Herbert Kaufman

What You'll Learn In This Chapter
- ❏ The vital importance of performance communication;
- ❏ How to decide whether formal performance appraisals are right for your organization;
- ❏ Evaluating whether your firm should tie performance appraisals to compensation;
- ❏ The three most common problems with appraisal systems and how to solve them;
- ❏ How to design an effective appraisal process; and
- ❏ Tips to improve informal performance feedback.

Who is most responsible for developing talent in your company? Is it HR? The training department? Top management?

The person most responsible for developing talent in any organization is the first level leader. He or she has the best line of sight for determining development needs. They are in the best position to provide "just in time" performance feedback and coaching. They should know the best development path and the long-term desires of employees (by

---

[94] This chapter contains material from two of our Approachable Leadership™ modules, *Growing Potential: Coaching High Performance* and *Assessing Performance: Growing Your Team*. You can learn more about this training at http://ApproachableLeaders.com or by calling us at 800-888-9115.

asking the "Where are you going?" Approachable Leadership™ question).

Performance feedback and development is a high leverage activity. It improves productivity and business results. But the payoff for talent development goes beyond productivity. In employee surveys and focus groups, employees consistently state their desire for training and skill development. People feel better about themselves, their co-workers, the company, and the first level leader when they regularly get help to improve.

Lack of performance feedback, on the other hand, is a common employee relations complaint. Many organizations only discuss performance and development on formal performance appraisals. In the best circumstances, supervisors meet with employees formally once every few months to deliver appraisals; most systems only require one meeting a year. This is completely inadequate.

You don't need to be a training specialist to get great results in this area. If you ever helped teach a kid to walk or swing a bat you can be an effective coach for your team. This chapter gives you some tips on how to create a development culture. It also provides some basic tools your first level leaders can adopt to do a good job of coaching their employees on performance and development. If your organization already does formal performance appraisals, there are some tips on how to improve those processes.

Performance Feedback and Coaching

Start by asking this question: Do your employees know the performance standards for their jobs? If not, how will your employees (or you) know if they are improving? Some supervisors are great at the mechanics of coaching (which we'll discuss soon), but don't communicate clear standards. You can avoid a lot of confusion and wasted time by making sure the standards or the behavioral goals of the job are made clear. Once those are set, you've got a target to shoot for – a benchmark.

First level leaders are more like a basketball coach on the sideline – helping to shape the way their "players" interact with each other and their jobs in a constantly moving work environment. An occasional "time out" is needed to re-group the team, and sometimes to provide individual coaching to one of the team members.

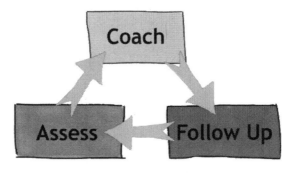

Figure 22.1 – Coaching Model

The diagram above illustrates the coaching model. Coaching comes down to three basic components: assess, coach, and follow-up. You first assess your employee and identify performance gaps against the standards. Next, you coach your employee toward desirable performance, using those standards as the target. Finally, you regularly follow-up to make sure they aren't having any problems and to identify additional development steps.

Earlier in this book we talked about one of the key assumptions of successful first level leaders: you assume your people want to be great. Think about this for a second: How do you feel when you know you didn't meet the standard you hold for yourself? This could be because of a misunderstanding, lack of experience, lack of resources or a lack of skill. Were you frustrated? Maybe a little embarrassed? Were you looking forward to a chat with your leader about what went wrong?

These feeling create stress. That stress can cause a lot of bad things to happen. Ignoring performance gaps can really hurt your work environment. It can lead to long-term declines in productivity and quality, starting a horrible downward spiral.

However, when a performance gap is addressed, that stress is relieved. Your employee knows that you've taken the time to notice the issue. You have cared enough to make sure the employee understands this isn't a discussion about blame, but about development. You've worked together to identify a gap and a course of action to close it. Each of you has agreed to give feedback about how those improvements are coming along. There is nothing left unknown, which allows the employee to reengage and "swing for the fences" again.

There are two main performance gaps: task performance and contextual performance. Task performance relates to the formally defined aspects of a job. Knowing the daily tasks of the job or understanding systems or processes are examples of task performance. Contextual performance is the social aspects of performance. Communication or problem-solving skills are examples of contextual performance.

You must also define the behavior gap. What specific behavior is desired? What exactly is the gap? When coaching you should be able to describe and teach specific behaviors. Sometimes you should identify steps, with the "best possible target" as the ultimate objective but with improvement goals along the way. If the distance from "where we are now" to "where we want to be" is too far, your coaching will demotivate and be unsuccessful.

Finally, your personal observations are important. Don't coach until you have verified the behavior in question with your own eyes. If you haven't, then you are really still in an investigative stage and not ready to begin coaching.

Once you have properly defined what the performance issue is, it is time to discuss the issue with your employee. Coaching a performance gap should be:

- Private,
- Positive, and
- Goal-oriented.

Keep it private. Many employees can get defensive or embarrassed when confronted with a performance gap. Put yourself in your employee's shoes. Do you like to be coached on gaps in front of your peers? Your employee is no different. Keep the conversation between yourself and the employees. Showing sensitivity and respect in this conversation keeps everything focused on the end goal – closing the gap.

Stay positive. Your employee may be embarrassed or surprised by their performance gap. If so, they may engage in one of two escape behaviors. The first is to be defensive, denying the problem. This is where defining a specific, observable behavior gap is key. If you can describe a behavior gap you have personally observed, it is very hard for the employee to dispute it. Some employees take a different tack. They quickly agree to everything you say hoping you'll move on from the conversation as quickly as possible.

It helps if you stay positive and demonstrate confidence that you know your employee will shrink the gap. It also helps if you assume responsibility, as the coach, for the gap in performance ("Boy, I blew it when I didn't show you this trick to doing this task"). If you stay positive, the defenses come down and the employee will be more willing and engaged in closing the gap.

For coaching to really work it is important that the employee *own* the behavior being addressed. You need to describe the behavior that needs improvement and see if the employee agrees. If not, you may need to describe additional examples until they do *own* their behavior. Don't start coaching until you have this agreement. Until they own the behavior and agree there is an opportunity for growth, no amount of coaching will help. In fact, it will backfire.

Once the gap is defined, it's time to define the path to progress. Together, you can decide what the ideal target it and then develop the steps needed to reach it. Many people get this part wrong. To construct effective goals, use the SMART Goals acronym.[95] The acronym stands for:

- Specific: What exactly is the next step to reach the ideal endpoint? Make sure the employee can restate the step in their own words.
- Measurable: How will you know whether the goal is reached? This should be observable and tracked.
- Achievable: Does the employee have the necessary skills and resources to reach the next step? Consider any accommodations you need to make to help the employee reach their next target.
- Realistic: Are other people able to meet the target? Make sure you are asking the employee to reach a reasonable goal.
- Time-Constrained: Finally, set a time target. When will we have the data we need to measure progress? When should this goal be reached?

For most goals it is good to use a SMART Goals worksheet to document the action steps, measures and timeline. Keep it simple, but cover each of the SMART categories. Committing it to writing ensures that the plan is taken as a serious

---

[95] For more information about goal-setting and problem solving check out our Approachable Leadership™ module *Finding Solutions: Problems & Decision Making.* You can learn more about this training at http://ApproachableLeaders.com or by calling us at 800-888-9115.

commitment. It helps remind both the employee and the coach of exactly the steps and measures agreed to.

Set some reminders to check up on progress. This may be simply observing the employee or taking a few moments to check in with the employee and ask how it is going. Are there any challenges or problems? Can you help fix them?

When the employee improves, make sure they know you've seen the results of their effort. Encourage them to the finish line. When the deadline arrives, it's time to take stock and measure progress. In most cases your employee will have closed the gap. In other cases, they may still be a little off the mark. In either case, it is important to find success, capitalize on that success and refine goals as necessary, perhaps diagraming another plan with new details and deadlines.

Should You Conduct Formal Performance Appraisals?

I think performance reviews in most companies are a complete waste of time and counterproductive to a positive work environment. There, I said it. Here are my reasons:

First, supervisors hate them. Humans avoid conflict situations whenever possible. A set-in-stone performance evaluation, especially one tied to a pay increase, is one of those situations. Your lizard-brain comes up with every possible avoidance strategy (from just forgetting about it to not taking it seriously to out and out lying to avoid a negative conversation). Managers waste valuable time writing out reviews that have little basis in reality. They then have a meeting where they share the results with an employee who knows the reviews aren't "real." What a complete waste of time.

Second, employees hate them. Performance review meetings are usually inauthentic and excruciating for both parties. The employee leaves feeling lied to, unappreciated (or at least under-appreciated) and they will remember little if any of the constructive suggestions actually made. If the appraisal is tied to a raise they will pay no attention until they hear a number... at which time they will pay no attention because they know the number.

What to do instead? I am not saying to abandon performance feedback, just the ritual of "performance review" meetings. Try giving real, honest feedback on a regular basis (every week or so). One of the best ways to start that conversation is asking the approachable leadership question, "Where are you going?" Then continue that development conversation over time. Where you see gaps between the present state and the destination, you've found a great place for a coaching conversation.

Make your feedback specific and spend most of your time maximizing an employee's strong points and not trying to change their weak areas. Focus on behavior and don't work on too many things at once. One is a good number to start with. Making a ritual out of the appraisal process just adds unnecessary stress for both parties.

What If We Already Conduct Formal Performance Appraisals?

I am not suggesting that every company should ditch its performance appraisal process, and there are many companies where the formal appraisal process works fine. But if your company is committed to using formal performance appraisals as part of your performance feedback process, you have to make sure you are fully committed to doing it well. You must make sure you hold line level leaders accountable for taking it seriously, making it a priority, and executing it right.

Making an effort and taking the time to conduct the performance appraisal right can motivate employees. To be effective, the appraisal should provide an opportunity for employees to help set their own goals for closing any gaps between either their current performance and their "ideal" performance, or reaching the next step in their development goals. As we've discussed, setting and reaching goals is one of the highest internal motivators. It charges up high performers to reach for the next rung and gives direction to lower performers about where they need to improve.

On the other hand, completing appraisals late, doing them inconsistently, or "dialing them in" can have the opposite effect and de-motivate employees. Giving a satisfactory rating to a low performing employee basically says that low performance is acceptable. It kills company pride.

A poorly conducted appraisal process also kills motivation for high performing employees. They feel like their efforts aren't recognized or valued. Their motivation spirals downward. They stop engaging in Organizational Citizenship Behaviors and instead only do what it takes to get by and no more. There are a few individuals who are, by-nature, highly motivated no matter what system they find themselves in. But even these individuals will look to move on to their next opportunity if they're in a company that doesn't recognize their efforts.

Performance appraisals also create another avenue for employee communication. Many of the companies we work with have serious, company-wide communication problems. As discussed starting in Chapter 14, there are no simple solutions to communication problems. Only a consistent and continuous effort to communicate across many different "channels" will help to relieve problems in a company. Appraisal meetings are an opportunity to open another channel for communication.

Performance appraisal meetings can also be an effective place to standardize communication around important company initiatives. During individual meetings, managers have an opportunity to communicate with employees about a number of issues. In addition to job performance, they can include the employee's role in the company, personal development, important company initiatives, and any other important matters on the employee's mind. These meetings can be highly motivational to employees and are an important piece of a total communications program.

Preparing managers to conduct effective appraisal meetings is also a great way to develop leaders. One reason many appraisal processes fail is because leaders do a poor job of execution. Numerous factors contribute to this, including lack of training, poor communication skills, or simply lack of priority given to the process.

Preparing leaders to execute this process well is also a great development opportunity that teaches communication skills, observation skills, Approachable Leadership™ and more. Leaders are required to objectively identify:

- Performance behavior and performance gaps of individual employees;
- Performance metrics of individuals, the department and the business overall;
- Gaps in their own performance and ways they can improve their own communication skills.

Leaders also must confront and manage performance problems. They have to help identify development opportunities. These are critical skills for leaders. Mastering them can have a dramatic effect on the performance of a company.

A final reason to conduct performance appraisals is to increase the profitability and performance of a company. The more effectively the performance appraisal process ties to business goals, the better the business will perform. But the question still remains: Should you tie performance appraisals to raises?

Should I Tie Performance Appraisals to Pay?

I don't think it's a good idea to tie performance appraisals to pay. It can be done, but it is very difficult to do right. Most companies (particularly if they have communication problems in general) are best served by keeping the two processes separate. Tying performance appraisals to compensation highly charges the process. This, of course, is why it can be a good thing if it is handled well.

Unfortunately, leaders (like most humans) want to avoid painful (negative) experiences. Telling an employee their performance is sub-par and that as a result they won't be getting a raise is a negative, high-stress experience. In an effort to avoid pain, these leaders will often look for the path of least resistance. They'll stall or even "game" the process to avoid the conversation altogether. These predictable reactions destroy the effectiveness of any performance communication program.

Employees may engage in similar conflict avoidance behavior. As mentioned earlier, if they know that their raise amount will be announced at the end of the meeting, they may not talk much during the meeting trying to get to the "finish line" so they can find out their raise. They won't pay attention to much until the raise is announced. Once the raise is announced, they will be consumed with their reaction to the raise (positive or negative). If it is negative, they will likely express this by becoming defensive and arguing about the raise amount. Sure, some may keep their composure, but even these won't hear another word of the meeting.

While a skilled leader can overcome these reactions, it is difficult. The average leader spends the meeting wondering if the employee is angry with them. The average employee spends the meeting wondering what the raise is going to be. It is very difficult to have an effective performance discussion in this environment.

This is why I think the best course it to divorce pay raises from the performance communication process. Before tying performance appraisals to pay, take a good long look in the mirror. Do you have the leadership talent to do it effectively? Are your processes defined and measurable enough to adequately differentiate performance fairly? Will the significant costs of tying it to pay earn a solid return?

I think in the vast majority of cases annual appraisals are tied to pay for one reason: it makes sure managers actually complete the review. This is the dumbest reason of them all. I'm serious about this. If the only way to get leaders in your organization to conduct reviews is because it's a step in the pay raise process, you should get rid of the performance review altogether. I guarantee it's not effective and is working against your goal of improving performance. It is a red flag. Your leaders are not making the connection between performance feedback, development conversations and their role as leaders.

In the remainder of this chapter, I discuss systems that tie performance to pay. If you feel your organization is not ready for this step (or if this is just not consistent with your philosophy) then just ignore the parts about tying it to pay – the remainder of the advice remains valid.

Common Problems With Appraisal Systems

There are four main problem areas common to performance appraisal systems:
- Timing or regularity of reviews;
- Fairness and objectivity of reviews;
- Disconnect between performance, compensation and business goals; and
- Lack of a development component.

To design a more effective appraisal program, look at these common faults and avoid them. Each one is examined below.

The timing and regularity of reviews is critical. Employees who receive reviews irregularly, or not at all, will be demotivated. Employees often look forward to the review process, especially when the review is tied to a raise and they feel they are performing well. They think about what they want to discuss during the review and are disappointed if the review does not occur.

Reviews completed in a half-hearted fashion or are deferred send an important signal to employees: leaders just don't care that much about the appraisal process. It's very de-motivating and is often a reason employees turn to unions. Inconsistent appraisals are also of little use as a motivational tool, no matter how well they are designed. Therefore, any effective appraisal system tracks reviews and holds leaders accountable for regular and consistent delivery.

Unfair or subjective standards, along with a lack of objective performance criteria based on observable behavior, are other critical problems with many review programs. Employers, in the interest of simplicity, will often give very subjective criteria for performance reviews. It is easier to draft opinions rather than to do the harder work of actually observing and documenting behavior in an impartial and objective way. Many times, even objectively measurable issues are dealt with in a subjective way on performance reviews.

Take a simplistic example like attendance. Many companies review attendance as a performance-related factor, without identifying what level of attendance is considered "good" performance and what level is considered "poor" performance. This creates ambiguity. In these companies it is quite common that two employees with equal attendance records are rated different.

Subjective "systems" like this not only raise questions of fairness, but even creates potential legal liability. If an employee doesn't get a raise because of poor attendance and other employees with similar or worse attendance records get raises, you face a serious risk of a discrimination claim. Defending this claim by saying, "we just do a crappy job of executing our performance appraisal process" is not a winning strategy.

Subjective criteria also fail to motivate employees. If you (and more important your employee) can't explain the difference between good and bad performance, you have a bad performance measure. The more subjective a performance measure, the more likely your leader will not know how to rate employees' performance. Subjectivity also increases the chances for unintentional discrimination. Unintentional discrimination is nearly as bad as the intentional kind. It's also a very common complaint cited by union supporters.

Many readers may object at this point that, "hey, there is a lot of stuff that we want to talk about that is subjective, like employee attitude and motivation." No question. Don't ignore these issues in performance discussions; instead, try to save them for coaching conversations. If you are going to rate them on performance appraisals, you must make them objective. Just like with your hiring process (discussed in Chapter 18), you should train leaders to identify specific behaviors that lead them to conclude an employee has a poor attitude or is unmotivated.

Instead of saying, "you have a bad attitude" a supervisor could say, "when a coworker asks for your help I have noticed that you roll your eyes and sigh – that behavior can be perceived as having a negative attitude." Picking out specific behaviors to discuss is much less judgmental; you can discuss the employee's awareness of the behavior (if they deny doing it), the impact of the behavior or the reasons for the behavior. It is not subjective. It is something you notice and that you (and perhaps other coworkers) react to. It is something the employee can start to notice themselves and work on.

If you tie performance to compensation, it should also be carefully tied to business goals. Otherwise, the system may not motivate employees to improve the performance of the company. At its worst, a poorly designed performance appraisal system can actually encourage employees to "game" the system and take action contrary to the business interests of the company ("yeah, we produce a lot of out of spec stuff since we just get measured on throughput but not on quality").

Companies should regularly review their performance communication program with an eye toward business goals. What can an individual do each day that impacts company performance. If you thoroughly apply this to every job performance review factor, you'll have everyone rowing in the same direction. Employees will be encouraged and motivated by their own self-interest to help the company reach its business goals.

How To Design Performance Appraisals That Work

Start by analyzing the current performance appraisal system to identify any gaps. While you sometimes will end up starting from scratch, it is still a good idea to review what came before and to keep any pieces of the existing system that work. Many times the problems with a performance communication system have nothing to do with the structure of the system, but merely its implementation.

This review process can use a number of tools. An engagement survey is a good place to start. Look specifically at complaints from employees regarding the appraisal system. Are there any patterns or common complaints? If you don't have survey data, you can try focus group sessions on the performance appraisal process. Get employees and leaders to suggest improvements to that process.

The next step is to identify the various job positions that are going to be part of the performance appraisal system. Depending on the size of the company and the number of positions involved, these jobs may be grouped according to similarity of tasks involved. The idea is to get a broad picture of the different types of performance criteria that need to be measured.

Next, identify the key indicators of company performance to measure. Most successful companies already have a set of key business indicators that they use to judge the performance of the company. This can vary depending on the type of business, but examples include scrap rates, reject rates, quality control measures, number of units produced, and the like. Financial measures like cost per unit can also be used. Customer complaints, on-time delivery and warranty rates are other possibilities.

The ultimate aim is to line up as many objective, measurable business criteria as possible to help drive the appraisal process. This is not to say that other, more generic performance appraisal criteria cannot be used. Certainly issues like attendance, team orientation, motivation, attitude etc., can be part of the process. Again, the key is to include as many objective measurements as possible.

The next step is to identify the performance criteria that best apply to each position category. Not all positions have a readily identifiable impact on every factor listed. You should look at particular job positions and identify how to best measure that job's impact against the important business criteria identified. This step can be the most challenging part of developing the performance appraisal program.

At this step in the process, avoid getting bogged down in questioning what is the most convenient or what applies best across job categories. Simply identify how each job impacts the bottom line. This may require you to identify new methods of measuring performance. In companies that are not heavily driven by reporting in numbers, this will certainly be the case. The key to a good appraisal program, however, is the ability to tie the measurable job performance factors to an underlying business goal. This will assist both in communicating the importance of the performance factors to the employees and ensuring that the appraisal process is in fact driving the company toward reaching its stated business goals.

Once the job-specific measurements are identified, the next step in the process is to simplify the appraisal system as much as possible. Then create the forms. In some companies, the same form may be appropriate for all job positions. However, most of the best systems have a two-part form. One part of the form may cover generic job responsibilities applicable across the company (attendance, team orientation, discipline during the review period, etc.). A second sheet includes job-specific performance criteria applicable only to workers in a particular job classification.

With the use of carefully crafted forms, a company can truly drive performance toward its business goals. Additionally, employees will benefit from a very specific, easy to understand road map of their performance goals. These performance numbers should be easily tracked and communicated throughout the year, not just at the time of the performance review. The performance review process should never surprise an employee; he or she should be able to constantly track progress.

Employers often say that this process sounds good on paper, but that the jobs in their company require too many subjective performance traits to use a specific measurement. This, they claim, makes specific levels of measurement for performance goals impossible. Most of the time these employers are simply too lazy to work through the performance appraisal process in order to find optimal methods. Every job has some type of measurable impact on the bottom line and productivity of the company – otherwise it shouldn't exist! The key is to identify the specific behaviors that drive these business results.

The next step in the process (if you choose to do this) is to tie the performance appraisal program to the compensation system. If you do this, clearly state the relationship between compensation and job performance. What aspect of pay is tied to performance? How does improving performance directly impact the pay increase? Make sure this is easy to understand and that it is made clear to both leaders and employees.

The final and vitally important part of the process is to establish a system that ensures performance appraisals actually happen when they're supposed to. Track appraisals and make sure they and the communication sessions are completed on time, every time. One way to do this is to require a review of appraisals before communication meetings happen (although this can sometimes slow the process down). Getting signed copies of performance appraisals from the employees appraised is another method. Spot-checking the scheduling and follow-through of the communication meetings is a good practice. Finally, you can tie performance ratings (and compensation) of leaders to how successfully they deliver performance appraisals on schedule to their work groups.

The performance appraisal process can be a great opportunity for companies to communicate expectations and development opportunities to employees. But done poorly it can rob the company of an important way to improve business performance. Worse yet, it can become a source of frustration for employees, who may later turn to outsiders (like government agencies, plaintiff's attorneys, or unions) for assistance with employment problems.

Bringing It All Together – Coaching and Performance Appraisals

Formal performance appraisals provide regular, "serious" moments to reflect on performance. However, this is not a substitute for the regular coaching discussions discussed at the beginning of the chapter. Your leaders should be constantly communicating about performance and development with employees all the time. These regular coaching discussions should provide the context for the annual performance appraisal meetings. The two should work hand in hand.

Leaders who use the formal appraisal process as a substitute for regular informal performance communication are not doing their job. Both types of communication are important. Regular coaching lets an employee know whether they are "on-track" or if they need to improve. It gives the leader opportunities to know about the concerns of employees before those concerns become major issues. They keep employees and leaders connected.

If an employee is surprised by a formal performance review, then the manager has failed. Regular coaching should keep each employee aware of his or her strengths and areas for improvement. Most important, those discussions will outline key areas for development. In this context the annual performance appraisal process becomes a "stake in the ground" where the leader and employee can take stock, review progress and start charting a course for the next year.

Conclusion

Remember what Herzberg and Maslow said about internal motivation? The most motivating thing you can do as a leader is help employees grow and develop. But remember that poorly communicating about performance and development is a common frustration among disgruntled employees. Getting this right can do more than anything else you do to improve morale in an organization. Your performance communication program should be among the first areas you consider when identifying projects for your Left of Boom program.

Take Action

- ☐ Establish a consistent performance appraisal process using objective, measurable business criteria for each of the various job positions within your organization.
- ☐ Hold a training session for your leadership team introducing them to the coaching model. Review how they may already be applying this model and how they can improve upon it.
- ☐ Think about some recent performance gaps you have noticed in your organization. It could involve a single employee, a whole department, or the company in general. Utilizing the SMART Goals acronym, construct a path for improvement

Chapter 23

Dispute Resolution and Peer Review

"It is not he who gains the exact point in dispute who scores
most in controversy, but he who has shown the better
temper."
Samuel Butler

What You'll Learn In This Chapter

- ☐ How dispute resolution programs can often "pre-empt" claims that normally would go to a union organizer, government agency or a plaintiff's lawyer;
- ☐ Cost reductions that can be achieved through reliance on dispute resolution;
- ☐ Strategies to reduce the amount of time and energy your firm currently spends on disputes;
- ☐ Using your dispute resolution program to begin discovery and improve your chances in litigation;
- ☐ Legal issues to consider when implementing a dispute resolution program; and
- ☐ The main types of dispute resolution programs.

Unions claim to offer an alternative to a workplace where "what the boss says, goes." While the reality is quite different, the fact remains that unions do win the right to bargain over significant changes when they win the right to represent employees. While most of the big promises organizers make are false (big raises, better benefits, job security), unions do almost always provide representation during disciplinary investigations or other disputes at work. The quality of this representation is often suspect, but it is an actual deliverable they can sell to workers.

There are other types of third-party intervention that you have to consider. Most third-party interference can be successfully avoided using dispute resolution. When employees turn to outside agencies or attorneys to resolve disputes, you can be sure it probably wasn't their first step. Employees prefer to resolve their disputes internally and without the hassle and grief of going to an outsider.

When employers ignore internal opportunities to resolve disputes or, worse yet, have no effective internal mechanism for dispute resolution, employees are left with few viable options. They feel forced to turn to the EEOC, DOL, NLRB or the "hate your boss, click here" plaintiff's lawyer on Google. Any time an employee arrives at one of these doorsteps, the dispute is no longer in control of the parties best capable of resolving it – the employee and the company.

Informal Dispute Resolution and the Myth of Resolving Conflict[96]

Many leaders think it is their job to resolve conflicts between two or more employees. That's a big mistake. The only people who can resolve a conflict are the people engaged in it. There is a role for the supervisor, but that role is not resolving the conflict.

Conflict in the workplace saps valuable time, resources and energy from your organization. Ironically, the typical way leaders try to resolve conflict can actually create more problems than it solves! When you attempt to solve your employee's problems for them you often make the problem worse. However, when you create conditions where your employees can come together and work through their differences you empower them and reduce the likelihood of

---

[96] This section is based on our Approachable Leadership™ module *Mending Fences: Mediating Conflict*. For more information about this and other leadership training modules in the Approachable Leadership™ training series go to http://ApproachableLeaders.com

future conflicts in the workplace. Mediating conflict is about helping others resolve differences themselves.

Mediating conflict is a process where you assist your employees finding their own solutions to work issues. The key to helping your employees "mend fences" is understanding that <u>you do not have the answer</u> for them. Because you are not a party to the conflict, your role is to assist your employees toward resolution, <u>not</u> fix their problems.

Conflict mediation is not solving a problem for your employees or imposing a solution upon them. In fact, trying to do that just creates more problems. Consider this diagram:

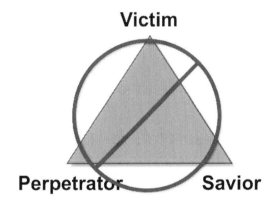

Figure 23.1 – The Triad Diagram

The Triad

This is the victim-perpetrator-savior triad. It is a common but ineffective way to address employee conflicts. When this cycle begins there are two employees in some sort of dispute. They feel unable to resolve the dispute between themselves so they reach out for a third party (their boss/savior) to settle the dispute.

The boss serves as a referee and "solves" the problem. This leaves one party feeling satisfied with the result and the other unhappy. It's a no-win situation. No matter who the savior sides with, they have created another victim and the cycle continues. The leader is now transformed into a perpetrator and creates a new victim. That victim will then seek a new savior. In this cycle, conflict escalates and generates <u>more conflict</u> as victims attempt to balance the score.

The reason that the victim-perpetrator-savior cycle doesn't work is because you are always creating a new victim. It is a win-lose situation. In order to turn the situation into a win-win situation you have to stop picking a winner and a loser and empower your employees to solve their own problems. That means that you have to stop solving your employee's problems for them. Instead of the triad, consider this model:

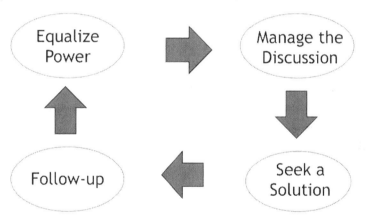

Figure 23.2 – The Facilitation Model

You want to step out of the triad and create a situation where your employees solve their own problems. After all, they are the only ones who can decide what a satisfactory solution to their situation looks like. The facilitation model has four main parts.

Step 1. Equalizing Power: The first step in bringing employees together is to equalize the power. In many cases one employee has some sort of leverage over another employee. The leader's job is to move out of the power relationship into one where equals work together to resolve the issue. You want to find neutral ground. You want to reduce risk and emotion. Reassure participants that addressing the issue will not result in additional negative consequences. Find a location where neither employee will feel threatened. Ideally, the location will not be in the leader's office or in either of the conflicted employees' work areas.

Step 2. Managing the Discussion: This step starts with setting out the ground rules for the discussion. Common rules are:
- One person talks at a time;
- Facts only (specific observable behavior, not assumptions, speculation or opinion);
- Facilitator summarizes and everyone agrees on the common facts; and
- Process repeats for the other person.

Step 3. Seeking a Solution: This step is done by your employees. Your role in seeking a solution is to ask solution-focused questions and keep your employees focused on the reason for the discussion. It is up to the employees to decide on a solution that is fair and equitable to them both.

Step 4. Follow-up: Once your employees have agreed on a solution and the discussion has ended you should set a time to check back. Give them a reasonable period of time to see if the solution is working. Sometimes the first attempt doesn't fully resolve things and resentment begins to build. Checking back allows you to bring the parties back together to modify their agreement if it is necessary. If things are going well then checking back lets your employees know that you care about their issues and are willing to help them where you can.

There are some things that the leader should be aware of before mediating an issue. First, the leader should be aware of their own emotions and avoid becoming emotionally involved in the conflict. If you find yourself siding with one employee over another, take a second and settle yourself down. Remember that you are not a party to the conflict and your job is to help your employees solve their problem, not take sides and remove the perception of fairness from both parties.

Second, the leader should be alert for defensive behavior. A common reaction to a conflict is the "fight or flight response." When one employee is dominating the conversation they may be exhibiting a fight response. If this happens, slow them down and allow the other person to respond to what they are saying. When an employee is agreeing with everything the other is saying then they may be exhibiting a flight response. Challenge them to state their side and make sure they feel heard and understood. Failure to respond to either reaction is a barrier to fairly resolving the conflict.

Third, listen to what your employees are saying. If something sounds unclear, ask clarifying questions. If things get a little confusing, stop the discussion for a minute and paraphrase what you are hearing. This helps foster clear communication.

Fourth, observe your employee's body language. Pay attention to defensive behavior and cues that something is being left unsaid. Prompt your employees to completely explore their issue so that their solution is a full reckoning of your employees' conflict. Be careful not to expand the conversation far beyond the scope of the conflict.

To be a successful leader you should remember that mediating conflict is valuable to you, your employees and your organization. The vast majority of conflict in an organization can be resolved using this model. But occasionally you'll run across a conflict that can't be worked out between the two participants. In these rare situations, you should consider more formal dispute resolution methods.

Formal Dispute Resolution

There are several important reasons companies should consider dispute resolution as part of their employee relations strategy. These reasons can be summarized in four categories:

- Union pre-emption;
- Reduced expense;
- Quick resolution;
- Early and less expensive discovery for litigated claims.

Let's look at each one in turn.

Union Pre-emption

If a union is lurking around your company union pre-emption is an important reason to consider using formal dispute resolution. Unions insist that employees cannot trust management and argue that without a neutral outsider employees will never get a fair shake. Since unions still persuasively argue that employees need a third party for grievance representation and settlement, Alternative Dispute Resolution (ADR) can substitute for this perceived need.

If your company does not have an effective way for employees to get legitimate complaints heard and appealed, the union argument is quite persuasive. The vast majority of collective bargaining agreements contain a grievance procedure, typically including a binding arbitration provision. With a history of over 40 years, these arrangements are well entrenched. There has been recent litigation over whether labor contracts can cover statutory discrimination claims, but the Supreme Court seems ready to allow collective bargaining agreements to cover even these rights, so long as the language is very specific on the issue.

A grievance process is appealing to many employees because it affords guarantees that their grievance will be resolved.

Whether or not the union fulfills other promises made during the campaign, employees latch on to the idea of having someone in the union available to represent them if they are ever wrongfully accused or disciplined for something at work.

Of course, this oversimplifies the grievance machinery in most collective bargaining agreements. In practice, these systems can be unwieldy, and take significant time and energy to resolve complaints. Many times employees are left at the mercy of union politics or the good-will of a shop steward.

Nevertheless, while grievance procedures in collective bargaining agreements often leave a lot to be desired, they can be better than what many employees have in their workplace today. The challenge for forward-thinking employers is to create a system that avoids the disadvantages of grievance handling in union contracts while improving on the informal "open door" policies so prevalent today.

Therefore one reason for setting up a system for dispute resolution is to take away this "deliverable" from the union. Employees who feel their workplace disputes are handled fairly, where their side of the issue is represented and a decision is made in a neutral fashion, will not feel the need to turn to a union for this service. Such a system can also be an effective recruiting point for prospective employees. But in my mind, while this is a valid consideration, it's also the least important reason for an ADR system.

Reduced Expense

A far more important reason for an ADR system is that it will likely save your company money. If your company has ever had the misfortune of becoming embroiled in an EEO charge or other employment law claim, you are well aware of the time and expense involved. There are legal fees. These will typically run into the tens of thousands of dollars even on a run-of-the-mill discrimination claim. These fees often escalate into hundreds of thousands of dollars as the complexity of the claim increases. In addition, there is lost time and productivity spent in gathering documentation and attending depositions and hearings.

Further, the system is just simply not designed for efficient or inexpensive resolution of claims. Even if a claim doesn't make it to court (the vast majority don't), being involved in an agency proceeding or litigation regularly results in large legal expenses. From the drafting of letters of position to responding to information requests and attending agency proceedings and hearings, many agency claims today approach the expense of a trial.

Mediation, arbitration and other dispute resolution procedures can be significantly less expensive than agency or court proceedings for several reasons. First, they can sometimes be handled without the expense of legal counsel. Second, they are typically handled much more quickly. You do not have to wait 300 days for an agency to act on the claim, only to find out they are issuing a right-to-sue letter that starts the whole process again. A mediation or arbitration process is (usually) quicker and cheaper.

The cost of a typical arbitration (which is generally the most expensive ADR solution on the menu) is significantly less expensive than the simplest agency hearing. If your firm has the capability to handle the hearings and brief writing internally, your costs can be under $25,000. Even a more complex arbitration, conducted by a law firm, is still considerably less expensive – if for no other reason than an arbitration does not last as long as the alternatives.

Finally, the awards in alternative forums are typically less extreme than those that go to a jury. This is true even though arbitration agreements must provide the same remedies and awards available through statutory claims (such as attorney's fees and punitive damages) to help get them upheld. Even if your arbitration agreement is challenged (the EEOC and the

NLRB don't like them and they may conduct agency actions in parallel to an arbitration case) you still speed up the time that it takes to get a plaintiff to want to settle all of their claims. And you rarely hear of arbitration awards (outside of baseball contract negotiations) for millions of dollars in punitive damages.

The reasonability of arbitration awards is due to several factors. The biggest factor is that there are no juries involved. Juries often base awards on emotional responses to the evidence presented during a trial. By contrast, arbitration relies on an arbitrator or mediator (or panel of arbitrators or mediators) with greater expertise in employment matters who are less likely to be swayed by emotional pleas that have nothing to do with the facts of the case.

Another reason, sometimes cited by companies as a disadvantage to arbitration, is that arbitrators and mediators often try to find a "middle of the road" solution to problems. While this can often mean that an employer's decision is not upheld, it also tends to reduce the likelihood of huge, unrealistic awards. Therefore, while the awards in the alternative forums may go against companies more often, they also tend to be more realistic.

Quick Resolution

Another reason companies use alternative dispute resolution is to quickly resolve employment law disputes, which can often take years to resolve in agencies or the courts. Alternative dispute resolution resolves disputes more quickly than even mediation and arbitration procedures as those typically require time measured in months. Most employment law cases heard in agencies or courts are lucky to be resolved inside of a couple of years; if appeals are involved, it can easily be four years or more.

There are a number of advantages to resolving disputes quickly. As discussed, the faster you resolve a dispute, the less your legal fees. Another advantage is that a quick resolution results in less down time for management employees in preparing for and testifying during the arbitration, mediation or other hearings. Finally, if there is a systemic problem that led to the dispute, the employer becomes aware of the issue sooner and can respond more quickly in order to avoid additional liability.

Client Story: Dispute Resolution Makes the Six O'Clock News

One client I worked with was plagued with the typical poor employee relations practices that we often find in clients with union issues. Additionally, the company was a very large employer whose every move was a newsworthy event. This company had suffered through two very public union organizing drives in a large pro-union city. It also had been painted, unfairly, as a rogue employer by the union and the press.

Over the course of the year, many efforts were made to improve working conditions and perceptions of the employees about the company. This included a revision of policies and procedures that were flash points during the prior organizing campaigns. A number of other efforts were made to improve employee communication during that year.
One of the major complaints related to the fairness and application of policies and procedures by supervisors. After reviewing the complaints, it looked like there was inconsistent application of the rules, especially the attendance policies. We decided on a proactive process to attack the problem, ultimately employing a combined approach.

First, we revised the policies that resulted in the largest number of complaints. We focused on making them easy to understand and administer. Leaders were retrained and a new attendance policy was implemented – the revisions based on a review of what other organizations in the industry were doing.

In addition, a peer review process was developed that empowered a group of hourly employees to review termination decisions made based on issues like attendance or violation of company work rules. Employees who were disciplined under these policies could have their claim reviewed by either company management or the peer review board, their choice.

The peer review board began reviewing termination decisions and, not even a month later, the local news called to do a television story on the procedure. I was not enthusiastic.

In order to heighten interest in the story, the television crew decided to wait until a day that the peer review board was actually meeting. The news crew received permission (from someone other than me...) to interview an employee who was appealing his termination decision. Reporters also interviewed a couple of the members of the peer review board. At the conclusion of the hearing, the peer review board decided to uphold the termination of the employee and the television crew left.

While anxiously awaiting the news telecast, I was filled with dread. I figured we were dead. While completely behind the concept of peer review (after all, I wrote the policy and trained the panel members), I was not hopeful that the news crew would understand what we were doing. This was a very "union" town, and our client was not exactly popular. There were just too many angles from which to pound the company.

The news anchors led the story by talking about how our client was letting co-workers decide whether or not to fire an employee. My heart began to sink.

Ultimately, however, the story was a great success for the company. The democratic nature of the process was commended in the story – even by the employee who was terminated!

Legal Issues

Some courts (following the suggestion of a few government agencies and plaintiff's lawyers) are limiting the ability of employers to enforce binding arbitration agreements. Many decisions hold that employees are unable to waive their right to litigate employment disputes, particularly if asked to do so in advance of an actual dispute. While this battle is far from over and its details well beyond the scope of this text, there are some general principles worth noting.

Although Congress (with the support of the Supreme Court), does favor arbitration of claims,[97] lower courts and agencies are reluctant to allow employees to waive remedies for state and federal employment law claims. While some courts will allow waiver of statutory employment rights, they normally require a number of factors to be present, including: specific notice to the employee of the rights being waived; ample time for employees to read and understand the agreement and policies about arbitration; a fair and neutral forum for hearing the dispute; and a provision for the same remedies available

---

[97] See *Southland Corp. v. Keating*, 465 U. S. 1, 16 (1984), holding that Congress intended the FAA to apply in state courts, and to pre-empt state anti-arbitration laws to the contrary. See also *Allied-Bruce*, 513 U.S., at 272; see also id., at 282 (O'Connor , J., concurring) (Court explicitly declined to overrule *Southland*).

under the statute in question (including punitive damages and attorneys' fees).[98]

Despite the favorable Supreme Court treatment of the general concept of arbitration of employment claims, some jurisdictions remain very inhospitable to these agreements. This is also the standard position of the EEOC and NLRB. Suffice it to say, requiring employees to arbitrate statutory employment law claims, particularly if you ask them to do so as a condition of employment before any claim arises, may not hold up in some circumstances.

In addition, many employers fear that employees might get "two bites at the apple" due to this legal complexity. Some argue that, due to the uncertain legal environment surrounding alternative dispute resolution, the likelihood is that an employee will use the procedure and then turn around and sue later for the same set of complaints. In essence, they get to litigate any issue twice and, if lucky, might even recover damage costs twice for the same dispute. Many employers who have not thought carefully about the issue dismiss ADR for this reason alone.

Should employers be concerned with these potential problems? As you might guess, my conclusion is that the advantages of ADR far outweigh any potential legal issues or double recovery possibilities. First, it is important to understand that the vast majority of cases resolved through

---

[98] See, e.g. *Shankle v. B-G Maintenance Management of Colorado*, 78 FEP Cases 1057 (10th Cir. 1999) (arbitration agreement requiring fee splitting between claimant and employer invalid due to restricting access to forum); *Gonzales v. Hughes Aircraft Employees Federal Credit Union*, 79 FEP Cases 65 (Cal. Ct. App. 1999) (arbitration clause invalid where time limits, discovery rights are less than provided by law and where employer not required to arbitrate); *Michalski v. Circuit City Stores*, 79 FEP Cases 1160 (7th Cir. 1999) (agreement to arbitrate valid where employer agrees to be bound by arbitrator's decision).

alternative methods work exactly as designed – without a court case. Thus, forcing all aggrieved employees to go into an agency or a court to resolve their dispute is an extreme overreaction. While there may be a case or two where employees want to get into the agency or the court system and avoid ADR, the vast majority will not.

Second, for that minority group of employees who are trying to get to court, you will probably not avoid a lawsuit no matter what system you have in place. In other words, you do not save yourself a lawsuit by failing to use ADR.

Another advantage of ADR is that you put an additional legal hurdle in front of those employees who are committed to a lawsuit. Many courts and agencies will require the employee to exhaust the ADR system before hearing their claim. This may reduce the attractiveness of the claim to potential plaintiff's attorneys and gives you an opportunity to see the employee's full case before they get to court. In some cases, you may even be able to improve your defense by catching the employee in inconsistencies or outright lies.

Further, the chances of double recovery are quite limited (courts will almost always offset any damage award by prior payments through the ADR system). If there is a great fear of fighting two suits for each dispute, employers can give employees the option of ADR at the time of their dispute. The law is much more settled where employees choose ADR after having knowledge of their claim. In addition, the likelihood of additional suits is very unlikely if the employee volunteers to try ADR in the first place.

Ultimately, there is very little legitimate fear of ADR by either employers or employees. Implementing a system where disputes can be settled early, quickly and inexpensively is an advantage to both companies and employees. Let's face it – employment disputes are inevitable, and resolving them is never simple or pleasant. The quicker and more cheaply these disputes can be resolved, the better for all parties. ADR, while not perfect, is simply the best way to accomplish this.

Which Type of ADR Process Should I Use?

There are a number of excellent options for alternative dispute resolution available today. While I have mentioned each of them, it is worthwhile to describe the processes in detail and outline the comparative advantages and disadvantages of each program. Further, it is good to remember that these dispute resolution processes can be used in combination with one another. For example, many successful programs combine mediation and arbitration and even peer review as steps in their dispute resolution process.

Mediation

Mediation is the least formal level of dispute resolution. Here an independent third party, usually an individual in no way associated with the company, listens to both sides of a dispute and attempts to encourage a resolution. Mediation within a company can be handled either through a Human Resources department or, better yet, through outside "ombudsman" programs or formal mediators. The problem with mediating within a company, particularly as a final step, is that the mediator may not be viewed as a neutral party by the employee. A critical aspect of any successful dispute resolution program is that the mediator be perceived as neutral.

Nevertheless, mediation still has several advantages. First, it is nonbinding. This means that mediation can be used without significant risk to either party. Mediation has the additional advantage of getting each party's side of the story on the table early on in the dispute. It also has the advantage of being informal. Informal proceedings normally result in reduced expense and also reduced time commitment.

The main disadvantage of mediation is that many times the dispute remains unresolved. Since mediation is non-binding, it has little coercive impact on the parties. If the parties have widely divergent views regarding the facts or a desirable resolution, mediation can be a waste of time for them. Ultimately, however, there is little reason to avoid mediation because of its low cost and effort, and its ability to move the parties closer to settlement of the issue.

Peer Review

There are a number of variations of peer review. The basic concept is that a group of employees is assigned to review specific decisions of the company. This group of employees can be strictly peers (hourly employees review decisions regarding other hourly employees), or a combined board of both hourly and managerial employees. The types of decisions reviewed by a particular board are also varied. Peer review boards can be very limited in their scope or can be empowered to review literally all termination decisions and other complaints.

Prior to establishing a peer review board, draft a specific procedure for appeal. Train peer board members on the process and record keeping procedures of appeal meetings. Finally, it is a good idea to give employees the option of appealing directly to management for those who are uncomfortable going through peer review.

The primary advantage of a peer review board is that it empowers employees to make decisions about their employment relationship with the company. They bring a tremendous amount of expertise regarding the day-to-day operations of the company that can be helpful in resolving disputes. However, because of their closeness to the issues being reviewed, most companies' experience is that the peer review board is often harder on employees than management.

Many employees feel much more comfortable with the decision made by a peer review board, even if that decision is the same as would have been made by management. Utilizing peer review of management decisions creates a system of checks and balances that many employees seek when they feel that management has been unfair.

However, there are some potential disadvantages to peer review. First off, allowing hourly employees into the decision-making process often raises confidentiality concerns. These concerns can usually be dealt with during the training process; but still, they reinforce the importance of making appeals to a peer review board a voluntary action. One can imagine potential liability from poorly trained or untrustworthy review board members freely discussing employment decisions regarding their peers. The same, of course, is true of supervisors or managers who handle employment issues.

Another potential problem (although one I have not experienced) is that peers may unjustifiably overturn every management decision. For this reason, it is very important to include fair-minded, conscientious and mature individuals on the peer review board. Nevertheless, if this – like any review system – is abused, it becomes ineffective.

Arbitration

Perhaps the best-known dispute resolution method available is arbitration. Arbitration can be either binding or non-binding. The arbitration process is much like a trial, although instead of occurring in a court of law in front of a judge or jury, it occurs in front of an impartial "expert" in an informal setting.

The advantages of arbitration are many. If the decision is binding, arbitration creates a final conclusion to disputes that, except in the most extreme circumstances, cannot be overturned on appeal. Arbitration proceedings are informal, so there is less expense. The proceedings also require much less time than a trial.

The biggest disadvantage of arbitration is that, because it's easier to use, arbitrations may occur more frequently than court cases. This can result in increased expense for the employer if care is not taken to deal with disputes prior to the point that they are appealed to arbitration. Nonbinding arbitration, while an effective way to bring issues to resolution, can be more than an expensive mediation in cases where the parties are simply not going to agree. Finally, if the company policy severely limits the remedies or responsibilities of an arbitrator, the award won't take the place of agency decisions. Thus, you could be giving employees two bites at the apple.

An incredible number of opportunities exist for resolving disputes before litigation. Each company needs to examine its own current dispute resolution process and retain what is working in that system. At the same time, it is also very valuable to look at other options for dispute resolution as part of an overall plan. New approaches can be valuable, not only as ways to resolve the inevitable disputes that occur during the employment relationship earlier and less expensively, but also as a way to help employers win those disputes that do end up in front of an agency or in court.

Take Action

☐ Think about five of the most recent workplace disputes you were asked to step in on. How would each of those disputes have been best resolved: mediation, peer review, or arbitration?

Chapter 24

Where Do We Go From Here? Living Left of Boom

"Men who are occupied in the restoration of health to other men, by the joint exertion of skill and humanity, are above all the great of the earth. They even partake of divinity, since to preserve and renew is almost as noble as to create."
Voltaire

What You'll Learn In This Chapter
❑ The six keys to a successful Left of Boom program;
❑ Why mapping out your plan of attack is essential;
❑ The importance of including employees in the development and review of the program;
❑ Tips to keep your Left of Boom program fresh and on track.

When I first wrote this book I called it *The Next 52 Weeks*. The idea was to provide companies that had been through a union campaign a one-year program to turn their company around. But as I said then, the idea of a "52 Week" program is a misnomer (which is a big reason this book is now called Left of Boom).

Becoming an employee relations leader does not end at the conclusion of a year of transformative work. It requires constant effort, forever. Living Left of Boom is not a fad program – it must be a habit. If you let yourself slip back into bad habits, you will end up with the same problems you face today. You have to consistently apply the principles discussed in this book.

The rewards for this hard work are great. Increased productivity, engaged employees, and higher profitability to name a few. Just as the negativity of a poor work environment continually reinforces itself, so do the positive feelings that are generated when a group of employees feel connected to the mission of their organization and feel good about the place where they work. This is the mountain that, with your hard work, your organization will scale.

In this final chapter I give you some tips about living left of the boom. Just like the military learned that the real leverage comes from attacking problems before they become "boom" events, you will be attacking employee relations problems way before they spin out of control. These are some of the most important steps you can take to transform your organization into an employee relations leader:

Assess Your Position and Make a Plan
The first and most important step in this process is to figure out where you stand today and map out a plan of attack. I've covered a number of tools you can use to do this. Most of our clients start with a combination of employee surveys and focus groups. You also want to get a good idea of the development opportunities for your supervisors (an Approachable Leadership™ workshop is a great place to start). Once you know where you stand you can begin thinking about where you want to be. Then you figure out just a few steps you can take that move you in the right direction.

Your plan will be unique. While many companies share similar problems, none of them share the same individual personalities. Those personalities (both in your employee and leadership ranks) will have a significant impact on how particular details of your plan will be implemented. You'll need to account for your unique situation as you map out your next steps.

This initial map is something you should refer to over the course of the year, both as a means of checking your progress and also as a foundation for the celebrations of success that you will have as you reach your employee relations goals.

Be Creative

Once you have identified the areas that you wish to attack, get creative with responses. There are a number of starting points outlined for you in this text. There are many, many others outlined in other books on this subject. Study and come up with things that you think will work given your particular complement of employees and your organization's own specific mission.

There are many ways to approach employee relations issues that are weakening your organization. Often your first attempt to deal with a problem will not be successful. Therefore, it is very important to think of as many possible angles to attack an issue as you can.

Get Help

It is also very important to remember that you are not in this alone. No one person can change an entire organization. In fact, the only person you can change is yourself. Your goal is to create conditions in which your co-workers decide on their own that they want to join with you on your journey.

While in the beginning it may be difficult to get people to join you (particularly those who are extremely negative or who have been hurt by the organization in the past), you still should be constantly reaching out for assistance. If you feel stuck call me – I'm dead serious about this (my number is 800-888-9115). While your particular path will be your own, there are many who have gone before you. I would love to talk about your situation and see if we can't think of a creative way to break through any obstacles you face. .

The fastest and most reliable route to get people on the path with you is to get employees feeling it is a part their own journey. Include them very early in creating the vision. This is particularly true of the leadership group. Your leaders will have the best line of sight to whether you are making progress. They are often the source of issues, so working with them gets you ahead of (left of) those potential problems. They will be responsible for dealing with many of the employee relations issues that will come up.

In addition, it is very important to try to get employees involved in attacking issues that come up whenever possible. As you now know there are many matters that are not suitable for "team" solutions, but there are many more where employees can and should help.

We would be happy to put you in touch with organizations who have used this model as the basis for their employee relations planning. This gives you an opportunity to bounce ideas off of other leaders who have "been there, done that." We have a number of people who done a terrific job in improving their employee relations and who are excited about talking to others about their experiences.

Check Your Progress
Don't be afraid to survey throughout the year. While you will not want to conduct a 70 plus statement survey more than once a year, you can always conduct what we call "pulse-surveys" on particular issues. You for sure can ask our three "net promoter" statements.[99] You could also ask the 10 statements in a category area that you have attacked as a pulse survey and compare those results to your earlier survey results. In some cases, you may ask completely different questions over issues that come up during the course of the year. You may simply want to conduct focus group sessions or sessions to gauge your progress.

In any event, it is vitally important to make sure that you are making progress on the issues that you have decided to attack. This also gives you an excellent opportunity to

---

[99] You can learn more about "net promoter" statements supra at p. 158.

communicate to employees the progress that you have made and to celebrate the changes that have been made in the employee relations environment.

Be Flexible and Expect Challenges

There will be a number of unexpected challenges. It never fails that at just the time an organization decides to spend significant resources on improving its employee relations, it will find out that its insurance costs are going to increase by 50 percent or that a huge customer is taking its business elsewhere. Challenges like these will come up. Boom events like these are opportunities for an employee relations leader to really show their stripes.

It's much easier to manage in the good times. The best companies do a good job of managing even in the bad ones. Look at these challenges as opportunities to prove the organization's commitment to its employee relations. This normally means concentrating heavily on communicating and explaining exactly why the company is making the decisions it is making.

In an union organizing environment, these challenges are all the more evident because there is typically a large group of people looking to put the negative spin on anything that management does. In the worst cases, these employees look to sabotage every move that management makes. Once you get better at predicting the expected challenges that you will receive from these employees, your response will improve. Nevertheless, it is vitally important to be very flexible when challenges arise.

Celebrate Your Success

The most valuable use of the data that you collect to benchmark your current status and to identify growth during the year is to celebrate progress. The survey results provide an excellent objective benchmark of where your organization is. A month or two after working on the issues of concern that came up during the initial survey, communicate your progress to employees.

Also communicate a list of all the actions that have occurred in response to that particular area. Many employers forget to remind employees of things that they have done to respond to issues. This is the biggest communication mistake that you can make.

Employees who are busy working on day-to-day tasks cannot be expected to remember all the different things that management has done over a 6- or even 3-month period of time. In addition, some people take these changes for granted. A particularly negative employee might simply say, "look, that's management's job." However, when given the opportunity, it is important for management to remind employees that in the past these things were not handled as well, and that based on its renewed commitment to employee relations, they now are effectively responding to those issues.

This honesty and candor with employees is appreciated. If you act like there was never a problem to start, you lose credibility with employees. This information also creates common ground for employees. It is a common point of reference that you can and should use to talk about employee relations concerns. You should point to the survey results and then identify things that you have done to respond to those particular issues. This should become a habit not just for top management in the organization but for all leaders.

What's Next?
Living Left of Boom is a lifetime commitment and as you progress you will want to reassess where you are, figure out your next goals, and draft up a new road map. Each organization is different and your path will depend on how much you have accomplished during the first year.

Some organizations conduct a brand new survey and start the process over each year. Other organizations continue working on the initial survey for 18 to 24 months before conducting another survey. Some conduct focus group sessions regularly on the issues that are talked about in the survey and do not conduct a formal survey on a regular basis. The ultimate answer is to do what works for you.

While for many organizations an objective survey is the best method to judge progress, it's not for everyone. If you felt the survey process was effective with employees, then it should be continued. If employees did not engage with the survey, or if it was too negative and not that helpful, then your organization should consider other alternatives like focus group sessions or Appreciative Inquiry.

It is my sincere hope that your organization will be able to find some useful tools in this book to help live Left of Boom and transform its employee relations environment. There is nothing more satisfying to me than seeing a company whose employees have completely lost confidence in management transform itself into an organization where employees feel connected, proud and positive about their company. It is possible. I have seen it happen in situations that even I felt were impossible. The best news is that it is not a magical or extremely complicated process. It is hard work, but not difficult work. In fact, if you've lived Left of Boom for a while you will find it is one of the most rewarding things you have ever done.

Appendicies and End Material

Appendix 1.1 – Sample Employee Opinion Survey

Statement	strongly disagree — strongly agree
1. Considering the work I do, my work area is orderly and clean.	1 2 3 4 5 6 7
2. My present job makes good use of my skills and abilities.	1 2 3 4 5 6 7
3. I am proud to be an employee here.	1 2 3 4 5 6 7
4. The benefits offered here are fair and reasonable when compared to similar jobs at other companies.	1 2 3 4 5 6 7
5. The most capable employees are always the ones selected for promotions.	1 2 3 4 5 6 7
6. When assigned work I've never done before, I get the necessary instructions to do a good job.	1 2 3 4 5 6 7
7. Generally speaking, my immediate supervisor is doing a good job.	1 2 3 4 5 6 7
8. Communications from top management are adequate for me to know what is going on in the organization.	1 2 3 4 5 6 7
9. The people here are pleasant and cooperative to work with.	1 2 3 4 5 6 7
10. Today this organization is headed in the right direction to be successful.	1 2 3 4 5 6 7
11. My work area is safe and accidents are infrequent.	1 2 3 4 5 6 7
12. I feel I am valued by the company.	1 2 3 4 5 6 7
13. I would recommend the company as a great place to work.	1 2 3 4 5 6 7
14. The benefit plan provides adequate protection for me and my family in case of accident or illness.	1 2 3 4 5 6 7
15. For a person of my abilities, there are many opportunities for advancement.	1 2 3 4 5 6 7
16. I feel I receive the training necessary to keep me productive in my present job.	1 2 3 4 5 6 7
17. My supervisor listens to my ideas and suggestions when I make them.	1 2 3 4 5 6 7
18. I have a clear understanding of my job responsibilities.	1 2 3 4 5 6 7
19. The company places a high value on treating employees fairly.	1 2 3 4 5 6 7
20. The management team does what they say they are going to do.	1 2 3 4 5 6 7
21. I have the proper materials and equipment to do my job effectively.	1 2 3 4 5 6 7
22. I find my present job challenging and interesting.	1 2 3 4 5 6 7
23. Morale here is high.	1 2 3 4 5 6 7
24. I am paid fairly for the work that I do.	1 2 3 4 5 6 7

Appendix 1.2 – Sample Employee Opinion Survey

Statement	strongly disagree strongly agree
25. Around here, "what" you know is more important than "who" you know.	1 2 3 4 5 6 7
26. I feel I receive the training necessary to prepare me for advancement.	1 2 3 4 5 6 7
27. My immediate supervisor makes me feel like part of a team.	1 2 3 4 5 6 7
28. The channels of communication between associates and management are working satisfactorily	1 2 3 4 5 6 7
29. No one here is discriminated on the basis of race, age, sex.	1 2 3 4 5 6 7
30. I have great confidence in top management.	1 2 3 4 5 6 7
31. I have the resources (e.g., equipment, tools, supplies, information) I need to do my job effectively.	1 2 3 4 5 6 7
32. I have no problem keeping up with my workload.	1 2 3 4 5 6 7
33. Our policies and procedures allow me to provide great service to our community.	1 2 3 4 5 6 7
34. I believe the annual raises are equal to, or better than, other area company's.	1 2 3 4 5 6 7
35. Whenever possible, promotions are made from within.	1 2 3 4 5 6 7
36. People here are given the chance to cross train for other jobs.	1 2 3 4 5 6 7
37. My immediate supervisor provides the support I need to do a good job.	1 2 3 4 5 6 7
38. When changes are made that affect how to do my job, the reasons are explained to me.	1 2 3 4 5 6 7
39. I am not aware of any instances of workplace harassment.	1 2 3 4 5 6 7
40. Top management is available to listen to employees.	1 2 3 4 5 6 7
41. The company provides a safe working environment for employees.	1 2 3 4 5 6 7
42. I am very satisfied with my job.	1 2 3 4 5 6 7
43. We have a lot of good people here working hard to make us successful.	1 2 3 4 5 6 7
44. The way raises are determined here are fair.	1 2 3 4 5 6 7
45. People here get terminated only for good reasons.	1 2 3 4 5 6 7
46. New employees receive adequate training as soon as they start to work.	1 2 3 4 5 6 7
47. I am able to talk openly and honestly with my supervisor about my work.	1 2 3 4 5 6 7
48. I feel comfortable talking with my supervisor or someone else in management about my personal problems or complaints.	1 2 3 4 5 6 7
49. Our rules and regulations are uniformly administered.	1 2 3 4 5 6 7

Appendix 1.3 – Sample Employee Opinion Survey

Statement	strongly disagree strongly agree
50. My management team explains the reasons for their decisions.	1 2 3 4 5 6 7
51. When suggestions are made to improve working conditions, those suggestions are given careful consideration.	1 2 3 4 5 6 7
52. If I had to do it over again, I would still go to work here.	1 2 3 4 5 6 7
53. We have an excellent reputation in the community.	1 2 3 4 5 6 7
54. I feel like I completely understand our benefit program.	1 2 3 4 5 6 7
55. My plans are to remain here for many years.	1 2 3 4 5 6 7
56. Management seems sincerely interested in training everyone to do the best possible job.	1 2 3 4 5 6 7
57. My immediate supervisor treats me with dignity and respect.	1 2 3 4 5 6 7
58. I believe top management knows what employees think about most major issues.	1 2 3 4 5 6 7
59. There is very little friction between co-workers in my department.	1 2 3 4 5 6 7
60. I believe management measures performance fairly.	1 2 3 4 5 6 7
61. Overall, the working conditions here are good.	1 2 3 4 5 6 7
62. The amount of work expected of me is fair and realistic.	1 2 3 4 5 6 7
63. When I tell others about where I work, my comments are always positive.	1 2 3 4 5 6 7
64. Considering the type of work I do, I feel my pay is fair for this area.	1 2 3 4 5 6 7
65. This organization has a great future.	1 2 3 4 5 6 7
66. Everyone here seems to be well trained for their present job.	1 2 3 4 5 6 7
67. My supervisor judges me based on facts, rather than opinions, rumors and personality judgments.	1 2 3 4 5 6 7
68. When management gives out information, I can always believe it.	1 2 3 4 5 6 7
69. Everyone here does their fair share of the work assigned to them.	1 2 3 4 5 6 7
70. My management team listens and responds appropriately to issues and ideas raised by employees.	1 2 3 4 5 6 7

The things I like most about my job:

The things I like least about my job:

Appendix 2.1 – Sample Employee Survey Report

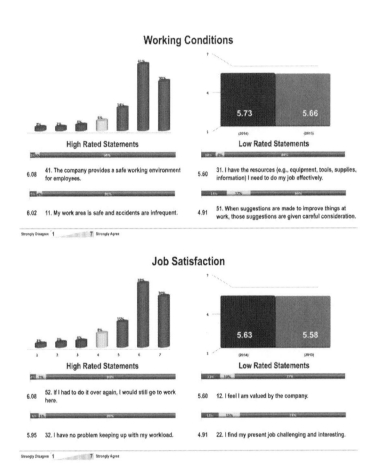

Working Conditions

High Rated Statements

6.08 — 41. The company provides a safe working environment for employees.

6.02 — 11. My work area is safe and accidents are infrequent.

Low Rated Statements

5.60 — 31. I have the resources (e.g., equipment, tools, supplies, information) I need to do my job effectively.

4.91 — 51. When suggestions are made to improve things at work, those suggestions are given careful consideration.

5.73 (2014)   5.66 (2015)

Strongly Disagree 1 — 7 Strongly Agree

Job Satisfaction

High Rated Statements

6.08 — 52. If I had to do it over again, I would still go to work here.

5.95 — 32. I have no problem keeping up with my workload.

Low Rated Statements

5.60 — 12. I feel I am valued by the company.

4.91 — 22. I find my present job challenging and interesting.

5.63 (2014)   5.58 (2015)

Strongly Disagree 1 — 7 Strongly Agree

Appendix 2.2 – Sample Employee Survey Report

Company Pride

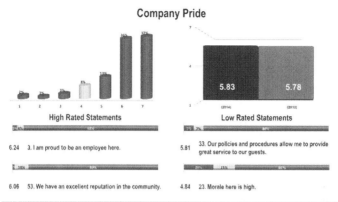

	High Rated Statements
6.24	3. I am proud to be an employee here.
6.06	53. We have an excellent reputation in the community.

	Low Rated Statements
5.81	33. Our policies and procedures allow me to provide great service to our guests.
4.84	23. Morale here is high.

Strongly Disagree 1   7 Strongly Agree

Advancement

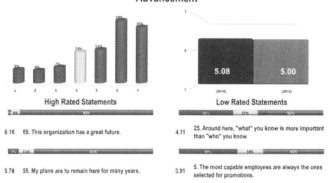

	High Rated Statements
6.16	65. This organization has a great future.
5.78	55. My plans are to remain here for many years.

	Low Rated Statements
4.11	25. Around here, "what" you know is more important than "who" you know.
3.91	5. The most capable employees are always the ones selected for promotions.

Strongly Disagree 1   7 Strongly Agree

Appendix 2.3 – Sample Employee Survey Report

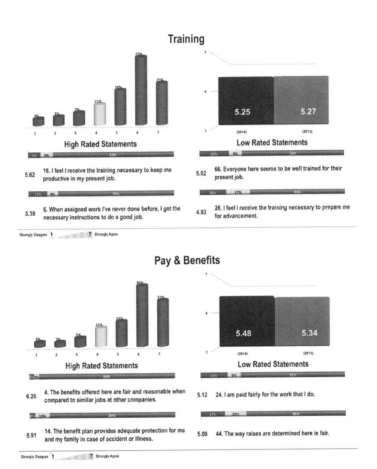

Training

High Rated Statements

5.62   16. I feel I receive the training necessary to keep me productive in my present job.

5.39   6. When assigned work I've never done before, I get the necessary instructions to do a good job.

Low Rated Statements

5.25 (2014)   5.27 (2013)

5.02   66. Everyone here seems to be well trained for their present job.

4.93   26. I feel I receive the training necessary to prepare me for advancement.

Strongly Disagree 1   7 Strongly Agree

Pay & Benefits

High Rated Statements

6.26   4. The benefits offered here are fair and reasonable when compared to similar jobs at other companies.

5.91   14. The benefit plan provides adequate protection for me and my family in case of accident or illness.

Low Rated Statements

5.48 (2014)   5.34 (2013)

5.12   24. I am paid fairly for the work that I do.

5.09   44. The way raises are determined here is fair.

Strongly Disagree 1   7 Strongly Agree

Appendix 3.1 – Sample Employment Audit

EMPLOYMENT AUDIT

_____ My firm has audited its employment policies with the assistance of labor counsel in the last 12 months.

HANDBOOK - POLICIES

_____ We have an employee handbook.

_____ The employee handbook is distributed to all employees.

_____ The employee handbook contains an acknowledgement form that is signed by the employee.

_____ The employee handbook contains a valid "at-will" disclaimer at the beginning and on the signature page.

_____ The employee handbook contains summaries of sexual harassment/discrimination, injury reporting requirements, FMLA, no solicitation, statement on unions, and progressive discipline.

_____ The policies in the employee handbook are consistently applied by all managers/supervisors.

SEXUAL HARASSMENT - DISCRIMINATION

_____ Our firm has a sexual harassment and nondiscrimination policy.

_____ Our policy is posted.

_____ Our policy is well communicated - employees and supervisors receive regular training on the policy and the complaint procedure, and this training is documented.

_____ Our firm has an effective reporting and investigation procedure (including multiple routes for complaint/investigation).

FLSA - WAGE AND HOUR

_____ Our firm has a clearly defined method of designating exempt and non-exempt employees.

_____ Our exempt employees are paid on a salary basis for all hours worked.

_____ Our non-exempt employees receive overtime for all hours worked over 40 in a week.

_____ We have reviewed our state laws regarding wage payment, lunch and break periods, accrual of vacation pay and pay on termination and our policies are consistent with those regulations.

OSHA

_____ Our firm has a well-designed safety program, including lockout/tagout, hazard communication and MSDS materials.

_____ Our firm conducts regular training on safety issues as part of our safety program and this training is documented.

_____ We have an effective reporting procedure for injuries.

WORKERS COMPENSATION, ADA, FMLA

_____ Our firm has a consistent return-to-work policy for employees who are away from work due to injury or illness, whether work related or not.

_____ Our firm has a policy for determining when light duty or other accommodations should be made for injured or ill employees.

NLRA

_____ Our supervisors are trained to recognize the early warning signs of union organizing as well as their rights and obligations under the NLRA.

_____ Our firm has a valid, consistently enforced, no solicitation policy.

Appendix 4.1 – Sample Exit Interview

Appendix 4 – Sample Exit Interview Form

JOB CONTENT

1. What factors contributed to your accepting a job with COMPANY NAME? Have your feelings changed?
2. Did you understand the job expectations when you were hired?
3. Did you receive sufficient training to meet those expectations? Did you know how or where to get information you needed to succeed in your job?
4. How would you rate your own performance on the job?

COMPANY AS A PLACE TO WORK

5. How would you rate the following aspects of your employment here?

Aspect of Employment	Excellent	Good	Fair	Poor
Opportunity for Advancement				
Performance Appraisals				
Physical Working Conditions				
Your Salary				
Vacation/Holidays				
Other Company Benefits				
Feeling of Belonging				

6. If you were leading this company, what would you do differently?
7. What made your employment enjoyable?
8. What would make you interested in returning to work at COMPANY NAME?

QUALITY OF SUPERVISION

9. How would you rate your supervisor in the following areas?

Supervisory Area	Excellent	Good	Fair	Poor
Demonstrates Fair & Equal Treatment				
Provides Appropriate Recognition				
Resolves Complaints/Difficulties In Timely Fashion				
Follows Policy & Procedures				
Informs Employee of Matters Relating To Work				
Encourages Feedback				
Is Knowledgeable In Own Job				
Expresses Instructions Clearly				
Develops Cooperation				

10. If you came back to work for the company, would you work for the same supervisor?

REASONS FOR LEAVING

11. Are you leaving for a similar job?
12. How is your new job different from the old one? Are you staying in the same industry?
13. What part does salary play in your decision to leave?
14. What made you begin looking for another position, or, if appropriate, what made you listen to the offer to interview for another position?
15. What could COMPANY NAME have done to prevent you from leaving?
16. If you are going to another job, what does the job offer you that your job here did not?

Employee
Signature_____ Date_____

FREE CONSULTING CERTIFICATE

This certificate entitles you to <u>one FREE 30-minute Left of Boom Consulting Session</u> with Phil Wilson ($250 value) PLUS a FREE Supervisor DNA Assessment ($650 value).

Use the code below to schedule your free 30-minute session with LRI President Phil Wilson (limit one session per company). You set the agenda – Phil provides the insight. Nothing's off the table. What do you want to discuss...

☐ Approachable leadership?
☐ Best first step to get your company Left of Boom now?
☐ Best tool (there are many) to gauge the attitudes of <u>your</u> workforce?
☐ Assessing and training supervisors (they are <u>the</u> key to a healthy environment)?
☐ Vulnerability to a union campaign?
☐ Getting buy-in from the C-Suite?

To set up your session, call Tammy at 800-888-9115 and give her this code: LOBSession15

Supervisor DNA Assessment: Should you invest in soft skills training for your front-line supervisors? Do you need to justify the expense to the C-Suite? The Supervisor DNA Assessment can help. A quick, on-line questionnaire that will reveal the level of competency in a handful of core skills. Once you have this data your can organize your training plan to tackle the highest payoff training efforts first.

To set up the assessment for your company, contact **Greg** at **800-888-9115** or gkittinger@lrionline.com

Labor and Positive Employee
Relations Expert Phillip Wilson

About Labor Relations Institute, Inc.
LRI helps clients create positive and productive workplaces
while strengthening direct relationships with employees. LRI
is best known for educating employees during NLRB union
election campaigns. LRI also helps companies create positive
workplaces by assessing vulnerability, directing workplace
improvement, and training line-level leaders to create healthy,
high-performing organizations.

About Phillip B. Wilson
Phillip B. Wilson, President and General Counsel of Labor
Relations Institute, is a national expert on labor relations and
creating positive workplaces. He is regularly featured in the
business media including Fox Business News, Bloomberg
News, HR Magazine, and the New York Times. He has been
called on multiple occasions to testify before Congress on the
subject of union financial reporting and labor law reform.
Wilson graduated magna cum laude from Augustana College
in Rock Island, Illinois, and went on to earn his J.D. from the
University of Michigan Law School.

Wilson is a highly regarded lecturer and an adjunct professor
at Northeastern State University. Phil delivers workshops and

webinars regularly for business executives and managers. Some of Phil's favorite and requested topics include:

☐ Approachable Leadership™ (learn more at http://ApproachableLeadership.com)
☐ The role of front-line managers in maintaining a productive employee relations environment
☐ How and what to train front-line managers to create and maintain a positive employee relations environment
☐ Measuring the right things in your employee relations environment
☐ What makes a company vulnerable to a union organizing campaign
☐ Labor law and the impact of legislative and regulatory changes on American businesses
☐ Making a company bullet-proof to union organizing campaigns

Phil is the author of multiple books and publications, including:

☐ *The Next 52 Weeks: One Year to Transform Your Work Environment*, Broken Arrow, OK: LRI Management Services, Inc.
☐ *Managing the Union Shop*, Broken Arrow, OK: Labor Relations Institute.
☐ *How to Investigate Grievances*, Broken Arrow, OK: Labor Relations Institute.
☐ *Model Contract Clauses*, Broken Arrow, OK: Labor Relations Institute.
☐ *Model Reprimands for the Union Shop*, Broken Arrow, OK: Labor Relations Institute.
☐ *We Won Our Election, Now What?* Broken Arrow, OK: Labor Relations Institute.
☐ *The Case for Reform of Union Reporting Law: How Financial Transparency Could Have Prevented ULLICO and Other Abuses*, Washington, D.C.: Labor Policy Association
☐ *Corruption: A study of the Problem, Its Sources, and its Remedies*, Fairfax, VA: John M. Olin Institute for Employment Practice and Policy, George Mason

University (LR-40 in the Labor Relations and Public Policy Series) with Kendrick, D., Thiebolt, A.J.

☐ *Current Section 13(b) Exemptions From the Overtime Requirements of the Act in The Fair Labor Standards Act in The Fair Labor Standards Act* (Chapter Contributor, Ellen C. Kearns, ed., Washington, D.C.: The Bureau of National Affairs).

☐ *Reporting Union Finances* in Labor Watch, Washington, D.C.: Capital Research Group.

Contact:
Phillip B. Wilson
pbwilson@lrionline.com
(800) 888-9115

Labor Relations Institute
7850 S. Elm Place – Suite E
Broken Arrow, Oklahoma 74011
(918) 455-9995

Order these publications for <u>your</u> team today!

- ❏ Comprehensive—essential labor topics covered
- ❏ Thorough—written by a labor lawyer and practitioner
- ❏ Handy—designed to be used, not sit on a desk
- ❏ Understandable—no jargon, covers key concepts
- ❏ Inexpensive—beginning under $10 each

CALL 800-888-9115, FAX the form below to 918-455-9998, or order ONLINE at www.LRIonline.com

For details about these and other publications below, visit:
www.LRIonline.com/store/publications/

YES! Send me the following tools for my team	Copies	Price	Total
Left of Boom: Putting Proactive Engagement to Work		$49.99+ shipping	
Managing the Union Shop –74-page guide for supervisors		$9.99+ shipping	
How to Investigate Grievances – 68-page guide for supervisors		$9.99+ shipping	
Model Contract Clauses – Over 200 model clauses (strong company & union proposals) plus drafting guide		$39.99+ shipping	
Reprimands for Union Shops – Nearly 100 sample letters of reprimand; document problems and win grievances		$29.99+ shipping	
Name			
Company Name			
Address	City/State/Zip		
Phone	Email		

Method of Payment ($20.00 minimum for credit card orders)

- ☐ Check (order shipped upon receipt)
- ☐ Visa
- ☐ MasterCard
- ☐ American Express

Card No:

Expiration Date: _____   3-Digit Security Number: _____

Signature

If <u>one leadership behavior</u> predicted high performance <u>88% of the time</u> would you want to know what it is?

Watch the Approachable Leadership™ Keynote and learn:

- <u>What many "experts" get wrong about engagement</u> – and why "happy" employees often aren't the most productive;
- The <u>clear signal</u> to watch for to tell if your employees are really engaged;
- Why some leaders fail and others – who you think will fall on their face – succeed;
- How <u>3 simple questions</u> can transform your leaders (and maybe even *improve your love life!*)

Call 800-888-9115 to learn more about bringing the Approachable Leadership™ workshop to your company

Do you think Approachable Leadership™ is right for your company? Here's what to do next.

Bring our compelling Approachable Leadership™ Keynote Presentation to your company. Engaging, interactive, and delivered with Phil's unique blend of humor and hard research, your team will walk away moved to begin their own approachability journey.

The Keynote can be delivered as a stand-alone speech during a corporate retreat or learning event, or as part of our customizable half-day workshop delivered by LRI's approachability experts. Call us at 800-888-9115 to learn more.

"Phillip's discussion on what makes an Approachable Leader and what motivates people in the workplace today, demystified what connecting with another human being – whether an employee, client, or spouse – can be like. I've used his 3-question strategy every day, both in my personal and professional relationships, to become a better coach, sister, and friend."

Lori A Broyles, Business and Entrepreneurial Services Coordinator, Francis Tuttle Technology Center

Made in the USA
Charleston, SC
08 December 2014